Values and
Human Experience

American University Studies

Series V
Philosophy

Vol. 188

PETER LANG
New York   Washington, D.C./Baltimore   Boston   Bern
Frankfurt am Main   Berlin   Brussels   Vienna   Canterbury

Values and Human Experience

Essays in Honor of the Memory of Balduin Schwarz

Edited by
Stephen Schwarz
and Fritz Wenisch

PETER LANG
New York Washington, D.C./Baltimore Boston Bern
Frankfurt am Main Berlin Brussels Vienna Canterbury

Library of Congress Cataloging-in-Publication Data

Values and human experience: essays in honor
of the memory of Balduin Schwarz /
[edited by] Stephen Schwarz and Fritz Wenisch.
p. cm. — (American university studies. V, Philosophy; 188)
"Selected bibliography of the works of Balduin Schwarz": p.
Includes bibliographical references.
1. Ethics. 2. Values. I. Schwarz, Balduin, 1902–1993. II. Schwarz,
Stephen. III. Wenisch, Fritz. IV. Series: American university studies.
Series V, Philosophy; vol. 188.
BJ1012.V345   170—dc21   99-19447
ISBN 0-8204-4407-3
ISSN 0739-6392

Die Deutsche Bibliothek-CIP-Einheitsaufnahme

Values and human experience: essays in honor of the memory of Balduin
Schwarz / ed. by Stephen Schwarz and Fritz Wenisch.
–New York; Washington, D.C./Baltimore; Boston; Bern;
Frankfurt am Main; Berlin; Brussels; Vienna; Canterbury: Lang.
(American university studies: Ser. 5, Philosophy; Vol. 188)
ISBN 0-8204-4407-3

The paper in this book meets the guidelines for permanence and durability
of the Committee on Production Guidelines for Book Longevity
of the Council of Library Resources.

ACKNOWLEDGMENTS

We would like to express our grateful appreciation to Sherry Schwarz, who is Stephen Schwarz's wife, to his daughter Mary Schwarz, to Lori Mantia, and to Linda Josefson for all their help in typing and proofreading.

Further, we would like to express our gratitude to the University of Rhode Island's Department of Philosophy as well as to its College of Arts and Sciences for their support of our project.

A special word of thanks is also due to Lynn Pasquerella, URI Philosophy Department Chair, whose strong support of the project is deeply appreciated.

We would also like to thank Josef Seifert and the International Academy of Philosophy in Liechtenstein/Europe for a generous donation helping with defraying the cost of publishing this book in honor of the memory of Balduin Schwarz.

TABLE OF CONTENTS

Foreword

Virtue Ethics

Fundamental Dimensions of Axiology

In Defense of Objective Values and Morality

Existential Perspectives

Appendix

FOREWORD

Balduin Schwarz, May 1991 (age 89),
in Ainring, Germany (near Salzburg, Austria).

Balduin and Leni Schwarz, June 1977 (ages 75 and 80),
in Salzburg, Austria

THE LIFE AND WORK OF BALDUIN SCHWARZ

Stephen Schwarz, Otto Neumaier, and Michael Wenisch[1]

This is a Festschrift in honor of my late father, who died on November 25, 1993, after a long and productive life. It was a life that spanned the time before World War I until long after World War II, and spanned the European and American continents.

Balduin Schwarz was born in Hannover, Germany, on March 23, 1902. His early studies led him to Heidelberg, where he attended the lectures of Karl Jaspers and others. Later, he developed ties with Max Scheler and Nicolai Hartmann in Cologne. But his most important philosophical explorations were conducted in Munich. It is there that he first met Dietrich von Hildebrand who had a profound influence on him, not only for his philosophical orientation and development, but also as a person. It was in von Hildebrand's lectures, and in his private conversations with him, that he came to understand the true meaning and value of philosophy, as well as the general direction his own philosophical journey would take. His contact with von Hildebrand was the beginning of a deep, life-long friendship and philosophical collaboration. He studied a variety of subjects with von Hildebrand, particularly value philosophy, which von Hildebrand had developed extensively beyond the early contributions of Max Scheler in this domain. Through von Hildebrand, Scheler, Alexander Pfänder and others, he became intimately acquainted with realistic phenomenology as taught by the "Munich School" of phe-

---

[1] Prepared by Stephen Schwarz, son and only child of Balduin Schwarz, based on an essay by Otto Neumaier, which was written for a previous Festschrift in Balduin Schwarz's honor, *Vom Wahren und Guten* (About the true and the good), ed. Joseph Seifert, Fritz Wenisch and Edgar Morscher, (Salzburg: Verlag St. Peter, 1982), and translated for the present volume by Michael Wenisch. Used with the kind permission of the publisher, Verlag St. Peter, Salzburg.

nomenology. It was in this tradition that he pursued philosophical questions throughout his long, rich life. His main areas of interest were the history of philosophy—both as historical development and in its intrinsic significance for philosophy itself—and value theory, with a particular focus on gratitude during the last years of his life.

His first two publications came out while he was still a student. One was a translation of a short piece by J. B. Bossuet and the other a literary essay about Ravenna. In February 1927, he received his doctorate, writing his dissertation under Dietrich von Hildebrand, a philosophical work entitled, *An Analysis of the Psychology of Tears*. Ortega y Gasset thought so highly of this work that he translated it into Spanish. During these student times he also traveled through France, Italy, and Spain. These travels yielded further fruit in the form of a series of literary essays which he published under the pseudonym Anselm Stilling. This pseudonym reflects both his great esteem for St. Anselm of Canterbury, and his love for the work of his ancestor, Jung-Stilling, a contemporary and friend of Goethe who wrote a biography of Jung-Stilling.

On May 2, 1926, he met Leni Katzenstein in Munich. On April 30, 1929, they got engaged while traveling in Italy. And then, on September 6, 1931, they were married in Munich. On November 8, 1932, in Munich, their first and only child was born, Stephen. Dietrich von Hildebrand was his godfather. In the same year as his marriage, Schwarz received his *Habilitation* in Münster under the direction of Peter Wust, a representative of Christian personalism and existentialism who was influenced in his views above all by Max Scheler. The second reader was Heinrich Scholz, one of the founders of modern symbolic logic in Germany, who also worked intensively in the areas of the history of philosophy and the history of religion.

Schwarz's first teaching position was at the University of Münster in Germany during the academic year 1932–33. During the Spring semester of 1933, after Hitler had come to power in January of 1933, he met frequently with his close friend Edith Stein to discuss philosophy and the rapidly deteriorating political situation. At this time the government contacted all university professors and demanded an expression of support from them. He refused. In fact, he was always absolutely clear and unequivocally outspoken in his total and uncompromising opposition to Hitler and the Nazi regime. Requesting a leave of absence from the University of Münster, he taught at the University of Fribourg in Switzerland during the academic year 1933–34. In the summer of 1934 he delivered a series of lectures in Salzburg at the *Hochschulwochen* (a series of academic lectures held during the summer) about the biologistic world-view inherent in some of the newer trends in philosophy. Thereupon he was offered a guest professorship at the University of Salzburg for the academic year 1934–35. In the summer of 1935 he again lectured at the *Hochschulwochen* on St. Augustine. During the academic year 1935–36, he again taught at the University of Fribourg.

Despite the turmoil of the times, he published two books, *On Error in Philosophy* (1934), and *Perennial Philosophy* (1937). The former received an extensive and favorable review by Nicolai Hartmann, who praised it for (among other things) making explicit the various sources of philosophical error. Schwarz also wrote a series of penetrating analyses attacking the ideology of National Socialism (Nazism), which were published under the pseudonym Johannes Ilen in *Der Christliche Ständestat*, a journal edited by Dietrich von Hildebrand in Vienna. In Switzerland his life came under increasing difficulties. The government was growing more and more hostile to foreigners, especially those holding academic positions. And so he came under increasing pressure to seek a position outside Switzerland. In 1938, when the Swiss government refused to extend his residence permit, he was forced to move to France.

This new settlement meant an interruption of his philosophical activities in the academic sphere. He found a job teaching Latin and German at a high school for girls in Limoges—of course in French! When World War II broke out in Europe in September 1939, he was brought to an internment camp for "foreign enemies," despite the fact that he had left Germany in protest against the Nazis, had explicitly renounced his German citizenship, both for himself and his family, and that the Nazi regime had officially acknowledged this and stripped him of his German citizenship. Thanks to the influence of his friend Jacques Maritain (he had been the first to translate a work of this philosopher into German), he was released after three months and returned to his family. Immediately thereafter, the day before Christmas 1939, he left his family again in order to fight the war against the Nazis with an infantry company of the French army. He had volunteered for military service out of the deeply felt conviction that this was a war, not between two countries, France and Germany, but between the forces of justice and injustice, liberty and tyranny.

During his time on the front in northern France, he narrowly escaped capture by the Germans, which would have meant certain death, since they considered him a traitor. He finally managed to make his way south and was reunited with his family. Through the kindness of Edmond Michelet, the family was able to find security and lodging at a farm near Brive-la-Gaillarde, in central France. Michelet worked heroically to save refugees from the Nazis and thereby saved the lives of countless persons, including Dietrich von Hildebrand and his wife. Michelet was among the first to organize the French Resistance, but was later betrayed by French traitors and was imprisoned for eighteen months in the German concentration camp at Dachau. After the war, he became one of the first architects of reconciliation and dialogue between Germany and France and served in the cabinet under De Gaulle.

In the meantime, some friends of Schwarz who had emigrated to America, among them the onetime Salzburg professor Fr. Thomas Michels, O.S.B., obtained for him a grant from the Rockefeller foundation. Another friend, Waldemar Gurian, was able to obtain a teaching position for him from Mother Grace Damman at Manhattanville College of the Sacred Heart, a college for girls in New York City administered by the nuns of the Sacred Heart. Thus, the Schwarz family was able to leave Europe for the United States in May of 1941. They arrived in New York City on June 27, 1941, and took up residence at 448 Central Park West, in the apartment immediately below that of Dietrich von Hildebrand and his wife, who had saved it for them. In the fall of that year, he started teaching at Manhattanville College. Even though the adjustment to teaching in English cost him a great deal of effort, it also bestowed on him a considerable intellectual enrichment, as was also previously the case with the transition to French. Because of this difficult linguistic transition, his possibilities for publishing were at first greatly limited. Not until 1947 was he able to publish a short essay on Book I of Aristotle's *Politics*, which he followed up in subsequent years with a number of essays derived from his lecture notes.

After four years at Manhattanville College, his appointment was terminated because of a new requirement that only members of the religious order affiliated with the college be allowed to teach there. He subsequently taught on the undergraduate level at numerous other colleges, including Hunter College, Manhattan College (both in New York City), and Seton Hill College in Greensburg, Pennsylvania (near Pittsburgh). In 1951, he received an appointment to teach philosophy at the Fordham University Graduate School. This enabled him at last to resume fully his activities as an academic philosopher. At Fordham, his teaching was devoted mainly to the history of philosophy, especially ancient philosophy and modern philosophy.

The post-war period saw the re-establishment of contacts to the "European Motherland." Several German Universities, among them Münster, Göttingen, and Cologne, inquired whether he would be interested in accepting a teaching post. He declined all these offers, preferring to stay in the United States. But he did return to the *Salzburger Hochschulwochen* in the summer of 1949, and gave a lecture series on the theme of human rights. During these *Hochschulwochen*, he met Rene Marcic, who displayed a great interest in his lectures. As a gesture of redress from Germany, he was named Honorary Professor Emeritus of Philosophy at the University of Münster on January 1, 1954.

His ties to Salzburg, as well as his friendship with Rene Marcic, deepened over the course of a lengthy stay in 1960. When, in the early 1960's, the idea of reintroducing the old traditions of the University of Salzburg began taking shape once again, it was Balduin Schwarz who received the invitation to be the one to establish a Philosophical Institute at the University and to guide its development. The offer was unusual in that he was at that time already sixty-two years of age. Because this task greatly interested him and because he had long-standing ties with Salzburg, he accepted the offer with great joy. On July 28, 1964, he was appointed Honorary Professor and Director of the Institute for Philosophy at what was then called the Philosophical Faculty [Faculty of Arts and Sciences] of the University of Salzburg.

The commencement of his duties at the University of Salzburg was marked by two points of emphasis: the assembly of a library which was readily able to provide for colleagues and students the most important literature necessary for continuous progress in research, and a wide range of course offerings, with special importance attached to both the history of philosophy and specific content areas in the discipline. He began his lectures in the history of philosophy at the very beginning, with Thales of Miletus, and traced the witness of philosophy through the centuries. However, he never regarded the history of philosophy purely as history, but rather as an encounter with the object of philosophy. His approach rested on the insight that what we undertake today as philosophers stands in living contact with what our predecessors said and wrote. Soon, though, the emphasis of his lectures came to include a variety of areas related to value philosophy, such as ethics, aesthetics, and philosophy of community.

The period in Salzburg was once again an exceptionally fruitful one for him. Not only did he publish three short books and over sixty essays, he was also instrumental in the founding of the Philosophical Society in Salzburg, which held its first general meeting and established a constitution on December 9, 1966. This society was intended by him to be a place of encounter and exchange for those who "had the wish to devote themselves to the serious study of philosophy." In order to achieve this aim, both "native" thinkers from Salzburg and well-known philosophers and experts in other fields from places outside Salzburg were to hold lectures and seminars, and participate in conferences and workshops. A high point in the life of the society was an Austria-wide symposium for instructors of philosophy at various universities and other schools of higher education in Austria, an event organized and led by the Philosophical Society. Balduin Schwarz held a seminar at this symposium entitled "The Place of Ethics in the Instruction of Philosophy at Schools of Higher Education."

In 1972, he became Professor Emeritus. But he continued to direct the affairs of the Philosophical Society in Salzburg until 1978. And he continued to live in his lovely house in Salzburg, until January 1990. At that time he and his wife, Leni, moved to a fine retirement home, the Kurstift Mozart, in Ainring, Germany, just across the border from Salzburg. He and Leni were thus able to maintain personal contacts with the many friends they had in Salzburg. He continued his writings, publishing fifteen scholarly articles on a wide variety of topics.

But the focus of his interest during these last years of his life, both in terms of his scholarly work and his own life and thoughts as a person, was on gratitude. He had written about it earlier, but now it became the center of his life. He was hoping to complete a book on this subject, so dear to his heart, but he was unable to do this. What remains is a large treasure of notes which, hopefully, can be edited into a published work, or perhaps a series of works.

Gratitude for him was not only a topic for philosophical analysis, but something to be lived in one's daily life. And something to be shared with others. He would often stress, for example, that, if one starts to feel sad at an anticipated separation from a loved one, one can and should counteract this sadness with gratitude: not sadness at what I do not have, but gratitude for what I do have, for what I have been given. Sadness weighs us down, gratitude lifts us up, and enables us to see reality truthfully.

Though weaker and somewhat frail in the last years of his life, he was able to work and perform ordinary tasks, including cooking simple meals. His mind lost none of its sharpness, and he continued his philosophical writing until the very end. He died in the morning hours of Thursday, November 25, 1993, with his computer still on, in the midst of an essay—on gratitude. How appropriate that this day was a Feast of Gratitude: Thanksgiving Day.

In view of the central role of gratitude for Balduin Schwarz, it is fitting that this volume in his honor include some of his key thoughts on this subject. And so the second part of this Foreword is dedicated to this basic theme of his life and thought.

THE HEALING POWER OF GRATITUDE

Balduin Schwarz
(Edited and translated from the German
by Stephen Schwarz)

From gratitude there goes forth a healing power. The disposition of gratitude is a hidden door leading to the meaning of life; it liberates us from that which would hinder us from discovering the meaning of life. It dissolves our self-centeredness, it leads us out of selfishness and greed. Only a grateful person can be truly blessed with gifts. Only a grateful person can experience himself as a free being who is loved by his Creator. One who is ungrateful cannot truly give, that is, give out of love. Where gratitude withers, there withers also true joy; and with it, the power of self-donation. Gratitude liberates us to our true freedom: to be lovingly co-creative with God's love. In this consists the true meaning of our life.

Gratitude places us at that point where we are able to receive fully. It is the fertile ground in which the reverent recognition, the real "receiving" (with its aspects of humility) becomes actualized. Here there is a certain paradox. Gratitude as a response follows receiving, yet as a disposition, it precedes and intermingles with receiving. If reverence and hope are clearly anticipatory attitudes preparing the way for a fruitful contact with things that are really good for us, that are the sources of true happiness for us, gratitude arises at the point of contact and becomes an element of the bliss and joy in receiving.

The readiness to be grateful—this is the underlying attitude of openness, which alone places us in a position to receive a gift. This attitude is a basic orientation of the person, actualized and carried forth by the person's will (in the broad sense), a commitment of the whole person. It includes being awake and ready for obstacles that may come in the way of responding in gratitude.

Gratitude makes us humble. In being grateful, we recognize that we are beings whose essence includes not only acting, but also receiving. We are free creatures, loved by our Creator, and called upon to love Him and to love with Him.

Just as we can stand in the middle of a world full of bright colors with our eyes closed, so too, we can stand in the middle of a world full of beautiful gifts offered to us, gifts that can make us deeply happy, and not notice them because we are spiritually blind. Gratitude has the power to free us from such blindness.

Another person has made something important to me *his* concern; he has taken a concern that is "mine" and made it "his own," such as my health, my safety, the preservation of my property, and ultimately, my happiness. In this there is an affirmation of my person.

Gratitude is the response to this affirmation of my person by the other: it is "aimed at" it and "corresponds" to it. To really give this response of gratitude, I must allow the gift, the loving intention of the other, to reach that point in my being where the affirmation of my person becomes real, and is actually experienced as such. The healing power of gratitude is also manifested in the fact that the loving affirmation by the other person of my being represents a call, a call addressed to me to be a more loving, affirming person.

Basically, gratitude arises when another person makes my concern *his* concern. But my gratitude to him also establishes a proper relation between myself and what I possess, what "is mine." For I can "have" the things that are mine in different ways. I can "have" them as gifts entrusted to me; or, in contrast, I can "have" them by being possessive, greedy, clutching them as my own in a self-centered way. Gratitude enables me to rethink, to re-evaluate my relation to what is mine. Gratitude is a reminder that what is "mine" is not only given to me, but also entrusted to me. Gratitude is an inner power that counteracts the force of habit that blinds me to my true relationship to what I have.

Again, from gratitude there goes forth a healing power because gratitude corresponds to truth, because it belongs to the truth about the human person, because in it humility reigns. Gratitude is a recognition, a perception of the good that is given to me [*erkennen*]; but it is also more than that, it is a deep acknowledgment of this good, a real appreciation of it, a taking it to heart [*anerkennen*]. It is an awakened, responsive "recognition" of a good, a good given to me.

Gratitude belongs to the world of the real good, of genuine human value. And it is not just a small part of this world, it is a deep breadth of its true life. Gratitude should not remain by itself, as something that simply occurs at a particular time. Its healing power should touch our whole life. A grateful person feels himself called to place himself under the healing power of gratitude, in his inner being.

There is a power of conversion in gratitude. Gratitude is itself a form of conversion, a turning away from the false path of self-centeredness and its disjointed pursuit of immediate pleasure. Gratitude has the power of conversion, and is also a fruit and sign of conversion.

We must distinguish between a quick "thank you," not ungenuine but not fully thought out, not invalid but lacking the full measure of real gratitude—and the gratitude that really comes from the heart, that is "thought through," that is affirmed from the depth of one's being, that is fully conscious and articulate. This fullness of gratitude awakens our heart in manifold ways: it engenders humility, reverence, love, and many other responses of the heart. The word "heart" is taken here in its classic, very broad but also very precise sense, as the core of the person in his personal being. Gratitude is the voice of the heart, in which a person actualizes his ultimate status as a person, namely that his being transcends itself, that the meaning of his life lies beyond the confines of his individual self; and that his life falls into meaninglessness if he tries to find its meaning in itself.

The human person is essentially a being who receives, who is and lives by what he receives; and gratitude is an awakened, deep acknowledgment, a full appreciation [*anerkennen*] of one's essence as a being who receives. Gratitude is, in the last analysis, a "lived" readiness to believe in love. And by being grateful, this belief in love proves itself, since gratitude makes us capable of seeing a gift as what it really is, and seeing the love that is manifested in it.

Gratitude is also vital for each of us if we are to understand ourselves; for gratitude sees, and fully affirms, our dependency, our lack, our need to receive all that which we cannot provide for ourselves. Gratitude is to life what the keel is to the ship; it provides a steady course. Gratitude acknowledges the ultimate importance of the world of interpersonal relations, the world in which we exist essentially as persons. In gratitude we understand that we are truly at home in this world of loving interpersonal relations, in a way that is possible only in such a world. A grateful person does not repress what belongs to the given of his being—his essential dependency on others. He does not try to take refuge in the many illusions of self-sufficiency, in which we try to find the meaning of our lives in ourselves. The collapse of this attempt at self-sufficiency will be experienced as the disintegration of one's false sense of self, and with it the (perhaps still hidden) resentment and anger of despair.

Gratitude comes from the true depth of our being, our genuine core as persons. Gratitude strengthens and vivifies this deep core of our being. In some cases, a breakthrough to gratitude may enable us to find our way back to this depth of our being, and to live out of this depth again, and thereby to stand in the truth.

Gratitude is part of the "child-like" in the deepest sense of the term, which can be seen in the words of Jesus, "Unless you become as little children, you cannot enter the Kingdom of Heaven" (Mt 18:3). Gratitude is purity and innocence and it gives us back our purity and innocence. Its healing power flows out from this source: it places us in the truth. For this is the truth of the matter: we are receptive beings, dependent on the help of others, on their gifts and their good will. In gratitude we affirm this: yes, so it is. We recognize it.

But to really stand in the truth it is not sufficient to merely recognize something [*erkennen*]; we must acknowledge it, take it to heart, affirm it with our whole being [*anerkennen*]. That is, someone who knows what the truth is but does not want it to be true; who refuses to place himself under the truth because he refuses to bow down to it, because he is full of self-glorification and self-will, such a person does not stand in the truth, even if he is aware of it. He will try not to see that which he basically knows, or could know, were he to let himself be drawn to it. He will blind himself, or become blinded by his pride. In his being as a person he struggles against his creatureliness. He refuses to bow down.

But the grateful person bows down, and in that very instant, he is raised, because he has humbled himself. He is elevated from within, in his being as a person. He has had the courage to "let go" of himself, to "lose his soul"; and precisely in this, he has "gained it." Gratitude is experienced as peace, the opposite of being inwardly torn. It is experienced as the truth about our human situation—but in a pre-reflective way, in a pure, innocent way, as the grace of a gift received.

Pride means being inwardly torn and in a state of self-alienation, since it means a denial of a basic truth about ourselves. Pride is a rebellion against this truth, that we are receptive beings, called to be grateful for what we are and what we have. Pride is a loss of peace and spiritual power; gratitude is the key to these.

Gratitude is like the presence of a great light, the light of a profound truth about our life, in the midst of the bleakness and hardness of daily life. Gratitude is that seeming superfluousness that we so desperately need. Gratitude is "for nothing," free, as is the gift to which it is directed. It is, on a practical level, "useless" and "unnecessary"; and yet, on a higher level, absolutely essential and necessary. Humble and profound, gratitude is an acknowledgment [*anerkennung*] of the presence of God in an eminently human way. Gratitude is courage, as it dares to accept the way of the less powerful. It is believing in love, in God's love, a victory of God's grace. It is like a light in the darkness, a herald of the eternal.

Gratitude counteracts the general human tendency to take things for granted, to make the goods of our life a mere matter of course. We often realize this tendency with the sharpness of deep pain when we lose what we had taken for granted, for in our grief the regret that we have been ungrateful plays a great role. If we become blind, we feel that we have not sufficiently appreciated what a gift our eyesight was; or, if a beloved person dies, what a gift his presence was, although we may sometimes have been annoyed with him. Grief and sorrow over the loss of great goods tend at least to show us the level of depth to which we should have gone to receive them adequately when they were given, that is, in gratitude. The ungrateful matter-of-fact attitude to the significant gifts we receive in our life has a stifling general effect. Thus, gratitude proves its deep significance by its capacity to enrich human life.

Two attitudes stand in contrast to taking things for granted in an habitual, routine way: wonder and gratitude, and these are intimately bound together. Wonder is an essential element in our being grateful for the gifts received in our lives. The world, all of reality, is something so incredibly marvelous, and worthy of wonder, that if we do not wonder at it, we have not really seen it as it is. Wonder—a more general wonder than philosophical wonder—opens up our dialogue with reality; or rather, takes it up and continues it, since reality has already spoken the first word in addressing us as persons. There comes then into being a dialogue between that which "speaks to us" and our soul which "receives" it. For this to take place, we must open ourselves inwardly to what is given to us, cooperate with it, "go along with it," bring it to completion in ourselves, work together with it. We must even become co-creative with it, "recreating" it in ourselves, as when we become "co-poetic" in order to really appreciate a work of poetry. This dialogue sets into motion an active receptivity. So it is with all things that, in themselves, have the capacity to move us, to touch us, to affect us deeply:

they cannot do so unless there is this active receptivity, in which we become co-creative with the object. Sentimentality is characterized precisely in this way, that it lacks this inner active receptivity, this spiritual
co-creativity. It is a pure passivity that relishes a kind of inner dissolving
of oneself. It "uses" a work of art or thing of beauty, something in itself
genuinely moving, touching, and gripping, in order to bring about a
completely subjective experience of self-centered satisfaction. It lacks
that noble sobriety characteristic of genuine receptivity. It also lacks that
humility which is essential for our being co-creative with objects of
value; the humility that enables us to submit ourselves spiritually, and
intently, to the nature of the object as it is in itself.

Gratitude reveals itself as most important in the fruitful contact with
reality. It has an opening-up power. This can be seen with particular
force when considering its negative counterpart. The ungrateful, envi-
ous, complaining person shuts himself off from what he receives. He
cripples himself. He is focused on what he has not, particularly on what
somebody else has or seems to have, and by that he tends to poison his
world, and thereby poisons himself as well. *In gratitude we are spiritually awake, and thereby capable of truly receiving.*

There is a healing power in gratitude for the gifts of our life. When
assailed by envy or by self-pity, a person may turn inward to the good
gifts he has received and find again the "place of peace." In this power
of gratitude to bring us back to ourselves, to liberate us when the destructive forces in us push to the fore, the deep functional role of gratitude becomes apparent. *In gratitude we are spiritually awake, and
thereby capable of truly receiving.*

Gratitude has a liberating effect, in that it frees us from various
forms of inner paralysis, such as self-centeredness, selfishness, despair
and self-hatred. In gratitude we come to appreciate what we have received. In envy we have our eyes on what another has received and blind
ourselves to what we have received. *In gratitude we are spiritually
awake, and thereby capable of truly receiving.*

Gratitude is something simple and unpretentious. Where it is true
and genuine, a person who feels gratitude will himself become true and
genuine, simple and unpretentious. He will leave behind him for a moment all that which is distorted or repressed in him. One cannot, at one
and the same time, be both cynical and grateful, or sly, crafty, cunning
and grateful, or deceitful, fraudulent and grateful. These vices may return, they may even come to dominate a person; but in the moment of

true gratitude, they cannot be present. In such a moment, a person becomes truly genuine; genuine and simple and unpretentious like a child.

Gratitude cannot be combined with envy, which is directed at what another person possesses. Gratitude is diametrically opposed to envy. It enables us to rejoice with another person because of what he has received. Such an attitude is also an inner liberation, another aspect of the healing power of gratitude.

There are a number of attitudes that are incompatible with gratefulness, that cannot coexist with it in the soul at the same time. They are: envy, greed, false mistrust, complaining and murmuring, misplaced resentment, and hateful anger. Also, self-centeredness as manifested in pride, conceit, and vanity. The attitude of gratefulness also takes away the ever menacing danger of taking things for granted. Again, we see the healing power of gratitude.

There are situations, rare but of great significance, where a breakthrough is made to gratitude, and which thereby represent an inner conversion. For example, one person tries to make clear to another—in a loving, tactful way—that he (the other) has behaved wrongly. (The clearest case of this is when the person who points out the fault is not personally involved in the matter.) The one who is told of his fault is at first angry, and defends himself. But then comes the moment—the moment of breakthrough—when he sees the whole situation in a new light, the way it really is, in the light of truth. And he realizes: I owe you a debt of gratitude. You have opened my eyes, and now I see it for myself. In this way the deed of the person who points out the fault is seen in a radically new way; it is seen as that which it truly is: a deed of love, a spiritual help. Again, we see the deep connection between gratitude and humility.

There is in all forms of gratitude—the inner attitude of gratefulness and its manifestation as the giving of thanks among us humans—a power to change us, and also the power to change situations among us. A home in which appreciation and gratitude reign and replace complaining and arguing, will be a happy home, a blessed home.

The healing power of gratitude places me in the true reality from which pride and greed separate me. In receiving help and acknowledging my need for help, I enter the truth. Humility is truth. It is metaphysical truth. I affirm myself as a created self.

Gratitude is an antidote to sadness. If I feel sad because I am about to be separated from a person I love, instead of giving in to the sadness and being down, I can recognize the great gift that this person is for me and respond in gratitude. Gratitude is the true and fitting response, and it has the power to lift my spirits. If I lose a loved one through death, I will, of course, be overwhelmed with sadness and grief. But this should not be the last word. I can go to a deeper level and be grateful that this person was given to me, was part of my life. In gratitude I not only actualize my true relation to the gift that this person was for me; I also overcome and go beyond the negative effects of sadness that fill my soul, and thereby actualize the positive effects, the healing power, of gratitude. In a word: not sadness at what I don't have, but *gratitude for I what I do have*, or have had.

Before whom do I live? The true goal is to live before God, in the presence of God. The reality is that we are always before God, in His presence. The question is whether we come to a full, awakened awareness of this reality, a full acknowledgment, affirmation of it; whether we consciously place ourselves in the light of His presence, whether we want to live as children of our Heavenly Father in His House. The question is whether, like the Prodigal Son in the Gospel, we (spiritually) abandon our Father's House, squander and waste the rich inheritance He has given us in our being as persons, and in His many gifts—or return to Him, live before Him, consciously and explicitly, and receive His gifts in humble gratefulness.

Atheism is not only an intellectual denial of the reality of God, a way of thinking as if He did not exist, but also a lived denial of the reality of God, a way of leading one's life as if He did not exist. In this sense, atheism is a mortal threat to our inner life, our existence as persons. We are all exposed to this threat, the threat of a sickness unto death, a spiritual death. At the root of atheism is despair: an antithesis to gratitude.

The times of inner emptiness and turmoil are the times we are not grateful to God.

When you feel down, what can you do? Start thanking God! For what? Give yourself no rest until you find something. After you find the first thing, there will be a second thing, then a third, . . . and finally no end to all the things for which you can thank God!

In my gratitude to God for my being as a person lies the recognition, the full acknowledgment, of the reality of God as the creator of my being. In this gratitude I become freed to the "Freedom of the Children of God." This is the great freedom in which the deeds of love addressed to me become fully real and fruitful in my inner being.

Our soul is like a cup: if it stands upright, it can be filled; but if it lies on its side, our soul will receive nothing even if it is pouring rain! Only the soul that is opened through gratitude can be enriched by gifts. Through gratitude, I hold onto the gifts I have received. I remain awake to them. Gratitude is a form of remembering. *Gratitude is the way the heart remembers.*

TRANSCENDENT GRATITUDE

Balduin Schwarz
(Prepared by Stephen Schwarz)

Can there be gratitude where there is no human person to turn to? There is a correspondence between the loving intention of another human person towards us and the spontaneous feeling of gratitude. Gratitude arises out of a recognition of this loving intention and is the fitting response to it. How then are we to interpret the feeling of tremendous gratitude that arises spontaneously in us when a great good is given to us but there is no human person who has given it to us?[1] A soldier returns to his wife who had given up all hope of ever seeing him again. Here a great evil has been averted, the life of a beloved person has been saved. The response of deep joy is like a light leaping up. There is a deep correspondence between the joy and the event. But there is also another quality intermingled with the joy. The person who receives this great good feels a desire, an impulse, to do something—a desire, an impulse, to be grateful and to give thanks. But there is no human being to whom he can turn. Even where there is someone who has played some role in bringing about this great good, the person will still feel that his impulse to be grateful has not been fulfilled when he has thanked the other.

People who believe in God can turn to God at such a time and express their gratitude to Him. But even people who usually do not think of God may nevertheless, in such moments, turn to God to thank Him. Chesterton writes: "Rossetti makes the remark somewhere, bitterly but with great truth, that the worst moment for an atheist is when he is really thankful but has nobody to thank."[2]

---

[1] Editor's note: The type of gratitude in question here can be referred to either as anonymous gratitude—when the focus is on the absence of a human person as the giver; or as transcendent gratitude—when the focus is on God as the Giver. Josef Seifert employs the former term in his article elsewhere in this volume.

[2] G. K. Chesterton, *St. Francis of Assisi* (London: Tavistock, 1957), p. 88.

Gratitude can be a way of finding God. If I see my own existence and all the things in my life that are sources of true and deep happiness as gifts for which I want to be grateful, for which I realize I should be grateful, what can I do? There are really only two alternatives. Either this experience of being grateful for my life and for the good things in my life is meaningful—in which case these things really are gifts, and there is a Giver behind these gifts, God, and my gratitude "reaches" God as the Loving Giver of these gifts. Or such a gratitude is absurd and meaningless—because these things are not really gifts and there is no Giver; they just fall into my life accidentally, and my deep feelings of gratitude are utterly misplaced and absurd. If I believe that existence is ultimately meaningful, then this second alternative is ruled out. I can then really be grateful for my own existence and for the good things of life, a gratitude that reaches God, that brings me to God; a gratitude that enriches my life by opening my eyes and my heart to seeing all good things as gifts of God and to living my whole life as a continuous prayer of gratitude to God.[3]

---

[3] Editor's note: In part 2 of his article elsewhere in this volume (pp. 42–50), Josef Seifert offers a superb, penetrating and profound analysis of transcendent gratitude, in which he shows that it is present not only in the kind of case discussed above but also in every gratitude to a human person.

VIRTUE ETHICS

FROM A PHENOMENOLOGY OF GRATITUDE TO A PERSONALISTIC METAPHYSICS

Josef Seifert
(Translated by Andrew Tardiff)

Dedicated with deep gratitude and respect to Balduin Schwarz.

Without doubt it was Balduin Schwarz who, while I was still in high school, opened my eyes to the fascinating aspects of a phenomenology of gratitude as the foundation for a philosophical anthropology and personalistic metaphysics. Hardly any thinker before him has analyzed this topic so deeply. With my high school classmates, I often discussed cassettes of his lectures on gratitude, and in particular his discovery of the problem of an anonymous gratitude.[*] These ideas of Schwarz, which he has developed more fully in an unpublished book, are also uniquely characteristic of his personality, whose nature has been deeply formed by this forgotten virtue—a virtue which, moreover, played a central part in Scheler's essay on humility in *Zur Rehabilitierung der Tugend* (A rehabilitation of virtue). Just a few days before his 90th birthday, he shared with me, from his sickbed, some penetrating insights into gratitude, most notably that the awakening to the pivotal gift of the existence and loving presence of the person to whom we are grateful is always a determining factor in gratitude, and that gratitude represents such an awakening. Without this gift, we would be forever doomed to remain in the abyss of existential loneliness. I owe to Schwarz's later and ever more intense investigation of gratitude also the idea that the transcendent ordination of every person to a "Thou" is given special expression in gratitude. His earlier reflections have decisively contributed to my discovering the beauty and qualitative potential of philosophical and phenomenological investigations. This discovery motivated my decision to go into philosophy. Thus, in profound gratitude I dedicate to Balduin

---

[*] Please see Transcendent Gratitude, in the Foreword [the editors].

Schwarz my own reflections on gratitude.

The following reflections do not claim to investigate the phenomenon of gratitude comprehensively, covering the whole spectrum of acts and experiences which could meaningfully fall under it. Neither is it our objective to investigate all the subtle and phenomenologically relevant nuances embodied in the wisdom of the word meanings and roots of the words for 'thanks' and 'gratitude' of the various languages, however exciting such a linguistically oriented phenomenology and hermeneutic of essences might be. Finally, it is not our plan to investigate the manifold relationships between gratitude and other acts of the person, or even the many ramifications of the basic forms of gratitude. For, however fascinating such investigations may be, they do not seem to be necessary for revealing the metaphysics of the person which lies in the nature of gratitude.

This essay is devoted to a phenomenology and metaphysics of gratitude. To this end it seems best to consider a particularly clear and important type of gratitude, and to gain access to a personalistic metaphysics in light of its investigation.

In his work *De Beneficiis*, Seneca discusses benefaction and gratitude. After various reflections on gratitude—such as that the grateful person is happy in an abiding way for a gift, while the ungrateful person remembers it only once[1]—he poses a question of great interest, and in answering it he develops insights into the metaphysical make-up of the person which were especially formative for modern philosophy and the codification of human rights from the 18th century on up to the present. He mentions an objection to his view that a slave can perform good deeds, and therefore be the addressee of gratitude. Here Seneca and his interlocutor employ the same concept of benefaction (benefit). According to Seneca, "A benefit is something that some person has given when it was also within his power not to give it."[2] Now the slave has no power, and, in any case, no right to refuse to do anything (negandi potestatem). Therefore, he is not capable of giving a free gift or of doing a good deed to which his master has no right. Thus, any thanks by the latter would be groundless.

Without disputing the fact that gratitude and good deeds presuppose the voluntary character of the giver's gift, Seneca responds to this ob-

---

[1] See Seneca, *De Beneficiis*, III. xvii. 3–4.

[2] "Beneficium enim id est, quod quis dedit, cum illi liceret et non dare." Seneca, *ibid.*, III. xix. 1, trans. by John W. Basore in *Seneca: Moral Essays* (Cambridge, Mass.: Harvard University Press, 1964), p. 163.

jection by distinguishing internal from external freedom. He shows that not only is it within the power of the slave freely to give or not to give many things, but also that there is much to which his master has no right, and that in this legal sense he is also free. In explaining this, Seneca gives a moving example of gratitude.

> Meanwhile, tell me this, if I show you one who fights for the safety of his master without any regard for his own, and, pierced with wounds, pours forth the last drops of his life-blood drawn from his very vitals, who, in order to provide time for his master to escape, seeks to give him a respite at the cost of his own life, will you deny that this man has bestowed a benefit simply because he is a slave?[3]

Indeed, this gift of the life of the slave is all the greater and more worthy of thanks, Seneca argues, because the man is a slave, and could rid himself of his universally hated bondage by betraying his master. In order to give his life for his master, "his love (*caritas*) for his master has to conquer his hatred of being a slave." This victory of love over hatred also makes his action all the more worthy of thanks.

Thus, while Seneca recognizes freedom and perhaps a voluntariness—in the sense of an absence of legal or moral obligations to give a gift or do a certain good deed for one's master[4]—as conditions for gratitude, he also knows that every man is free, and that everyone can give freely. For this reason, slavery can never overcome the whole person. His better part remains untouched. Only with regard to the body, not the spirit, can the master possess the slave, precisely because the spirit is free, and therefore under its own law ("*mens quidem sui iuris*"). In fact, this spirit is so free that it cannot be held by any prison, and by its own spontaneous power (*impetu suo*) can accomplish tremendous things, even align itself with the infinite.[5]

The core of the person, his freedom, says Seneca, can neither be bought nor sold. What issues from this core is free. In this inner sanctum of personal freedom, the slave can also refuse to commit a crime, and act

---

[3] Seneca, *ibid.*, III. xix. 2. The texts contains another impressive example: "If I show you one who, refusing to betray to a tyrant the secrets of his master, was bribed by no promises, terrified by no threats, overcome by no tortures, and, as far as he was able, confounded the suspicions of his questioner, and paid the penalty of good faith with his life, will you deny that this man bestowed a benefit on his master simply because he was his slave?"

[4] I.e., the *donum gratis datum*.

[5] *Ibid.*, III. xx.

in a manner which the master can neither buy nor determine.

If the aforementioned objection—that an act must be voluntary to ground gratitude—included under "voluntary" not only an act's being free, but also its not being required and obligatory (i.e., no one's having a right to it), and claimed that only this latter sort could be a beneficial deed for which one should be grateful, still there is much in the conduct of the slave which is neither prescribed by justice nor by law. If the slave goes above and beyond the call of duty, one can be grateful to him.

Gratitude and its object, as Seneca shows us in this important example, are not mere facts. Still less are its governing essential laws dependent upon our arbitrary fiats or definitions. Rather, gratitude, its object and its addressee, present to us in Seneca's example and in his phenomenology of freedom, possess an objective and highly intelligible essence. We turn now to the metaphysical implications of this.

1. Metaphysics of the Person: How It Discloses Itself to Us Directly through a Reflection on the Subject and Addressee of Gratitude

When we consider the gratitude which the master feels (as opposed to his taking the act of the slave for granted or treating it with indifference), we realize that the subject of gratitude must be a person (even if there are powerful analogies to personal gratitude in the animal kingdom). That gratitude presupposes a person as subject shows itself in the diversity and performance of the spiritual acts which it requires.

Let us turn to Seneca's example. In order to be truly grateful, the master must first understand the act of the slave. He must explicitly recognize that the slave has given his life for him, and even be capable in principle of giving a linguistic-conceptual expression to this act. Moreover, he must know why the slave acted as he did. To be precise, he must recognize this act as one inspired by good will toward him, and not as simply self-serving. Furthermore, since the feeling of gratitude is not an immanent conscious state, but a stance (Stellungnahme) which must have an intentional object to which it is meaningfully and rationally related,[6] gratitude does not need to be experienced merely as an automatic

---

[6] Is difficult for me to see how Bollnow can speak of an objectless gratitude having nothing whatsoever *for* which one is grateful. See his contribution to *Danken und Dankbarkeit: Zur Rehabilitierung einer vergessenen Tugend*, ed. by J. Seifert (Bern: Peter Lang, 1992). Presumably, he is referring to that grateful and joyful mood which goes above and beyond the object-directed gratitude, and which, as it were, fills our soul in the wake of an overwhelming feeling of grati-

affective state, but can be freely sanctioned as an object-directed feeling. This "cooperative freedom" unites the inner "yes" of freedom (in which Aristotle saw the essence of freedom)[7] with the voice of the heart, the affective response of gratitude. This freedom to sanction and this free, inner response of gratitude elevate the proper feeling of gratitude to the level of a free response.

The personhood of the subject of gratitude reveals itself still more clearly when one looks at the object of gratitude and recognizes, in light of its distinctiveness, that only a person has the kind of rational approach or relationship to the world and the ability to possess the manifold knowledge which are presupposed for gratitude. The object of gratitude is complex, having at least two parts. First of all, gratitude has an object for which one is grateful. The master is grateful for his life, for his rescue, and for other consequences of his servant's fidelity. All these goods for which he is grateful must be understood. Second, he can only be grateful if he understands these as objective goods and benefits which are not—like the pleasure of smoking a cigarette—merely subjectively satisfying, but which are objectively valuable, or objectively beneficial to him. The richest, deepest sort of gratitude occurs when a person is grateful either for something which is intrinsically valuable,[8] or for an

---

tude. But such a gratitude as mood is completely dependent upon the intentional object-directed sort, and can neither be freed from, nor made sense of without direct reference to, the latter. Gratitude as a general and superactually existing attitude in the person—supposing this is what is meant by "objectless gratitude"—is also, in fact, object-directed, even if its object is universal (the embodiment of all goods for which we are thankful), and not an individual good.

[7] See Aristotle, *Nicomachean Ethics*, 1113 b 5 ff (III. v. 1–2), where he describes the free act as an ability to say "yes" or "no." Dietrich von Hildebrand has more precisely worked out the notion of freedom as inner stance, as responding "yes" or "no," and has shown its unique role in relation to the affective response. See Hildebrand, *Ethics* (Chicago: Franciscan Herald Press, 1972), chap. 15, "Cooperative Freedom."

[8] Kierkegaard, in the *Edifying Discourses* on Job's "The Lord giveth; the Lord taketh away; blessed be the name of the Lord" (especially in the last of these sayings), has impressively analyzed the dimension of gratitude which culminates in a pure gesture of praise. See S. Kierkegaard, *Edifying Discourses*, trans. by David F. Swenson and Lillian Marvin Swenson (Minneapolis: Augsburg Publishing House, 1943), vol. 2, pp. 7–26. Although Hildebrand himself and Balduin Schwarz see in gratitude a response primarily to objective goods *for* the person and not a value response, it seems to me no accident that Hildebrand, with the discovery in *Die Idee der sittlichen Handlung* of the idea of

objective good for the person which grows directly out of the intrinsic value of a good, and is, as it were, the very face and turning toward us of a good which is intrinsically precious. However, even if a person afflicted with lung cancer is grateful for the destructive pleasure of deadly cigarette smoking, still he must at least interpret this pleasure as an objective benefit in order to be grateful.[9]

The knowledge of the objectivity of this good *for the person*, which has as its object either the gift or the good deed, once again presupposes the personhood of the one thanking as well as the one thanked.

The personhood of the subject of gratitude reveals itself also in the investigation of fundamentally different kinds of acts of gratitude which are at the same time closely connected with each other within the broad domain of gratitude. First, there is gratitude as the inner, affective or willed stance. It can exist in the solitary life of the soul without the person who is the object of this gratitude knowing anything about it. However, this inner gratitude normally pushes on to an expression of thanks. This expression of thanks—a second kind of act, the act of thanking someone—is a social act which, as such, is in need of being heard.[10] Third, gratitude exists also in the form of reciprocity, i.e., of actions which return a gift to the giver. It is this form of gratitude which Thomas Aquinas especially emphasizes.[11]

And yet gratitude presupposes more than just the personhood and directedness of the grateful party to the gift for which he is thankful. It also involves a second "intentional directedness" to the person whom he

---

value response as response to an intrinsically precious good, used the expression "to thank the object for its value character" to describe the concept of value response. See Dietrich von Hildebrand, *Die Idee der sittlichen Handlung: Sittlichkeit und ethische Werterkenntnis* (Darmstadt: Wissenschaftliche Buchgesellschaft, 1969), p. 40. Moreover, the liturgy of the Catholic Church, in the *Gloria,* views the majesty of God as the primary object of thanks ("gratias agimus Tibi propter magnam gloriam Tuam"). Here, too, light is shed on the close connection between thanking God and praising Him.

[9] See Dietrich von Hildebrand, *Über die Dankbarkeit: Nachgelassene Schrift* (St. Ottilien: Eos Verlag, 1980), pp. 8–11.

[10] See A. Reinach, "The Apriori Foundations of Civil Law," trans. by John Crosby, ed. by Josef Seifert, in *Aletheia* (Irving Texas: International Academy of Philosophy Press, 1983). There, the social act as such, and its fundamental characteristic, *Vernehmungsbedürftigkeit,* or its "need of being heard," was for the first time clearly seen and analyzed.

[11] See Thomas Aquinas, *Summa Theologica,* II-II, Q. 106, art. 4–6; art. 107, art. 1

is thanking or to whom he is grateful. This person can never coincide with the subject of gratitude. Gratitude is thus an other-directed act, since it is impossible to thank oneself.[12]

Someone could question the person-directedness of gratitude by citing examples which supposedly show that there are instances of it which are not directed to anyone at all.

First, there is what Schwarz, in pondering an example of Chesterton's, calls "anonymous gratitude." An atheist might experience a gratitude for the recovery of his wife which is not applicable to any human giver, but bound up with the painful awareness that he knows no one toward whom it could be directed. Such an experience is possible. But the pain of the atheist over the missing addressee of his gratitude clearly points to an addressee. Thus, this example, far from being an objection against, is an argument for, the necessary directedness of gratitude to a person.

Second, one can think of a simple state, say of joyful exhilaration and delight, which is bound up with a feeling of gratitude and in which one does not experience any directedness to another person as addressee, not even in the form of painful absence. However, such a feeling turns out to be at best a "joyful mood," which does not, in fact, have a person as addressee, but which cannot be called gratitude either.

One could also include under the heading of "gratitude having no addressee" the object and person-directed feeling of gratitude insofar as it *becomes* a general attitude of gratitude, which, as it were, goes beyond any specific object and person-directedness, and may give rise to a "grateful attuning" of the mind. (This is similar to the way joy *over* a certain event can lead to a cheerful mood which has no object.) This general attitude, however, is completely dependent on the object-directed gratitude, which has a person as addressee, and could not be described as gratitude without reference to its origin.

Finally, one might take a real instance of gratitude and call it "without object" and "without addressee" if there is no more than a vague directedness to a person to whom one is grateful. What prevails in consciousness in this case is rather the directedness to the world, a thanks to

---

[12] See Thomas Aquinas for this (*Summa Theologica* III, Q. 106, art., 3; art. 1). Here, with reference to Seneca, *De Beneficiis*, v, Thomas clearly affirms the other-personal structure of gratitude. "[N]emo sibi ipsi beneficium dat . . . unde in his quae sunt ad seipsum non habet locum gratitudo et ingratitudo." Cf. *ibid.*, art. 1, "sed homo sibi ipsi non potest gratias agere, quia gratiarum actio videtur transire ab uno in alterum."

things. When one considers such gratitude more closely, however, one finds that it is impossible to be grateful, in the true sense of the word, *to* the air, *to* the water, *to* the bees, etc., however much one may be thankful *for* them. To say that one is grateful to them is to speak in a purely metaphorical or highly analogous sense or to have in mind a gratitude which has a hidden person as addressee. For, as we saw, one cannot even meaningfully be grateful to persons if one is unwilling to recognize them as free in the metaphysical sense. This by itself excludes the possibility that one could be grateful to the air or water, which are certainly not free.

The essential person-directedness of gratitude might also be lost sight of by being forcibly driven out of consciousness by a religion like Buddhism or pantheism. One could speak here of a reinterpretation or renaming of the original experience, or even of a watering down or falsification of gratitude though human consciousness and human error. In any case, the arch-datum which confronts us when we thank another person presents itself as a fundamental human experience which upon closer analysis either does not tolerate, or, at best, only in a purely analogous sense tolerates, being experienced as addressed to a non-personal being.

Within the scope of their object-directedness, therefore, gratitude and thanking possess those two dimensions of the "thanks for something" and the "thanking someone." Indeed, one must speak of an inner intertwining of these two intentional directions. In fact, the "gratitude *for*" does not apply exclusively to the benefits the other person bestows upon us or to his beneficial deeds as such, but also, and primarily, to the goodness of the person himself. Indeed, we would feel no gratitude for a good which was simply forced from another person and not freely willed. Thus, gratitude possesses a directedness to the person of the giver even in its being a thanking "for a gift."

The giver must, however, not only will these benefits and be the free source; he must also will them for the sake of his receiver, and not for his own, for one to be grateful to him. If we think carefully about the various aforementioned interrelations, we will find that we are not primarily thankful for the helpfulness of the gift as such, but rather for those elements of personal solidarity, kindness, and goodwill which are made manifest in the gift.

It should be clear by now, not only with regard to the addressee, but even with regard to the object for which we are thankful, that thanks is first and foremost a response to the other person. We thank the other person not only for something distinct from him which he may give to us. Rather, "gratitude for" is also a response of thanks for the Thou of the person, his goodwill and—in Thomas Aquinas' sense—his love itself. "Love is the first gift (Ur-Geschenk). Everything else which is undeserved that may be given becomes a gift through it."[13]

In fact, just as the persons only actualizes and expresses himself in the proper use of freedom and in the morally good act or stance, so is he always the primary and true object of gratitude.

And yet, at the same time, we also realize that gratitude not only has the other person and his goodness as the object *for* which we are grateful, but that it also responds in quite a different way to the person who does the good deed by "thanking *him*," not as the object of "gratitude for" something, but as the addressee of gratitude *to whom* we are thankful, and whom we expressly thank or, at least, want to thank *for* some benefit.

The slave owner in Seneca's example thanks his slave *for* his life, and is thereby not only grateful for him but also *to him*. The unique relationship between the person, his act, and what it brings about is first recognized in this "thanking him." The benefit is not only seen and responded to as something coming from a person, but it is also related back to the one who originated it such that he is recognized as person, as free, and as author of the benefit. Thus, in "thanking him" for his action, there is also a thanks for his goodness, a goodness which expresses itself in the gift, and which is often in some sense a greater gift than any imaginable non-personal benefit.

The love or goodness of the giver, however, is not exclusively perceived in terms of its being a gift for me, but always also as good in itself, and as something which the integral goodness of the person himself brings about. In every instance of gratitude there is in this sense a pure value response to the person, a moment of selfless praising of this person, the author of the gift. This praise finds a powerful musical expression in the final chorus of Beethoven's *Fidelio* in which Leonora is praised by Florestan, whom she saved, and by all others. It achieves a lofty religious height in the "we give you thanks for your great glory" of the Gloria in the liturgy of the Mass of the Catholic Church.

However, whereas the praise and glorification of the person are pure value responses, we are thankful, in the most marked sense of the word, for gifts which are addressed to us, for objective goods for us or for

---

[13] See J. Pieper, *Über die Liebe* (Munich: Kösel Verlag, 1972), p. 13.

those we love. Thus once again we are thankful primarily for the love and kindness of the person insofar as these are directed to us in his desire for our good. We always thank the other for the gift of his love as well, however, even more than for what it brings about. Thus, even in the object of "gratitude for objective goods *for* us," the person in his love reveals himself as a greater good than anything received through him, and as something *for* which we are grateful.

In fact, even when the gift is something external to the person, such as an objective "good for me," there is something like an objective element of love in the objective benefit of the gift. This love first becomes conscious and finds its full embodiment in personal love.[14]

And yet, as we said, we only thank a person exclusively for himself when the gift he offers is his good will or his love. In being presented with the non-personal gifts of a person, we are grateful also for something which is not the person himself, but his gift distinct from him. And yet at the same time, even in this context we respond to the other as the personal, free, and benevolent giver of the gift.

Thus, the various sorts of object-directedness of gratitude stand in dialectic, dynamic, manifold, and reflexive relationships to each other. When we are grateful to another, we praise his goodness. At the same time, our gratitude turns from the person to whom we are grateful toward the gift (in our case, one's life and successful escape) which we receive from him, and *for* which we are grateful. However, while the gratitude arrives and resides at the gift, it does not simply remain with it, but also directs itself back to the person *to whom* we are thankful.[15] Finally, from both of these the gaze of gratitude turns back to the recipient of the gift and good will, either oneself, or someone we love. Thus, gratitude, as a response, consciously establishes the various interrelationships and reflexive relationships in which giver, gift, and recipient stand together. In view of these relationships among the three points of reference of gratitude, one could speak of a threefold and Trinitarian

---

[14] For this see Hildebrand, *Über die Dankbarkeit: Nachgelassene Schrift* (St. Ottilien: Eos Verlag, 1980), p. 11; *Moralia* (Regensburg: Habbel, 1980), chap. 5.

[15] In the phenomenon of anonymous gratitude analyzed by Schwarz, this gratitude can pertain to an unknown person. In such a case the gratitude can neither realize itself in thanking as a social act (which is in need of being heard), nor in external actions in which the gratitude expresses itself. For knowledge of the addressee is a condition for these dimensions of gratitude.

relationship of gratitude.[16]

Thus, "being thankful *to* someone" is at least as important as "being thankful *for*." The master is at least as thankful *to the slave*, to whom he owes his life, as he is *for* his rescue. In fact, the act of gratitude should be directed in an even more pronounced and deeper way to the person whom we have to thank for the benefit and his kind action. For this person is as much the source of the kind deed as his deed is the embodiment of his goodness.

By reflecting on the fact that gratitude always pertains to a person, we discover a further truth, one which points to a personalistic metaphysics by overcoming determinism. The addressee of gratitude is always understood to be a *free* person. Were we to suppose that there was no freedom in the world, and that the other person was forced to act by God's predestination or by some eternal series of material causes, we could no longer thank him, but, at most, be thankful for him. For to thank another person is to affirm him as the ultimate author of a gift. If the slave in Seneca's example had acted only because he was forced to by a certain configuration of some eternal chain of causes,[17] then he would no longer deserve thanks. Indeed, we could not be grateful to him.

Not only does the willed response of gratitude follow a logic of the heart, but even the feeling of gratitude, which is not itself a free act, but which, as Schwarz says, wells up in our soul—even this feeling follows a logic of the heart. We can only have this feeling toward another person insofar as we really think he is free. As the great skeptic of the Academy, Carneades, rightly emphasized in opposition to the stoics, a genuine recognition of the metaphysical reality of freedom forces us to deny an eternal chain of causes in which a free act would be just one determined link among others. In order to be thankful and express thankfulness, we must accept the truth of Aristotle's assertion about freedom in

---

[16] As a Christian one may certainly see in this Trinitarian structure of gratitude—as Augustine did in many threefold structures within the world of our experience—an image of the Holy Trinity.

[17] One will suppose that Seneca himself is not far from this typical stoic understanding, since he is himself a stoic of the third period of the Stoa during the age of the Caesars. In the foregoing and heated discussion between Chrysippus and Carneades, the skeptic of the Academy, it was even discussed whether the doctrine of the *heimarmene* as a kind of fate—which was identified by the ancient Stoics with the dependence of every external and internal movement of things, including the mind of man, on the eternal series of material causes—is compatible with freedom.

the *Eudemian Ethics*: "Man is the master over the being and non-being of his acts."[18]

At the very most we could, with Poseidonius and Cicero, accept "causes" of human freedom which are not totally determining, which would not have an inherent, complete causal efficacy, but which would allow for freedom and be mere conditions and motives for free acts.

Thus, gratitude, inasmuch as it turns to another person as its addressee, bears witness to the ultimate, intrinsic freedom and source-character of the person with respect to his acts. For gratitude must perish, or at least be robbed of its metaphysical foundation, without the freedom of the one who performs the benevolent deed. Only when we, with Aristotle, view the person as an ultimate source of his acts, in the sense that the being or non-being of his acts depends on himself, can we thank him and view him—as the boy Bip at the end of Dickens' *Great Expectations* views the felon to whom he owes his happiness—as the genuine, ultimate source of a good deed. For the fact that a person is the ultimate source of his act is what makes it possible in the logic of gratitude to thank him. Otherwise, though we could be happy that we received something good through him, or, in a spirit of social hypocrisy, could perhaps even disingenuously and half-politely offer him thanks, we could not feel any real gratitude.

Yet the necessarily voluntary character of the benefaction presupposes not only freedom, but also knowledge. In the third book of Aristotle's *Nicomachean Ethics*, we discover that along with the freedom of the subject and his power over his actions, knowledge of his object and other determining factors are presupposed for the voluntary character of his acts. Only this knowledge enables him to act voluntarily and intentionally. Thus, not only is the free, conscious intending of a good deed and the good will of the person presupposed for such an act, but also knowledge of the nature and object of the act. If a person wants to poison us, for example, but accidentally exchanges the poison for some medication which makes us well, we could be thankful *for* the cure, but not grateful *to* the person. For such gratitude would erroneously ascribe to him a benevolent intention and knowledge of the beneficial effect of his action.

Moreover, if a person helps us purely out of self-interest, if there is no genuine good will, no action for our sake and our well-being, gratitude is impossible.

---

[18] See Aristotle, *Eudemian Ethics*, 1223 a 5 ff. (II. vi. 9).

These anthropological dimensions within the foundations of gratitude also have metaphysical implications and bear witness to the existence of that higher being and that higher self-possession of a being which is only possible through consciousness, knowledge and freedom.[19]

Yet, in a philosophy which starts from the analysis of conscious acts, one might catch the scents of certain unmetaphysical and subjective ideas, and suppose that gratitude presupposes no more than a purely "subjective opinion about" freedom and real benevolence, but not their objective existence as such. It is quite correct that we might be in error in a particular case. This person may not have acted freely, for example, or may have only accidentally done us a good deed when he really wanted to poison us, and in our gratitude we falsely assume his freedom or his good will or both.

Nevertheless, in opposition to the subjectivism of this interpretation, we should see that the accidental error here does not exclude the truth that such benefactors are free. Furthermore, we should ask ourselves whether an analysis of the nature of personal acts might not make metaphysical discoveries possible, and whether the nature of gratitude in general might not allow us to make metaphysical discoveries about freedom and the person, and whether gratitude might not bear witness to the actual existence of freedom and the ability of the person to be genuinely benevolent. Are we not led by the things themselves to the conclusion that it is so?

First, gratitude presupposes the freedom not only of its addressee, but also of its subject. In neither case is this accidental or arbitrary. Gratitude, in its intelligible essence, is anchored in the free being of the person, such that its own highly intelligible and essentially necessary structure would be impossible without the truth of the essential freedom of the person. And, in considering our own experience of our present acts of gratitude in light of its necessary union with freedom, we are assured of the existence of personal freedom by knowing of our own existence and, thus, of that of one person.

Besides this conviction about, or even insight into, the freedom of the person necessarily presupposed for gratitude, there is also in gratitude the insight into the intrinsic possibility of benevolence issuing freely from one person to another. For gratitude is not possible under a radically hedonistic theory of motivation, or even under a purely eude-

---

[19] For more on this see the main thesis of my book, *Essere e persona* (Milano: Vita e Pensiero, 1989), chap. 9.

monistic one. If we suppose that another person acts merely for his own pleasure, and views us as no more than a means to this, or if we suppose that the other person considers us and his act of giving as a mere means to his own happiness, then we cannot be grateful.

In this respect, the objective, intelligible nature of gratitude reveals the possibility of good will among persons, for without it, gratitude would be impossible. Yet gratitude thereby also reveals something important for a metaphysics of the person, namely, that the person cannot be understood as pure entelechy striving for the self-fulfillment of his own potential and his own happiness. Rather, the person must be understood as having a transcendent structure such that he only finds himself when he loses himself by affirming and caring about goods and persons for their own sake.[20]

If the other person were to possess only an entelechy, and not a transtelechy,[21] i.e., if he would always have to be stuck only in himself and in his own interests, then that bond between persons, presupposed for gratitude, and thus the intelligible foundation of gratitude, would not exist. And this is no mere anthropological or even psychological state of affairs. Here is disclosed a deep metaphysical truth about the perfection of the person, who can direct himself to the real (to being as such) and the true and the good for their own sake, and is capable, and, thus, called to a transcending *adaequatio* of the mind, the will, and the heart to the true and the precious in itself. That we *should* be grateful points also to the absolute inherent value of gratitude and to the transcending value response contained in it.

2. Personalistic Metaphysics of Absolute Being in the Light of Gratitude

Gratitude, however, not only bears witness to the personhood of

---

[20] I have in mind here the value response and the interest in another person's objective good as such. Such an anti-eudemonistically understood affirmation of another person for his own sake stands at the center of the philosophical anthropology and ethics of Karol Wojtyla and Tadeusz Styczen.

[21] See Seifert, *Essere e persona* (Milano: Vita e Pensiero, 1989), chap. 9, where the Aristotelian ontology of life as entelechy (that which has its end in itself), which pertains primarily to living organisms as such, is thoroughly investigated through a personalistic metaphysics of *trans-tel-echy* (of having one's end beyond oneself in the object of true judgment and due response, and of first finding one's fulfillment in conforming oneself to the true and the good).

human beings, towards whom it is often directed, but also to the personhood of the source of all things.

To appreciate this, we must reflect once again on the addressee of gratitude. If we consider that phenomenon which Balduin Schwarz analyzed and called "anonymous gratitude,"[22] or even if we consider gratitude directed to another person, we invariably find on closer inspection a dimension of gratitude which goes beyond the human person to whom we are immediately grateful.

We could speak of a transcendent surplus of gratitude and say that in gratitude there lies the following metaphysical insight, namely, that, along with the human person to whom thankfulness is directed, an ultimate and unquestionably free origin of any benefit is known and recognized, and that only on the basis of this recognition (*reconnaissance*) of some absolute subject who can also be the addressee of gratitude are we aware that not the whole of the benefit that we receive from another human being can have its ultimate source in man. This follows from the fact that no human benefactor can bring about his own being, and from the fact that he does not possess his being with inner necessity. Thus, along with the gratitude and thanks *to him*, there is an element of thanks *for him* as for a gift. The addressee of this ultimate gratitude, however, cannot be the human person of the benefactor himself.

These insights, that the human beings we thank are themselves gifts and that the good deeds they do for us invariably point to gifts for which we cannot thank them, can also, oddly enough, be found in the Stoic Epictetus (who defended the idea that we should devote our energies exclusively to what is within our power). The idea that other human beings and goods—which as gifts are clearly not within our control—are nevertheless important for us and can and should be objects of our gratitude seems hardly in keeping with the foundation of his ethics. By leaving open a path for gratitude, however, Epictetus breaks through the strict philosophy of stoic self-sufficiency and autonomy:

---

[22] See, for example, *The Human person and the World of Values*, ed. by B. Schwarz (New York: Fordham University Press, 1960), pp. 168–191, especially pp. 185ff. See also, by the same author, "Über die Dankbarkeit," in *Wirklichkeit der Mitte. Beiträge zu einer Strukturanthropologie. Festgabe für August Vetter* (Freiburg: K. Alber, 1968), pp. 679–704. See also the beautiful reflections of D. Henrich, "Gedanken zur Dankbarkeit," in *Oikeiosis: Festschrift für Robert Spaemann*, ed. by R. Löw (Weinheim: 1987), pp. 69–89, which talks about the gratitude for being and thereby the metaphysical dimensions of gratitude.

Never say of anything, 'I lost it,' but say, 'I gave it back.' Has your
child died? It was given back. Has your wife died? She was given
back. . . . But you say, 'He who took it from me is wicked.' What
does it matter to you through whom the Giver asked it back?[23]

The text "On Providence" from the *Diatribes* places the ideal of a
perpetual gratitude for the innumerable goods which we do not receive
from other human beings far more clearly at the center of Epictetus'
ethics: "If we had sense we ought to do nothing else ... than to praise
and bless God and pay Him due thanks."[24]

Apart from the all-important gift of the being of the human benefactor as the condition for all that is received from him, many other
things which are not in his control are also gifts. Thus, in Seneca's example, it was also a gift for the master that his slave was not sick or
weak, that he was present at the right moment, that the superior strength

---

[23] See, "The Manual of Epictetus," 11, in *The Stoic and Epicurean Philosophers*, ed. by Whitney J. Oates, trans. by P. E. Matheson (New York: Random
House, 1940), p. 470.

[24] The passage in its entirety is as follows: "Are these the only works of
Providence in us? Nay, what words are enough to praise them or bring them
home to us? If we had sense we ought to do nothing else, in public and in private, than to praise and bless God and pay Him due thanks. Ought we not, as we
dig and plough and eat, to sing the hymn to God? 'Great is God that He gave us
these instruments wherewith we shall till the earth. Great is God that He has
given us hands, and power to swallow, and a belly, and the power to grow without knowing it, and to draw our breath in our sleep.' At every moment we ought
to sing these praises and above all the greatest and most divine praise, that God
gave us the faculty to comprehend these gifts and to use the way of reason.

"More than that: since most of you are walking in blindness, should there
not be some one to discharge this duty and sing praises to God for all? What else
can a lame old man as I am do but chant the praise of God? If, indeed, I were a
nightingale, I should sing as a nightingale, if a swan, as a swan; but as I am a rational creature I must praise God. This is my task, and I do it; and I will not
abandon this duty, so long as it is given me; and I invite you all to join in this
same song." See "Discourses of Epictetus," book I, chap. xvi, in *The Stoic and
Epicurean Philosophers*, ed. by Whitney J. Oates, trans. by P. E. Matheson
(New York: Random House, 1940), p. 253.
Here the deepest use of freedom, which is possible even for the old and
lame, is seen precisely in the thanks and due response to goods which are in no
way within one's power, and thus the characteristic stoic reduction of interest to
that which is within one's power—in favor of an ethics which places gratitude
and the due response at the center of attention—is radically overcome.

of the enemy was not so great that the effectiveness of the slave's action was thwarted, etc. In this way there are innumerable factors which lie outside of the control of a human benefactor, and which are conditions for the gift received through him. On the basis of this metaphysical fact—one which is always co-given—the thanks to a human being also always involves a thanks that goes beyond him. Gratitude, therefore, is ultimately not simply an inter-human act; it is a fundamental metaphysical act in which the person is always also grateful for something whose addressee cannot be another human being.

Yet, we have seen that gratitude by its nature can only be directed to a person as the free and ultimate author of a gift. Thus, in every instance of gratitude there is a directedness to an addressee other than the human one. And, therefore, thanking a human being is always co-thanking, a *syneucharizein* (to recall an expression of Antigone, in Sophocles' play by the same name, in which she says to Creon that it is not her nature "to co-hate [i.e., hate both her brothers], but to co-love"). As Antigone speaks of a co-loving, we speak here of a co-thanking with respect to the addressees of gratitude. In fact, in the strict sense, we can never ultimately thank a human, contingent subject alone, but always only co-thank him, provided we do not forget his contingency and with it the fact that, in a radical sense, he is never the ultimate author of the gift we receive through him.[25]

Even reflection on oneself as subject of gratitude confirms this metaphysical dimension of gratitude as revealing an absolute person as ultimate addressee. For the human subject of gratitude and thanking is every bit as contingent. The thousand-fold experience of one's contingency (in the experience of temporality, mortality, etc.) is also co-given in thanking. If we existed necessarily from ourselves and were perfect and the source of our perfections such as to have received no good, we

---

[25] Kierkegaard has also profoundly expressed this in various works, for instance in *Edifying Discourses* 2, "Every Good and Every Perfect Gift Is from Above." Here he writes: "Is then every human life a continuous chain of miracles? Or is it possible for a man's understanding to make its way through the interminable ranks of derived causes and effects, to penetrate all the intervening events, and thus find God? . . . For the thanksgiving the apostle speaks about is not the gratitude which is offered by one man to another; and those teachers of false doctrines believed, too, that the believers, by transgressing ceremony (by being ungrateful), sinned against God. Would not the same hold true of every man's relation to God, that every gift is a good and perfect gift when it is received with thanksgiving?" *Edifying Discourses*, vol. 1, pp. 46–47.

could not be grateful. At the very least—even if we may not exclude gratitude as a pure perfection and the possibility of a divine gratitude (and within the Christian belief in the Trinity and its abundance of *caritas* we may not)[26]—the metaphysical insight that we possess neither our being nor our goodness purely from ourselves is always connected to human gratitude. We can be grateful only if we know and recognize our contingency. Thus, gratitude always contains an element of humility, and, as Epictetus says, is at the same time gratitude for the gift of one's own being, for the gift of one's person.[27]

In order to understand the connection between humility and gratitude better, we must also consider the particular personal structure of humility. Humility helps us to avoid taking things for granted, the arch-enemy of all that is truly great. It overcomes blindness to values, which prevents us from appreciating the innumerable, immeasurable gifts in our lives, and it opens up the mind in general.

Gratitude is thus also indissolubly bound up with humility, with the joyful acceptance of our contingency and the contingency of all human benefactors. It is from this starting point that Max Scheler launches his insights into the essential connection between humility and gratitude.

> To the extent that we, letting go, . . . truly "lose" ourselves, "give" ourselves, our whole self, all its potential value, its dignity and good repute—to which the proud one firmly clings—and "give" ourselves, . . . to that extent we are "humble." . . . Dare to wonder in gratitude at not not-being; that there is something at all—and not nothing instead. Dare to . . . renounce every claim to be "worthy" of any kind of fortune, and see it as a gift only. Then, only, are you humble. . . . Addison allows his "Stoic" to say: "We desire, my dear Lucilius, to prefer

---

[26] For the fundamental difference between pure and mixed perfections see Josef Seifert, *Essere e persona* (Milano: Vita e Pensiero, 1989), chap. 5.

[27] "You have received everything, nay your very self, from Another, and yet you complain and blame the Giver if He takes anything away from you. Who are you and for what have you come? Did He not bring you into the world? . . . And in what character did He bring you into life? Was it not as a mortal . . .? Will you not . . . when God leads you forth, go away with an obeisance to Him and thanksgiving for what you have heard and seen? . . . Leave it and depart, full of gratitude and respect." See Epictetus, *Discourses of Epictetus*, ed. by Whitney J. Oates, trans. by P. E. Matheson (New York: Random House, 1940), p. 416.

This idea of gratitude for one's very self as an element of every gratitude is reminiscent of the central discussions of T. Styczen on an ethics, philosophical anthropology, and metaphysics of gratitude.

to happiness the worthiness of possessing it," a sentence which conveys also a basic thought of Kant's Ethics. Indeed, this statement . . . is not half-true, not false—it is diabolical. Humility bids you accept *thankfully* all happiness, even the simplest, the most trifling pleasure touching your senses (Nerven), as well as the deepest bliss which, pervading your being, raises you and all being into divine light. It bids you never to delude yourself into thinking that you "deserve" even the smallest part. Is there a purer love than to *grant* to the other the blessedness of loving, and even to *allow* things, which come our way only by chance, the appearance of a certain goodness—even there where the world "in justice demands" services which are rendered by the other purely out of love, or provided accidentally by things—as by the chair which happens to be near when we wish to sit down, or by the sunshine when we do not have an umbrella? Is it not also deserving of gratitude that the world contains one just person, if he, by chance, acts "justly" towards us?

And as humility is the source from which gratitude can spring, pride is the source of value-darkness and ingratitude:

The proud one, whose eye is fixed, as if spellbound, on his own worth, lives, of necessity, in night and darkness. His world of values becomes darker from minute to minute, since each value which he beholds appears to him as a theft and robbery from his own worth (Selbstwert). Thus he becomes a devil and negator. Locked in the prison of his pride, the walls grow and grow, closing him off from the daylight of the world. Can you see the self-seeking (Ich-gierige), jealous eye as he knits his brow? Humility, on the other hand, *opens* the mind's eye to all the world's values. Only humility, which proceeds as if nothing is deserved and everything is gift and wonder, can win all things. She still allows one to perceive the magnificence of space in which bodies can spread themselves as they please without falling apart. And how much more wonderful and more deserving of gratitude is it that there is space, time, light and air, the ocean and flowers. Ever anew she joyfully discovers foot and hand and eye, as things whose value we seem capable of grasping only when they are rare and others do not possess them![28] Be humble, and you will immediately be

---

[28] Kierkegaard has delved deeply into this connection between humility and gratitude for the glory of being human. See S. Kierkegaard, *Edifying Discourses*, vol. 2, p. 62ff. Here Kierkegaard interprets the glorious raiment of the lily in light of the still more glorious one which man has received through human nature. He speaks of the glory of the human body as "visible garb," and his "spirit" as invisible garb. One is reminded of the poem by M. Claudius, "Daily to Sing":

rich and powerful. Because you no longer "deserve" anything, all things will be given to you, for humility is the virtue of the rich, as pride belongs to the poor. *All* pride is "beggar's pride." . . . [H]ow could the proud one, who "will not allow himself to give," and will not knowingly accept anything, feel and understand the *meaning* of the world?[29]

Only to the extent to which I joyfully accept and recognize in humility my not being God, my contingency, can I be thankful. If I suppose I possess my being and goodness from some inner necessity or purely from my own will, then I cannot be grateful in a human way, or would even refuse gratitude in a negative act. For the recognition which lies in the humility of my contingency is too much for my pride. This is captured in Goethe's poem "Prometheus," and in Schubert's song on the same.

If, however, one's own contingency must be an objective metaphysical condition of all human gratitude, and, at the same time, a metaphysical truth known and recognized by the subject, then in gratitude there is always also an implication of thanks for my own contingent being as the ultimate gift and condition of all other gifts. For without existence I could neither receive a gift from another person nor from nature. Thus, there is also in the awareness of one's contingency—which, as we have seen, is a condition for gratitude—an element of gratitude for one's own being as something which is given to one, and as the condition for the possibility of gratitude.

If, however, gratitude necessarily pertains to a person, then it is directed to someone other than a human person as its ultimate addressee in two ways: in its surplus regarding the human addressee, and regarding the gift that the subject is to himself. A super-human person as the ultimate addressee of gratitude is out of the question if he is also contingent, and thus also a gift to himself. Thus, the endpoint at which the move-

---

"Like a child over a Christmas gift
I thank God and rejoice,
That I am, am! and that you are mine,
Oh beautiful human face."

[29] See M. Scheler, *Zur Rehabilitierung der Tugend* (Zürich: Arche Verlag, 1950), pp. 18ff. [Translators note: A translation of Scheler's text by Barbara Fiand can be found in *Aletheia* (Irving, Texas: The International Academy of Philosophy Press, 1981), vol. 2, pp. 210–19. Slight changes have been made in Fiand's translation for reasons of flow to accommodate Seifert's editing of the passages.]

ment of gratitude toward the ultimate origin of the gifts stops can only be an absolute being.

Since, however, gratitude by nature can only apply to a free, personal being, then even gratitude towards human beings at its deepest level directs itself beyond human beings to an absolute and free person, who alone can bring a contingent person forth and give him to himself. Apart from an observation which we make with Descartes on the origin of the finite person in an absolute one, which, along with a proof for a personal God, shows Him to be the ultimate addressee of gratitude, aside from this we could come to know, from the metaphysical dimension of gratitude itself, that the absolute addressee can only be a personal and, at the same time, absolute being. If gratitude can only have as addressee a free benevolent person vis-á-vis me or a loved one, then the transcendent surplus and the dimension of gratitude which goes beyond every human and contingent addressee (because we as the subject of gratitude understand that such giving is also given to them as well as to us) is necessarily directed to a person who is loving and absolute.

Of course, from the evident phenomenologically discovered fact that gratitude subjectively necessitates an ultimate personal addressee nothing follows regarding its objective existence. For gratitude could be existentially absurd, implying something for consciousness which does not objectively exist. A purely subjective presupposition for consciousness that a divine person as author of my being also really exists (and with it the conditions under which the ultimate addressee of human gratitude can actually become the addressee of gratitude) does, of course, not prove the objective ontic reality of such a presupposition.

All the same, the choice remains: either we suppose that gratitude, in its innermost being and in its metaphysical implications, is groundless; either we declare a noble act—one that is constitutive for humanity, an act without which a human being would not be human, and one which is morally obligatory—either we declare such an act, gratitude, as absurdly frustrated with regard to its metaphysical foundations. Or we see in it the prophetic witness[30] for the existence of Him from Whom and through Whom all gifts and benefits come, and recognize an ultimate metaphysical and religious dimension in every instance of gratitude.

In addition, however, the analysis of a personal act like gratitude, which possesses an intrinsically necessary and uninventibly intelligible

---

[30] This idea is similar to Gabriel Marcel's argument for immortality, which takes its starting point in the prophetic voice of love and fidelity as evidence for the life of the beloved beyond the grave.

nature, is completely different from the analysis of merely subjective, conscious desires. The inner value of gratitude, its recognition of the person of the giver, along with its metaphysical implications, are thoroughly given to our mind. All that is included here springs from the inner, true nature of gratitude, and not from conventional rules of social behavior. Therefore, the conditions of the possibility of gratitude are not merely subjective conditions in Kant's sense, heuristic fictions like Kant's transcendental ideas, but objective, ontic conditions of the same, which, every bit as reliably as the analysis of more general ontic structures, can lead to the recognition of the objective existence of absolute being.

Moreover, those metaphysical discoveries which are not gathered from gratitude but which underlie it—the contingency of every finite subject and his ungroundedness in himself or in an impersonal or imperfect absolute being—are objective findings which can be discovered independently of the analysis of the experience of gratitude. Thus, the knowledge that in the absolute good—to whose most pure perfection even personhood belongs—resides the only possible and legitimate origin of every perfect gift, and that therefore only the divine personal being can be the ultimate addressee of every act of gratitude to whom all human thanks from its innermost depth ascends, this knowledge is not only gathered from the essence of gratitude, but ultimately grounds it.

The foregoing reflections may be understood as an exercise in Socratic maieutics.[31] They are only intended to bring to light commonly forgotten yet implicitly and universally known truths which every grateful person has himself already discovered in his experience of gratitude before philosophy makes them explicit. The reflections were intended to enable us to remember explicitly those eminently important metaphysical states of affairs which are co-given in the simplest experience of gratitude, but which are, for the most part, hidden before theoretical reflection uncovers them.

---

[31] As everyone knows, Socrates likened himself to a midwife, his mother's profession, and explained the task of philosophy in these terms. Just as the midwife neither begets nor gives birth, but only helps the mother to give birth herself, so, too, the philosopher does not produce knowledge in others, but only aids them in acquiring it themselves. Indeed, he only helps them "remember" such insights which they already possess, pre-philosophically, in their experience. So we may interpret Plato—short of a strict *anamnesis* theory of knowledge (that all knowledge is recollection) from a previous life. Besides Plato's *Meno*, see also his *Theaetetus*, 149ff.

COVETOUSNESS

Loretta Marra

Covetousness is a morally evil interior personal act or attitude involving an inordinate longing for some perceived good. It has several essential features, which we shall examine after making one brief psychological observation. In its "pure" form, covetousness is rarely encountered in adults, except in the case of a thievish man. In most cases, it is children who are truly, or "merely" covetous, for they are usually as yet too unreflective to allow covetousness to flower into envy. For example, a child will often desperately desire a bicycle like the one owned by a friend. He may think of it day and night, always asking his parents to get him one, always hoping to find it waiting for him when he returns from school. However excessive his desire may be, he need have no ill feeling toward his friend (this would be the beginning of envy)—he simply desires the bicycle for the pleasure it can afford him.

This observation leads us to see a first essential feature of covetousness, namely, that it is rooted in concupiscence rather than in pride. In envy, one may also frantically desire an object, but it is always desired with an eye to hurting or humiliating the present possessor. In contrast, covetousness is naive. The child mentioned above, like all true coveters, simply wants a nice toy "for its own sake."

A second important feature of covetousness is that the coveted object must be seen as "belonging to another." Even if the coveted object is a person, "John's wife Jane," this remains true. As "Jane, my lovely neighbor," she may be loved or lusted after, but the exact moment of covetousness is found only when she is looked at, not only as "something I want," but as "something I want *that belongs to someone else.*"

It is to be emphasized that no hatred, or even ill-feeling need be directed toward the person who now enjoys the good. In covetousness, one focuses specifically on the desired object itself, which is possessed by another, rather than on the possessor, "that cursed villain John," who has something I desire.

A third crucial feature of covetousness is that its object either be material, or somehow strongly symbolized by some material thing. It seems inappropriate to speak of one man "coveting" the holiness of another, or coveting his great virtue, nor could one exactly covet a man's intelligence or wit, though one can of course thoroughly envy a man on account of any of these things.

At this point it could be asked: Is it not possible to covet something that is non-material in quite another sense? For instance, could I not covet the love that my neighbor's wife bestows upon him, her husband? (Prescind now from any envy or jealousy on my part.) As such a man looks upon his neighbor's happy lot, his attitude might take one of two forms. He might say, "Would that *I* were loved this deeply by a woman such as she," or he might say, "Would that I were loved thus by this very woman—if she were only *my* wife!"

Let us investigate whether either of these expressions constitutes a covetous state of mind. In the first one of the attitudes mentioned, the man's longing is very unspecific. He sees that the love of this woman renders the neighbor happy, and considers that he too would like to be blessed by similar good fortune. This is so far a very natural, and indeed legitimate longing for affection. But even if the longing becomes inordinate, even if it begins to occupy all of his thoughts to the point where he cannot even go about his daily tasks, it still does not seem that he "covets" love. The term "crave" seems to apply much better to this all-consuming desire which obsesses him. This leads us to see yet another essential feature of covetousness: namely, that its object must be specific. Covetousness does not involve a vague longing for "something." It rather "latches on" and addresses itself to a determinate object. One cannot covet love or peace or anything of the sort; one can only pine after them.

We are now led at once to see an additional fundamental characteristic of covetousness, namely that the object to which it directs itself must already be in existence. This is best seen if we refer to the second of the possible attitudes the man in our example might take towards his neighbor's wife, wherein he desires the love of this specific woman, Jane. At first, this might appear to be covetousness, since the desired object is very specific, it is at least rooted in a material being, Jane, and the desire is inordinate. However, a closer examination shows the case to be otherwise.

The man does not exactly desire "Jane's love," but rather "Jane's love for *me*." This is going to be both a different *sort* of love from her loves for her friends, parents, etc., as well as a new and different *act* of love from any other acts of even this same spousal sort of love which she may have in the past bestowed on others. That is, he does not precisely desire "the love Jane has for her husband," but a new love, of the same sort, yet distinct from her present love for her spouse. In fact, he would most likely want to see her presently existing love die, to make room for her new-found love of him, the neighbor. This latter part of his attitude would belong to envy.

What he desires is something that does not exist: the love of a certain woman for him. His longing that it might come into existence is not the same as covetousness. The object of his desire is determinate in that he wants the love of a specific woman rather than "someone to love me," but it is highly indeterminate in that it simply does not exist. It seems improper to speak of a man coveting a good that is as yet a phantom and unreal.

A further essential characteristic is that covetousness, because of its essential orientation to self, is directed only at objects which are looked at under the aspect of being either subjectively satisfying or objective goods for the person. The object may of course have great intrinsic value, but this is by no means thematic in covetousness. One cannot covet an actual objective value *per se*, nor any object *in virtue* of such a value. For instance, I could not covet my friend's da Vinci masterpiece on account of its intrinsic worth as such, but rather because of its ability to please. The intrinsic worth may well be the ground of this ability to please, and it may be the object of my un-self-centered admiration, but the painting is specifically coveted for what it can provide *me*. *Objective value* as such lends itself easily to love or hate, but not to covetousness. This is grounded in the fact that value (as such) addresses itself to the spiritual center in man, the center from which sins of pride arise. As we have noted, covetousness is rooted in concupiscence, and is thus untouched one way or the other by objective value in the coveted object.

An additional feature of covetousness is that its object must be seen as being attainable in principle by the covetous person. In other words, it must seem possible in principle for me to acquire that which my neighbor has and I have not. This fact would exclude, for instance, the possibility of a person coveting divinity. One can envy God His divinity, but as it is in principle impossible for anyone to usurp His position, it is not subject to being coveted. This is easier seen in a more ordinary example: If I have recently lost my right arm, and I look about and see a person fortunate enough to have both his limbs, I can hate and envy him, and even hope that his own arm be lost, but I cannot covet the arm. Covetousness always contains some element of awareness or at least conviction that the object could be acquired. A merely covetous man, with no envy or bitterness in him, will turn simply to a regretful longing for an object, once he discovers that in principle, it can never be his.

One possible further characteristic of covetousness suggests itself here; however, it must be regarded as put forth only tentatively, because it is not entirely clear, as will be seen. It seems that covetousness can only arise in a man who has a relative lack of need for the coveted object. For example, it does not seem covetous for a man dying of thirst to wish desperately for the water in possession of his neighbor who has far more than enough. Here, it is not a question of his convenience or pleasure, but of his very life. His neighbor does not need the glass of water, and would in no way be injured by being deprived of it. Yet it does seem covetous for this same thirsty man to have the same desperate wish to get his hands on the glass of water just given to another whom he knows to be yet closer to death than he himself.

On the other hand, it could be argued that one can indeed covet something for which one has genuine need. In the film by Vittoria La Sica, *The Bicycle Thief*, a man in postwar Milan has at long last succeeded in obtaining employment by means of which he can keep himself and his family alive. The job absolutely requires that he own a bicycle. On his first day on the job, his bicycle is stolen on the street, and he spends days in a desperate, excruciating, and hopeless search for it. Finally, he sees thousands of bicycles parked outside a sports stadium while the owners are inside. Thanks to the genius of the director, we live through all of his turmoil with him: the injustice of the theft of his own bicycle, the predicament of his wife and son, and the profusion of bicycles parked there without owners—out of so many, what harm could the loss of one bring? It becomes impossible to think any longer of the fact that each of these is owned by someone else, who might also depend on the bicycle for his livelihood. The owners are entirely anonymous. Besides, if the owner can afford, in these hard times, to attend a sports event, he can probably live without his bicycle. After a terrible struggle with guilt and fear, the man steals one, only to be apprehended immediately by the police.

Although I doubt that covetousness could be said to be present in such a situation, I am not sure—I think a fairly good case could be made that he does covet the bicycle which he steals.

Rather than saying that it is an essential characteristic of covetousness that it arises only where there is a relative lack of need of the coveted object, we should look at it from a different point of view. In speaking of the relationship between need and covetousness, perhaps we should call those interior acts covetous which would inspire the person to commit a true theft; that is, to take that which belongs to another against the just wishes of the owner. In contrast, if the interior act is one which would inspire the person to take what is his by right, though not in fact, it would not be covetous. This leads us to reformulate our final essential characteristic of covetousness thus: Not only must the object of covetousness be seen as belonging to another—mentioned as the second feature; it must in fact belong to the other, and he thus be entirely within his right to refuse it to me, should I request it of him. Thus the man who is moments away from death from thirst is entitled by his greater need to keep for himself the water he may receive, even if he has a neighbor who is in a bad way from thirst, but not quite as bad as he himself. If the man suffering less is aware of these circumstances, he is guilty if he wishes to deprive the other of the water. In contrast, if a man is dying of thirst in the presence of another who has an abundance, his desperate wish is for something which is by right his already, by virtue of his great need on the one hand, and the other's surplus on the other. This just longing for something which in fact belongs to him already seems far removed from covetousness, which involves an unjust longing for something that belongs to someone else.

There is one further confusing question about the nature of covetousness. Is a covetous act necessarily directed at a specific individual object, or rather at the exact attributes which identify it? That is, if covetousness is to be satisfied, must the coveter possess the precise object which first aroused his longing, or would it suffice for him to have another which would be exactly similar? I suspect that this will vary according to the nature of the object in question, as well as the character of the coveter. Probably, in the case of an ordinary object, e.g., a bicycle, a substitute would suffice to quell covetousness. But in the case of an object whose very identity is partially inherent in the fact that it is unique or very rare, it would probably not satisfy the coveter even if an indistinguishable object were found. For instance, if I covet the Hope Diamond, it would probably do no good for someone to discover and present me with a diamond indistinguishable from it; in fact it would be likely to disappoint me deeply even to learn that such a duplicate existed. In this case, much of the lure is rooted in the fact that the gem is unique and irreplaceable, and my covetousness was not directed toward "an exquisite diamond" but toward the Hope Diamond.

It is, however, beyond the scope of this work to pursue this further; we leave it to some future investigation.

Covetousness is essentially opposed to generosity. It is a distinctly selfish attitude in which a person's own comfort and pleasure become disproportionately more important to him than the good of others. He need not actively desire that his neighbor's downfall result from his own acquisition of the coveted object, but if such a thing were to result, he would not let himself be hindered from taking the object if he were able.

A covetous man would freely take advantage of the liberality of an over-generous friend; covetousness contains an element of greed. The two are not identical, however, since greed and covetousness have quite different natures. The greedy man wants to collect all good things to himself almost as a matter of principle. He wants "things" as such. He need not see someone else owning a good thing before he wants it; rather, he goes through life "on the lookout," as it were, for more enjoyable things to acquire. The covetous man, on the other hand, desires this thing, or at least, "something exactly similar to this." He sees something and subsequently begins to thirst for it. He is not necessarily predisposed to covet every enjoyable thing because it is enjoyable. Rather, something good catches his eye, and he is infected with the inordinate desire for this particular enjoyable thing.

Covetousness can be the occasion of envy. Suppose I see the expensive new car of a casual acquaintance, and I begin to desire it more and more. Soon, my focus switches from the car to its owner, and a new and deeper poison enters my heart. I begin to dislike the owner and then hate him for no other reason than that he owns this wonderful car, while I am obliged to get about in a decrepit heap of rust. The situation is most unjust. Ultimately, I forget almost completely the car as desirable to me, and believe that I should be thoroughly happy if I could only learn that it had been in a devastating accident. And so on. Here, envy has been aroused by deprivation of a coveted object, and as the element of envy grows, that of covetousness tends to be pushed further and further into the background.

ON PITY AND SYMPATHY

William Marra

We all surely have our own joys and sorrows, and pleasures and pains, rooted strictly in *what happens to us*. Thus, *I* receive a coveted award and rejoice, or *I* am diagnosed with a serious illness and I worry and sorrow, or *I* suffer the pains of a broken leg and great damage to muscle and nerve tissue. But sometimes, *what happens to "others"* can result in a genuine emotional experience within us: we suffer *with* or *for* another; likewise, we are happy with or for another person. Also, even when the "other" is not a fellow human, or not even an animal subject to suffering, we can be profoundly moved by some event and say, at least to ourselves: "Ah! The pity of it all!"

This essay means to analyze in some detail the distinction between what I shall call *sympathy* and *pity*, respectively. What is common to both in my use of the terms is some *negative* feeling on my part somehow based on an "evil" *afflicting some other thing*.

We do well at the onset to notice, and then rule out, several counterfeits to genuine sympathy and pity. The first may be called "aesthetic revulsion." I may witness a fellow human undergoing great suffering and *I shrink from the sight*. It is not that I am unconcerned with him or with his ordeal. But my sensibilities are "offended" by the sight of ugly wounds, by the stench, and by the moans and strangulated speech of the victim. My one thought is "to get out of here"—to leave the hospital, or the war zone, and to surround myself with pleasant things.

Another counterfeit may be termed "future fear." My witnessing the plight of another serves only to torture me with the thought that "next time *I* could be the one painfully gasping for breath or writhing in agony." There is here, obviously, no hint of any genuine sympathy for the one suffering now. His plight is but the occasion for fearful reflections on my own vulnerability.

Still a third reality, by no means deserving the title of "counterfeit," must be mentioned and discussed briefly because in a certain way it might become confused with both pity and sympathy, and prejudice the exact understanding of their respective natures. I refer to *mercy* on the part of a "superior" who has the strict right and even obligation *in justice* to punish another or exact some payment from another, but who "takes pity on the inferior" who may be (but need not be) kneeling before him, begging for mercy.

Mercy, if indeed it is granted, comes from the *generosity* of the superior; he cancels a just penalty, he writes off a just debt. We may say that he *forgives* the other. Perhaps the reason for this generous canceling lies in a prior genuine feeling of sympathy or pity for the other, especially if the latter humbly pleads his cause and "throws himself upon the superior's mercy." Even so, the merciful act is neither pity, nor sympathy.

Sympathy

I use the term 'sympathy' to mean a strict *fellow-feeling*: I suffer *with* you. Your suffering somehow moves me to *com*-passion. No matter how well things go in my own life, a cloud of sorrow dims my interior sunshine, and at times totally eclipses it, simply because you now suffer greatly *and I suffer along with you.*

Of course, "sympathy" in its etymological sense need not be restricted to *suffering*; thus, I may *rejoice with you* when you receive good news and are jubilant and grateful. This "positive" sense of sympathy will be referred to a few times in what follows so as to help me draw the sharpest line possible between sympathy, positive or negative, and pity, *which is always something "negative."* In the greater part of this essay, however, I mean to restrict sympathy to its more common meaning—my *suffering* with you, my grieving when you grieve, my sharing your anxious concerns, and the like.

How is one to explain this touching solidarity of one person with another when the latter suffers? Is it really the case that *what happens to you truly happens to me also,* and that, therefore, my sympathy for you, my suffering with you, is rooted in my understanding—however implicit—that "the bell tolls for me," and that, in a profoundly true sense, *I am you*? Must we say, therefore, that the ultimate basis of all "fellow-feeling" is some metaphysical *unity* of all personal consciousness? Does some form of *pantheism* or of *panpsychism* offer the true explanation for genuine sympathy?

Before we consider such "explanations," we should explore sympathy a bit further. It is certainly not the case that all humans spontaneously grieve when they learn of the sad plight of some fellow human. Suppose that I *hate* N for whatever reason, and I learn that he has suffered a financial loss, a political defeat, or a serious and painful illness; or that his marriage is in ruins and he is despondent. Do I grieve with him? By no means. His plight rejoices me! I look upon his ill fortune as "something he well deserves," even as something which I should like to have inflicted upon him myself.

Or suppose that I am "indifferent to him." I look upon his sad plight with no greater interest than upon the results of some sports competition between strangers. Just why *should* his sufferings move me to suffer with him? If I even notice them at all, I might remark, "Better that this happened to him than to me." This is the classical word of *hardness of heart*. I shrug off the evils afflicting anyone except myself and the small circle whose interests I identify with my own.

Genuine sympathy is most clearly itself and most certainly identified when the one suffering *is loved* by me. But it can also occur if I am at least "tender of heart" so that the plight even of strangers, once it is brought to my attention, can move me to sympathize with them, and to take action to alleviate it.

In all cases of such genuine sympathy do I view the victim as *really identified with me?* Is my suffering with N to be explained as being rooted in some profound, even if dim, understanding that *it is I who really suffer*? Does my "tenderness of heart" really refer to my grasp of the "metaphysical truth" that *I and N are one?* Even more, when I *love* N, do I really simply *love myself*?

There are, to be sure, instances when a supposed love of mine for N is really a disguised self-love. I look upon certain other persons, whether family, friends, or even servants, as the prolongation of my ego. I react swiftly to any assault upon them as being an assault against my own person. Their successes and triumphs—their very pleasures and joys—are likewise interpreted by me such as to afford me *vicarious* experiences: as if it were *I* who triumph, *I* who am pleased, *I* who rejoice.

But what has this to do with real love, real concern for the beloved's trials, real joy because the loved one is happy? The unproved dogma, so widely believed in philosophical and psychological circles, that "all love is self-love" should be forced to produce its credentials and, failing this, should be abandoned as an unfortunate slogan which bars the way to a true understanding of love—and of sympathy and of many other profound data rooted in the mystery of personal relations.

We must be careful to distinguish sympathy in my sense from what may be called a "feeling in common": over some third reality. Real sympathy demands that first *you* suffer or rejoice; I, who love you or who at least have a tender heart, "enter into your life." My own feelings are engendered by *your* feelings. But suppose that you and I are both interested in the outcome of some sporting or political contest; or suppose that we both love a third person. The contest turns out favorably: *I* rejoice and *you also* rejoice. Or the beloved third person dies: *I* sorrow and *you* sorrow. In all these cases, we do indeed have "feelings in common," but not sympathy in any sense. *The same object* moves me to rejoice and you to rejoice; me to sorrow and you to sorrow. But *you* are not the object of my feelings here. It may also happen, of course, that after my primary response to the common reason for our grief—e.g., the death of the beloved third person—I notice your grief; and, of course, that following my primary response to the common reason for our grief—e.g., the death of the beloved third person—I notice your grief and *sympathize with you*. But this is another experience altogether, in no way essentially related to the original *grief in common* over the common beloved's death.

Pity

Whereas sympathy in my sense of the term demands that some other person *consciously suffers or rejoices*, so that I *suffer or rejoice with him*, pity has no such requirement. I may see a blind child, or a seriously handicapped or retarded child, happily playing with his friends. Just what is there to *sympathize* with? Again, I may come to know a man who seems to be prosperous and happy, but *who is a great sinner* and so inflicts grave damage upon his moral welfare, even to the point of possible eternal damnation. Can I "sympathize with him"?

There can be no fellow-feeling in such cases. But this in no way excludes our exclaiming: "How sad that this should be! The pity of it all!" We somehow "look negatively" upon the object or event that evokes our pity—quite apart from any *conscious suffering* on the object-side. Even when there is such a suffering to which we respond with sympathy, there can also be this "judgment of pity" which does not concern suffering *with* the other, but suffering "on account of the evil befalling the other."

Pity, therefore, is something different from the suffering-with another person or even perhaps with an animal. Pity is rather "the sadness of knowing" that *something is awry*, regardless of the presence or absence of suffering on the "victim's" part.

Thus, the correct way of speaking of my pity would be: I pity the child because he is blind, and the sinner because he injures himself.

Can I also "pity"—at least in some acceptably analogous sense—*the scenes of life*? It is sad: that the majestic oak tree must finally perish; that beautiful structures are abandoned and left to decay; that the strong become feeble; even that the wounded deer crawls into some sheltered forest space and awaits a lingering death. Are not all these scenes—and countless others still more lamentable—such as to excite a "negative feeling" within me akin to the pity I feel towards the blind but happy child and the prosperous sinner?

Let us look more closely at these last two cases. In both, we have supposed that the persons involved do not *consciously suffer*. Yet in both cases we recognize a serious "damage" to the person: the one physical, the other moral and spiritual; the one totally inflicted "from without," the other more or less *self-inflicted*. When, therefore, I *pity* either person, it is as if my heart addresses *him* with these words: "Alas! That you should bear such damages, that what *might have been perfect* is now seriously flawed!"

But could not pity exist and be fully real even if not addressed to the victim? In fact, do we not often try to hide our feelings of pity when we mix with "handicapped" people? Even thought *they* may not suffer, *we* feel a twinge within us when we grasp their plight, and we then usually try to mask the feeling lest they take offense. But the pity is real, even though addressed to no one. And the pity came into being just because we grasped some "damage" done to another, whether or not he knows it, and whether or not we address him about the damage.

Do I then "pity" the wounded deer? To the extent that I *personify* this injured animal, a certain analogous sense of pity might seem to obtain. But what of the majestic oak or the abandoned beautiful building? I cannot really personify either. And yet I do suffer at the thought of their perishing. I do think that there is something sad about their plight.

If I am disposed to "address" anyone in these cases, exactly who or what would the addressee be? Some or all of my fellow men? Perhaps God?

In his *Poetics*, Aristotle again and again insists on linking "Tragedy" with *pity and fear* in the observer. And he notes that "pity is occasioned

by undeserved misfortune." He wants the hero of every tragedy, therefore, to be "an intermediate kind of personage, a man not pre-eminently
virtuous and just, whose misfortune, however, is not brought upon him
by vice and depravity, but by some error of judgment . . ." Thus Aristotle
would not think it a reason for pity if "an extremely bad man is seen falling from happiness into misery." There has to be an *undeserved* plight.

Aristotle's concept of pity may be of some use to us here apart from
its intended use in literary criticism. We who observe the world in its
different levels cannot fail to grasp an essential note of death and decay—in everything. Nothing escapes Time's certain victory over every
earthly existent. The impersonal living things—the individual plants or
trees or insects or large animals—have different spans allotted to them
but each in its turn will surely die. And so will every man. The newborn
baby, as much as the bent-over ancient, has no way to cleave to this
earthly existence. So too the different dreams and plots of men, if ever
they enjoy even some temporal success, will in the end come to naught.

With Aristotle, we may ask: Is all this *deserved*? With pessimists
like Schopenhauer, we may further ask: Is there not something "tragic"
about earthly existence as such, and, much more, about *the sentence of
death* uniformly imposed upon every human life and plan and hope? And
does not all Nature seem to complain: "I might endure, I *should* endure—but I am helpless before decay and death"?

If we thus are entitled to "pity" everything in Nature just because "it
has been denied permanence," much more can we "pity" the child born
blind or retarded, and even the sinner who risks just punishment which
he does not desire, simply because he freely wills unlawful things which
he does desire.

"The pity of it all!" We exclaim this to no one person in particular.
But we mean to formulate, and perhaps outwardly express, "our judgment of sadness" on the plight of all things temporal because they seem
irrevocably condemned to pass away. We are also saddened over each
particular case wherein some thing fails to achieve even the relative perfection which Time might be expected to allow to happen.

Our pity, in the general sense suggested above, is surely well-
grounded in an objectively "sad" reality and to that extent is justified.
But it need not, and should not, be absolute. To those indeed who know
of nothing beyond Time, the "judgment of sadness" is simply correct—
and inevitable. The more such persons are sensitive to the secrets of
Nature, to the tender and frail existence of so many "little things," the

more saddened will they be when they focus on Time—which is but a kinder name for Death.

With still deeper sadness will they look upon the blind children, the lame, and the poor. Even those who suffer justly will be the objects of their pity. They will see the hundreds of thousands of criminals caged like animals in the prisons of the world, and they will exclaim: "What a waste! What a pity!"

Is there no relief for this judgment of sadness? Must we resign ourselves to "honest pessimism" as the only "realism"? Or, worse, are we entitled to nurture one or another "escape" lest we focus too hard on the sad realities of life?

Certainly, we must allow the *truth* of the *fact of evil* to register strongly in our consciousness. Virgil's poignant expression, "*sunt lacrimae rerum*," well describes an essential feature of our earthly lives: "There *are* things which call for our tears"—and our pity.

But if a personal, just, merciful, and holy God really exists, if *His* will must ultimately prevail, then we may permit ourselves the hope that all the evils of time can somehow be transcended—*redeemed*. This "ultimate redemption" is not now apparent to us "by sight," but it is unmistakably an important element in the Christian Gospel and is thus accessible to supernatural faith.

Meanwhile, genuine tragedy in great literature somehow manages at once to move us to profound pity *and* to "console" and even delight us with a mysterious hint that certain things exist which "are stronger than death"—and suffering and imperfection and evils of any kind.

St. Augustine in the *Confessions*, book 3, chapter 2, muses over his fascination with the sad narratives depicted in the theater: "In those days I used to share the joy of stage lovers and their sinful pleasure in each other even though it was all done in make-believe for the sake of entertainment; and when they were parted, pity of a sort [sympathy in our sense] led me to share their grief. I enjoyed both these emotions equally." He then continues: "But now I feel more pity for a man who is happy in his sins than for one who has to endure the ordeal of forgoing some harmful pleasure or of being deprived of some enjoyment which was really an affliction. Of the two, this sort of pity is certainly the more genuine, but the sorrow which it causes is not a source of pleasure. For although a man who is sorry for the sufferings of others deserves praise for his charity, nevertheless, if his pity is genuine, he would prefer that there should be no cause for his sorrow."

Pity and Merciful Actions

There is an essential feature of pity which we must now consider, that which moves us to what we might call "merciful action"—*to our doing something about* the reality which has called forth our pity. We desire *to do what we can* to cancel out the evil or, at least, to alleviate the suffering or destruction in question. Often, this desire is condemned to frustration. Can we restore sight to the blind, can we cleanse the immoral man from his sinful past and, even better, cause him *to convert*— to follow a profoundly different way of life? Can we restore the former glory and vitality of a ravaged institution?

Even so, whatever the degree of our impotence, genuine pity must include the *desire* to undo the present evils, to restore things to goodness and perfection, and *to do what we can, however little*, so that the object of our pity becomes objectively less tragic, less "entitled" to evoke from us that pity which exclaims, "Alas! That this should be so!"

We must take care, however, to distinguish "mercy" *in the strict sense* from what we have spoken of above as "merciful actions"—rooted in at least the wish to mold the world "nearer to the heart's desire." To repeat what we mentioned at the very beginning of this essay: Mercy in the strict sense must always be understood in relation to *justice*—as that "which overrides" justice. Thus, one finds mercy when a just judgment has been passed upon a malefactor *and a just penalty imposed*. Mercy obtains when the judge "cancels out the penalty," usually at the plea of the malefactor. Mercy always involves a "juridical superior" mitigating or even totally dissolving a just punishment.

Merciful actions in our sense involve no such superiority. In fact it is just because we so often sense our own helplessness that we are moved to exclaim: "The pity of it all!"

The Hard-Hearted Man

In contrast to the attitudes of sympathy and pity discussed above stands the empty response of the hard-hearted man. He is, of course, keenly alive to whatever evils threaten to afflict him, and he savors the pleasures and delights and victories which may come his way. But *he is unmoved* by the sufferings of others or even by their joys. Nor can he spare the slightest twinge of pity for death and decay and imperfections.

This type of man is in fact most pitiful. Simply by glancing at him, we can appreciate what we may call the *gift* of being open to the sufferings of others, of being tender, as well as the still different gift of *being moved to pity* over the many kinds of evil necessarily linked even to the temporal finitude of the creation, and still more, to the *bondage* of all things earthly because of some *moral* "falling out."

In the end, we must acknowledge that the *true* remedy to the costly sufferings of both our pity and our sympathy can never be found in our hardness of heart, or in our shrinking from any love or tenderness lest we suffer added miseries. Nor can any form of escapism supply the remedy. The real remedy can be based only on the conviction that limitation and suffering and death—and moral evil itself—do not have *and will not have* the last word; that there is indeed Someone *stronger than death*; that there is the real possibility of the ultimate "redemption" of evil and suffering.

LOVE OF TRUTH AS A MORAL VIRTUE

Stephen Schwarz

O Truth, Truth, how inwardly did the very marrow of my soul pant for you.[1]

In what way is love of truth a moral virtue? Is all concern for truth virtuous? Is a person who eagerly pries into the personal affairs of his neighbors, who can't wait to hear the latest items of gossip, interested in truth? He wants to know "how it really is." But his behavior and his attitude are hardly examples of a positive moral quality. Why is that? On the other hand, a person who is indifferent to the ultimate question of existence—What is the meaning of life? Do I exist before a Personal God? What will happen to me at death?—also represents the contrary of a positive moral quality. Clearly the latter fails in love of truth. What then is love of truth?

A classic expression of love of truth as it pertains to the ultimate questions of existence is that of Pascal:

> When I consider the short duration of my life, swallowed up in the eternity before and after, the little space which I fill, and even can see, engulfed in the infinite immensity of spaces of which I am ignorant, and which know me not, I am frightened, and am astonished at being here rather than there; . . . now rather than then. Who has put me here? By whose order and direction have this place and time been allotted to me?[2]
>
> This is what I see and what troubles me. I look on all sides, and I see only darkness everywhere. Nature presents to me nothing which is not matter of doubt and concern. If I saw nothing there which revealed a Divinity, I would come to a negative conclusion; if I saw everywhere the signs of a Creator, I would remain peacefully in faith. But, seeing too much to deny and too little to be sure, I am in a state to be pitied.[3]

---

[1] St. Augustine, *Confessions*, bk. 3, chap. 6, trans. F. J. Sheed (New York: Sheed and Ward, 1942), p. 47.

[2] Pascal, *Pensées*, no. 205.

[3] *Ibid.*, no. 229.

My heart inclines wholly to know, where is the true good, in order to follow it; nothing would be too dear to me for eternity.[4]

Surely then it is a great evil thus to be in doubt, but it is at least an indispensable duty to seek when we are in such doubt; and thus the doubter who does not seek is altogether completely unhappy and completely wrong.[5]

"My heart inclines wholly to know, where is the true good, in order to follow it; nothing would be too dear to me for eternity." This expresses the very core of love of truth as a moral virtue which I want to explore here.

I. Four Domains

I want to suggest that love of truth pertains to at least four domains.

First, there is love of truth because of the intrinsic importance of the truth at stake, in the sense of the *content* of truth. What is more important than the truth about God and the state of our soul, both now and after we die? We should lovingly long for the truth about these things because of their intrinsic importance and also because they are the most important things for us, for our ultimate happiness, our deepest happiness.

Included in this category of truth because of its importance are both truths about the universal human situation, about "the universe" in all its existential dimensions (God, life after death, etc.); and truths about one's own individual situation; questions such as, what is God's will for me? How do I now appear before God in terms of my moral status? What should I do with my life? Does this person whom I love, love me?

Second, there is love of truth because of its intrinsic importance as such; because truth matters *for its own sake*, as truth, and not only because of its content. During a conversation one person says that so-and-so was born in 1933. A second person politely corrects her and points out that he was actually born in 1932. One could ask, but does it really matter? In one sense, no it doesn't; and there are certainly occasions when it is best to keep quiet and not correct the mistake. Still, there is an importance at stake, the importance of affirming the truth just because it is the truth and not only for its content; the importance of conforming to

---

[4] *Ibid.* Emphasis added.
[5] *Ibid.*, no. 194.

reality because it is good to do so; intrinsically good and not just good for something else.

Correcting a minor factual error may be motivated in several ways. If one does the correcting as an act of self-assertion, to show others how well informed one is, how much better than others, as an expression of a proud "I know better" attitude, then we surely do not have any love of truth at all, and therefore also not the love of truth as a moral virtue. To be real love of truth, the correcting must be a value response to the intrinsic value of truth. One should correct the mistake because one wants to "re-establish" truth, and one wants to do so out of love, because one loves the truth.

The first domain of love of truth is love of important truths, the second is love of truth as important. The first responds to the content of truths, the second responds to truth simply as truth. The first concerns a kind of "material" object of love, the second a "formal" object.

The basic wrongness of lying comes under this second heading. I do not speak here of the wrongness of lying because the effects of a lie are injurious to the victim of the lie, and often to others as well. Nor do I refer to the utilitarian concern that lying tends to destroy the social bond of trust. Nor, finally, do I have in mind the evil of a lie that stems from its content, a lie about an important subject matter. Rather, the focus is on a lie just as a lie, exemplified in a trivial case as well as in a grave one. It is the wrongness of lying as a violation of truth, of the high intrinsic value of truth. Lying is a violation of truth in that I assert what I believe, or know, to be false, in order to bring about a false belief in the other person. It is this intention to say what I take to be false, to be contrary to truth, that constitutes the violation of truth inherent in every lie. This is so even in those rare cases where I lie and also—accidentally— tell the truth because the belief that I hold but contradict in my lie is false.[6]

In cases in which a lie is gravely injurious to another, and/or in which the lie concerns a matter of extreme objective importance, the wrong associated with the lie because of the injury caused or because of the disregard of the object with high importance "overshadows," as it were, in our perception at least, the wrong that stems simply from the

---

[6] For a brilliant analysis of lying, what it is and why it is wrong, see Charles Fried, *Right and Wrong* (Harvard University Press, 1978), chap. 3, "On Lying," pp. 54–78.

disrespect for truth. The result is that the latter is more difficult to see in such situations; this does not, however, cause the less conspicuous wrong to be absent.[7]

Lying violates both the value of truth and the dignity of the person who is the victim of the lie. "You lied to me!" the victim exclaims in horror as he confronts the liar. What is this horror? It is not simply the response of the victim to being affronted, as would be the case in a physical assault. It is a horror at the violation of truth, not in the abstract, but as it pertains to the relation between the two persons, liar and victim. "I expected the truth, you spoke to me as if you were giving me the truth, but you didn't. You violated the trust I had in you." That is, "You violated my trust in you that you would respect truth." The value of truth and the evil of disrespecting it are in the forefront here. The trust was the trust that the value of truth would be upheld, would be given its due response. The lie represents a violation of this value, hence an antithesis of love of truth as a virtue.

The degree of horror varies with the importance of the truth. To be lied to about something important causes a much greater horror than to be lied to about a trivial matter. But even in the latter case there is, or can be a horror, simply because what was said was a *lie*, and therefore a violation of the value of truth.

Third, there is love of truth which is the desire to see those things about my own person that are painful for me to acknowledge, that I subconsciously hide from myself because they are unpleasant or even painful. It includes faults which I would be ashamed to admit to myself, and of course to others as well. It also includes other things that I would like to leave alone and not allow the light to shine on. For example, I may have a certain relation to another person which I assume is one of genuine love, friendship, mutual support, the desire to help, etc. It is, but there are also other elements in it which are not so pure; which I am subconsciously uncomfortable with, and which I'd rather not face up to. I hide these from myself, I look the other way, I don't want to know the real truth. I do not have the virtue of love of truth in this respect.

When the psalmist prays "Ab occultis meis munda me, Domine" (From what is hidden in me cleanse me, O Lord), he prays to be freed from these things hidden deep in his soul.

---

[7] I am indebted to Fritz Wenisch for this point.

One thing that makes these *occulta*, these hidden elements, so difficult to see is that they are often very closely tied to good features in the person, to noble character traits. A mother deeply loves her child, she cares for him, she protects him. This is mostly good, a wonderful moral trait. And yet, mixed in with these moral virtues are some negative elements. Perhaps her own pride creeps in as she protects "*my* son." Perhaps she fails in charity towards others in defending his cause. Perhaps she is blind to the effect which her particular way of protecting him has on others. Perhaps there are negative motivational factors in why she feels as she does towards him. Love for person A may sometimes include, and conceal, resentment for person B. The beauty of the love as such and of all its positive qualities effectively hides the ugliness of the resentment. It is not easy to see it. Pride makes it really difficult. Only a genuine, deep, and strong love of truth can do so. We may say the prayer "Ab occultis meis munda me, Domine," but do we really mean it? Do we really *want* to see these hidden things? Do we really want God's help in uncovering them and facing them? Only if we have a deep and strong love of truth.

Fourth, there is the love of truth that counters our strong tendency to cling to our own opinions; to hold on to them because they are *ours*, rather than seek the truth, which is not ours but trans-personal. For example, what guides our thinking as we form our opinions on questions such as abortion? Is it a real love of truth? Or is it other factors? Factors perhaps hidden from us because we do not want to see them? Why would a person support the "Pro-choice" position? Could it be self-directed motives such as, "I want to preserve my freedom to choose"? Could it be clinging to what is familiar, where we feel at home? Could it be staying with one's circle of friends who all hold this position? I have selected the "Pro-choice" view on abortion as an illuminating example, but the kinds of factors involved are quite universal and can apply to any person. That is, all these kinds of factors differ from love of truth; they are in fact opposed to love of truth, and they tend to be present in all of us. In fact, I think they are present in all of us unless we counteract them with a real love of truth. Only love of truth as a moral virtue, the value response to truth, can protect us from these kinds of factors. They are strong, and we can escape them only by a strong counterweight, a strong and deep love of truth.

Real love of truth means a conscious willingness to let go of something which is "my opinion," even a strongly held opinion, a deeply cherished opinion, if there is a reasonable chance that it is false, or even inadequate; if, for example, it is challenged by someone I have reason to trust, or if new evidence comes to my attention that might undermine it. We are not always aware of our real reason for holding our opinions. We think it is because they are correct; they represent the truth. That may be a factor. But I think there is another factor that may enter, one that we do not usually notice, namely that we hold our opinions—and *hold on* to them—because they are "our" opinions. We cherish them as *our own*. We do so in the name of truth, of course. But the stronger pull is the one represented by "its *my* opinion," not the one represented by "because I love truth," and want only the truth. The reluctance people have of giving up their cherished opinions, or modifying them, or even questioning them, testifies to the strength of this "*my opinion*" factor. It is a factor that is specifically opposed to love of truth as a moral virtue.

Real love of truth loves only truth, it is concerned only with truth, in total disregard of whether an opinion is "mine" or "yours"; or perhaps a new opinion not yet held by anyone, the discovery of a new truth. For real love of truth, the "my opinion" factor carries no weight. This love is as ready to discard an opinion as false or inadequate which is, up to now, "mine," as it is to reject a false or inadequate opinion which is outside the realm of my opinions.

II. Does Truth Shine By Its Own Light?

"Truth shines by its own light," we like to say. But is this really true? Often it is, but there are also many types of cases where it isn't. Putting all these together, I suggest that there are three main areas:

1. Where truth does shine by its own light, where it is simply "given" to us in our experience, where we need only open our eyes and see; our physical eyes (and ears, etc.) or the eyes of our mind. Some of these truths are obvious at first sight, and can be seen with a minimum of effort. Others are evident to our minds because of their intelligibility; they are the *a priori* truths that shine by their own light, such as the truth that only a personal being can be the agent of morally good or morally evil actions.

2. Where truth does not shine by its own light, where we must "dig it out" by scientific research, or philosophical thinking, or other intellectual effort. Here the "non-shining" is due to completely *objective* factors, in the nature of the subject matter being investigated.

3. Where truth does not shine by its own light because of *subjective* factors, factors in the character of the person himself; where the truth is not evident but *occulta*, hidden from us because we do not want to see it, where we need the virtue of love of truth in order to be able to reach truth.

There is a sense in which truth by its very nature "shines forth"; and in this sense, truth always shines by its own light. That is, once we get to it, truth shines by its own light. But in both cases 2 and 3, we are prevented from getting to it right away, though for very different reasons. It is while we are at one of these two types of "distance" from truth that truth does not shine by its own light.

We can come to understand the nature of love of truth as a moral virtue, its beauty, its spiritual radiance, when we consider this: A real love of truth means that I have the same zeal, the same eagerness to see my own hidden faults and other *occulta*, as I have to see a truth about something external to me that interests me a great deal. Love of truth is, further, a desire to see my own inner state, in all its embarrassing negative features, with the same clarity, precision, and relative completeness that I often have in seeing the character of others.

It is, of course, my pride that constitutes the major barrier to my seeing my own inner state; and to overcome my pride I need humility. Humility is a necessary precondition; it enables me to leap over, or to break through, the pride that wants to "protect" and keep hidden the bitter truths about my inner state. But the actual "force" of the break-through is love of truth. I look because I want to see, because I want to know the truth, because I love the truth.

III. Two Problems: The Need for a Further Element

I turn now to two problems, each in a way the converse of the other. First, there is a kind of "love of truth," a desire to know things, which is not at all the genuine moral virtue of love of truth, namely the desire to poke into others' private lives, to know all the developments in their affairs, to be informed about the latest scandals, to be able to tell others and receive from them, to be a master gossiper. Second and conversely, I may have no interest in certain things, for example, who won last night's hockey game, detailed statistics about the lumber industry in British Columbia, and what the mayor said in his long dinner speech at the Elks Club last night. I may have no "love of truth" in these and other things without in any way failing against the moral virtue of love of truth. How are these to be explained?

Let me suggest as an explanation that it is never *just* the love of truth that constitutes the moral virtue of love of truth; there is always also some other element that is essential. Either it is (A) the **intrinsic importance** of the truth in its subject matter, its content, universal truths about reality that transcend any one individual, the important truths about God, immortality, morality, human nature, free will, the capacities and limitations of our intellect, and other ultimately important things. Or it is (B) the importance of the truth in its subject matter, its content **for the individual person**; the important truths about a person's soul, his moral character, his relationships to other persons, especially those who are close to him; the truth about the *occulta* that are initially veiled from him. Or it is (C) the **protection** of truth from errors, distortions and lies. The love of truth, it seems to me, is always directed at truth, and responds to truth, under one of these aspects. They provide, so to speak, the context in which love of truth is called for, and, hopefully, actualized.

If a person has absolutely no interest in hockey games and the standing of the various hockey teams, he is, in a sense, indifferent to truth. If team A defeated team B last night by a score of 4–2, then it is, of course, *true* that this is so. "I don't care," someone says. The truth here does not come under any of the headings, A–C, that constitute an essential context for love of truth as a moral virtue. I do not love truth any less—in the sense in which this love is a moral virtue—because I am not concerned with *this* truth. There are countless truths, in fact an infinite number of truths; clearly, no one can be concerned with each of them. And the choice of which ones I am concerned with is, in large part, up to me; I can make choices in accordance with my interests. Love of truth as a virtue means love of truth as it calls for a response; it does not necessarily mean an interest in this specific truth by itself. It means *protecting* a truth from attack (C), and here the hockey score might conceivably enter the picture, if someone got it wrong. It means love of truth because of its *importance* (A and B), where it is the importance of the truth (and not just truth alone) that is the object and concern of my love for truth.

Why are curiosity about the latest scandal, probing into the private lives of other persons, or reading sensationalist tabloid newspapers, not examples of love of truth? After all, one wants to know the truth, how it really is. The keen desire to obtain this truth is a kind of love. "I love reading about these things," someone will say. Why is this "love" not a moral virtue? Why is it rather a vice?

First, this "love" of truth does not approach truth under any of the headings we noted. The gossip items are not of any genuine, intrinsic importance (A); nor are they truths which are important for the individual person because they pertain to his soul, to his relations with others (B); nor is there a morally motivated desire to protect truth (C).

Second, this "love" of truth is in no way a value response. It does not take an interest in truth because of its intrinsic importance. It does not "look up" to truth as important in itself. It has no element of reverence, which is a necessary ingredient in every value response.

Third, this "love" of truth is in fact radically opposed to the spirit of value response, of reverence. It is nothing but a craving for a debased self-satisfaction. It appeals to morally illegitimate centers in a person, pride and concupiscence. It "uses" truths and the facts about which it is concerned for totally self-centered satisfaction.

In all genuine love of truth, we see a self-transcendence, a going beyond oneself for the sake of something important in its own right. Just the opposite is true of sensationalism and hungering for gossip. One does not care about truth because it is truth, and because truth is intrinsically valuable, but only because it serves one's base desires.

Finally, to see the difference between real love of truth and a debased curiosity about sensational things, consider a case where one and the same fact is approached in both ways. Suppose my child, whom I love deeply, is accused of a sex crime, causing a scandal in the small town where I live. Naturally, I take an interest in this. Are the charges true? What really happened? But *why* do I want to know these things? Because I love my child, and I want to know the truth, the real truth, no matter what it is. I shudder at the possibility that the charges might be true. But if they are true, I must face up to them. This is real love of truth. It is *repulsed* by the whole affair, but perseveres for the sake of the right response to truth, the love of truth. Sensationalism, in contrast, is *attracted* by the whole affair. It smells something appealing, and wants more; like a glutton, it seeks to devour its prey. This is not love of truth, but a horrible perversion; it is an abhorrent self-centeredness that cares about the affair only because of its subjective appeal.

IV. Two Dimensions

Two dimensions of love of truth should be noted. One concerns propositional truth. I want to know *that* such and such is the case if it really is. The other concerns the *true picture* of someone or of something. A Pascalian love of ultimate truth desires not only to know that such-and-such is the case about our ultimate metaphysical place in the world, that such-and-such is the case about the existence of God, but also (if God exists) to have, and to embrace, the true picture of God, to see Him (if that is what He is) as a Loving God, a God of Infinite Love and Mercy, and not to have (if that is what He is not) a distorted, one-sided picture of God, as a God of wrath and merciless "justice." So too, if I am concerned to shed light on my *occulta*, my hidden faults, what I want is a true picture of myself. And love of others, in its aspect of love of truth, desires to see the true picture of the other.

V. Scepticism and Relativism

How is scepticism related to love of truth? Scepticism is a vast and complex topic, beyond the scope of this paper. Let me only suggest two brief points. First, there is a scepticism that doubts or denies something which is really evident in its nature, that shines by its own light. I'm thinking here of a scepticism such as Hume's when he claims to deny the reality of the self.[8] Such a scepticism, I submit, is not simply a lack of love of truth, but something directly opposed to it. It is motivated by factors antithetical to the love of truth, such as the desire to say something sensational.

Second, and in sharp contrast to the above, I think there is also a noble "scepticism," or withholding of conviction motivated by love of truth; in fact implied by the love of truth, given the epistemological situation in which the person finds himself. Imagine a person who very much wants to believe in God but finds the reasons for such belief inadequate. He remains unconvinced. Given that this is his present state of mind (that is, prescinding from the question why this is his present state of mind), he is, I submit, doing the right thing in not accepting the belief. For his non-acceptance is motivated by a love of truth. "For the sake of truth, I cannot accept this belief"; that is, "I cannot believe something

---

[8] Hume, *A Treatise of Human Nature*, bk. 1, pt. 4, sec. 4

merely because I want to believe it, but only because it is true, only in the name of truth." The precedence which he gives to truth over desire is an example of a genuine love of truth. (Closely connected to this point is the fact that religious faith is a gift, not something we can bring into being by our own unaided efforts.)

On the other hand, relativism is a very different matter. This too is a vast topic beyond the scope of this paper.[9] I shall focus on one aspect of relativism, or one form that it can take, namely relativism as the denial of truth. This is the view—or perhaps the attitude—that "There is no truth" because "Who's to say what it is?" said in reference to divergent and contradictory opinions on various matters, especially morality and religion. This is at bottom a despair; first a despair at finding truth, then at its very existence. In sharp contrast to the "noble sceptic" mentioned above, who also does not find truth, but who maintains his deep and basic reverence for truth and his love of truth, the relativist, in his despair at finding truth, or finding it with the security (certainty) that he longs for, attacks truth. "Since I can't have it, it doesn't exist"; and, "Since I can't have it, no one can have it—it doesn't exist." This attack on truth out of a despair at finding it stands in stark contrast to a humble and reverent love of truth.[10]

VI. God, Truth, and Ultimate Meaning

What is the relation between God and truth? Specifically, what should our ultimate response be, to God or to truth? For a believer, there is no difficulty, there is not even a real question, for the truth is that God exists. Indeed, it is much more than this, for God *is* Truth, God is *the* Truth, the ultimate and Absolute Truth. "I am the Way, the Truth and the Life." (The difficult question of the relation between these two, between the propositional truth "that God exists" and the Transcending Truth, "God *is* Truth" and "God is *the* Truth" cannot be pursued here.)

But what is the situation for someone who is unsure about God's existence? As Pascal says, he should *seek*. "Surely then it is a great evil

---

[9] Please see the essay by Peter Kreeft elsewhere in this volume for an extensive analysis of relativism and brilliant refutations of it.

[10] For a brilliant and extensive analysis of various forms of attack on truth in modern times, and their philosophical roots and causes, see Dietrich von Hildebrand, "The Dethronement of Truth," in his book, *The New Tower of Babel* (Manchester: Sophia Institute Press, 1994), pp. 51–90.

thus to be in doubt, but it is at least an indispensable duty to seek when we are in such doubt."

But what should he seek, God or truth? For him they are not the same. For someone unsure of God's existence, it is an open question whether God and truth are one (God is and God is Truth), or there is a split (The truth is that there is no God).

I want to suggest that the answer must be, clearly and unequivocally, *truth*. One cannot believe in God, worship God, pray to Him, try to do His will, etc., unless it is in the name of *truth*. I must first believe that it is *true* that God is, before I can respond to Him in love and adoration. A love and worship of God outside the affirmation of truth is a sham. All religion is a counterfeit if it is not true; or at least, if it is not pursued in the name of truth, on the basis of truth. To genuinely worship God can only mean to worship a God who really is, or at least, whom I believe to be really existent. To say, "I will worship God, I will try to do His will; but if He doesn't exist, it doesn't matter," is the worst metaphysical and existential hypocrisy.

There is an important sense then in which, from our standpoint, the truth question is primary. *If* there is no God, if this unfathomably horrible state of affairs were really the case, then that is what I would have to believe. God, in all the many dimensions in which He is important, is nothing if it is not *true* that He is. This must be our starting point.

From this starting point, seeing all the signs in the world that point to God's real existence, the Pascalian seeker will hopefully find God. Or, God will find him! And the ultimate union of God and Truth will be actual. As Elisabeth Leseur expresses it, "Whoever seeks the truth will find God."[11]

But suppose the seeker hesitates. Suppose he says that he sees the positive side, the signs pointing to God; but also, he says, negative signs, for instance the terrible evil and suffering that God seems to allow, though He is all-loving and all-powerful. "How can there be so much evil and suffering, and also a God of Love?"

I would answer that this negative sign is outweighed by all the positive signs that point to God, such as: God as the ultimate source and ground for the world; the beauty of sublime music such as Mozart's *Ave Verum* and Bach's *St. Matthew Passion*; and the moral goodness exem-

---

[11] Elisabeth Leseur, *My Spirit Rejoices* (Manchester: Sophia Institute Press, 1996), p. 208.

plified in the saints, which point to God as the Absolute Good. Given these and other signs pointing to God, there is sufficient reason to believe that God exists. On this basis, the existence of evil, particularly moral evil and suffering, is a mystery. Why is there evil if God is good? The ultimate answer to this mystery cannot be given. It surpasses the human mind. But not understanding why something is, or how something can be, is not a reason to deny that it is if there are clear signs pointing to it.

Consider the biblical character of Job whose trust in God despite his great suffering makes him a paradigm example of what it means to have true faith. Although Job's question is not *How can a good God exist even though there is so much evil?* but rather *Why does an upright man have to suffer even though there is a good God?*[12] I think he can help us in our understanding here. In the midst of Job's pain he cries out to the Lord to answer and explain *why* he must suffer. But instead of answering, God asks Job questions, such as, "Do you have an arm like God's and can your voice thunder like his?"[13] which reminds Job that it is God alone who has the answers. Job realizes that God must be trusted above all, and that humility is essential to our faith, especially when we cannot fathom all of God's ways. In the last chapter, Job replies to the Lord:

> I know that you can do all things;
> No plan of yours can be thwarted.
> You asked, "Who is this that obscures my counsel without knowledge?"
> Surely I spoke of things I did not understand,
> Things too wonderful for me to know.[14]

Finally, one can reply to the sceptic by saying, "I'll tell you why there is evil in the universe if you'll tell me why there is a universe."

Perhaps the following considerations can be added in reply to the sceptic, the seeker for whom truth and God still remain distinct, who fears that perhaps the truth of the matter is that there is no God. I return to my basic thesis that our primary commitment must be to truth. *If* the truth is that there is no God, then that is what we must accept. Truth is primary, truth is the ultimately important thing, in comparison with which nothing else matters.

---

[12] I am indebted to Fritz Wenisch for calling my attention to this point.
[13] Job 40:9.
[14] *Ibid.*, 42:1–3.

If God is then He is the Truth, the Absolute Truth, the Ultimate Truth. If there is no God? Then the Highest Reality before which we must bow in submission in our love of truth is the state of affairs "that there is no God." Is this possible? Would this not be the greatest imaginable absurdity? All things that are meaningful in life, that provide the source of deep and genuine happiness for us, are things which transcend us, things to which we must look up. The beauty of music, the beauty and splendor of nature, a deep relationship of love with another person, all these are gifts which we must accept inwardly on our knees, in humility and gratitude, to which we must look up, in reverence. If God is, He is the culmination of this "looking up." If there is no God, then what exists above *us* and above *all these things* that give our life meaning and deep fulfillment and genuine happiness—beauty, moral goodness, love, deep truth—is ultimately nothing. These things would still be, they would be real and beautiful and meaningful in themselves, and for us. But if there is no God, they would be, so to speak, suspended in mid-air, with nothing above them as their ultimate source, and nothing to support them and give them the permanence that, in their inner meaning, they deserve, indeed that they promise. If this were the case, what would exist above us, and above all these deeply meaningful things, would be *nothing*, a mere negative state of affairs, "that there is no God." To *this* we must bow down? *Yes*, because (on the present assumption) it is the truth. *No*, because it is nothing! It is metaphysically infinitely less than, infinitely inferior to, one great piece of music, such as the *Missa Solemnis* of Beethoven, not to mention all the other great pieces of music and all the other sublime values that enrich our soul. This contradiction, indicated above by the *yes* and the *no*, represents the greatest imaginable absurdity.

The absurdity is so great that it throws into question one of the basic tenets on which this whole thought process is built. It is meaningful to believe what is true, because it is true. But in such a meaningless, absurd world in which the truth would be, "there is no God," is it still meaningful to conform one's conviction to reality, to truth? Yes and no, we are torn. Yes, conforming ourselves to the truth must always be the meaningful thing. No, because all is basically absurd.

Should we believe that existence is ultimately meaningful? If we were to *know* that it is not meaningful, we would of course have to accept this, in the name of truth, in the name of the love of truth. But then, we should also note the glaring, ultimate contradiction between, on the one hand, the *positive* value response to truth, believing what is true because it is true, responding because of our love for truth; and, on the other hand, the ultimate *destruction* of all value, including the value of truth in this ultimate absurdity. I submit no one *knows* this to be the case. In the absence of such knowledge, we can, I think, have the hope that existence is ultimately meaningful. We can follow the many signs that point to this; signs that can ground a confident belief that existence is ultimately meaningful.

What can be said to someone who doubts this? I suggest the following, based on Pascal[15] and William James.[16] Is it not better to believe (or at least seek to believe) that existence is ultimately meaningful with the risk that it is not, than to believe it is *not* meaningful with the risk that it *is* meaningful? Isn't the second error an infinitely more tragic one than the first? In either case we lose out on truth by being in error. But is not the loss of truth infinitely greater if that truth is, *existence is ultimately meaningful*, than if that truth is, *existence is ultimately absurd*? If we believe that existence is ultimately meaningful and we are mistaken, then our error is just one more absurdity in an already ultimately absurd world. But if we believe that existence is ultimately absurd when in fact it is ultimately meaningful, then we lose out on the most important truth there is!

Truth is always a value, and we should love all truth. But some truths are more significant than others, and our love of truth should increase accordingly. The truth that my spouse loves me is infinitely more significant than the truth about a trivial matter, such as that the stairway has eight steps. In a very different way, the truth that existence is ultimately meaningful—if that is the truth—is infinitely more significant than the truth—if that is the truth—that existence is ultimately absurd. For this reason, and in this sense, existence as ultimately meaningful has an absolute priority over its contradictory. In the name of meaningfulness, including the meaningfulness of truth, we should pursue ultimate meaningfulness as the truth. If existence is ultimately meaningful, and if I should love the truth, and seek the truth, especially the Ultimate Truth about God, then I can do this only by seeking God and loving God, for

---

[15] See Pascal, *Pensées*, no. 233 (The Wager) and no. 241. See also my article, "Faith, Doubt and Pascal's Wager," *Center Journal*, vol. 3, no. 3 (1984), pp. 29–58.

[16] William James, "The Will to Believe."

the Ultimate Reality must be the necessary and absolute coming together of the two aspects we have been pursuing, **Truth** and **God.** God is Truth, God is the Truth.[17]

---

[17] I am indebted to Prof. Fritz Wenisch and Prof. Mark Roberts for many helpful comments in the preparation of this article.

FUNDAMENTAL
DIMENSIONS
OF AXIOLOGY

TOWARD A CONCEPT AND A PHENOMENOLOGY OF THE GIFT

Damian Fedoryka

Tadeusz Styczen writes that during his Lublin years, Karol Wojtyla's discovery of the paradox of the fundamental role of existence in the structure of being and at the same time of the contingency of that existence led him into the very core of the metaphysics of the person as a gift.[1] This objective condition of being a gift is to be completed by the subjective act of the human person who is to "appropriate" that gift and, in a dialogue of love with its personal giver, to exchange gifts. The gift of self is the only possible way of receiving the gift of self.

Many years later, the teachings of John Paul II continue to echo this basic intuition. Thus, in a recent encyclical, he writes that man forgets that his capacity to transform the world through work is based on "God's prior and original gift of the things that are. Man thinks that he can make arbitrary use of the earth, subjecting it without restraint to his will, as though it did not have its own requisites and a prior God-given purpose, which man can indeed develop but must not betray."[2] And again, "Not only has God given the earth to man, who must use it with respect to the original good purpose for which it was given to him, but man too is God's gift to man."[3] There is no need to mention the frequent references in his teachings to the central role of the gift in marriage, the "mutual gift of self by husband and wife," which also finds its reference in the same encyclical.[4] The center of gravity in all these teachings is a concept in *Gaudium et Spes* # 24 which the Pope invokes frequently: "Man, who

---

[1] Cf. Tadeusz Styczen and Edward Balawajder, *Jedynie Prawda Wyzwala, Rozmowy o Janie Pawle 11* (Roma: Polski Instytut Kultury Chrzestianskiej, 1987), p. 35.

[2] Cf. John Paul II, *Centesimus Annus* (Vatican: Libreria Editrice Vaticana, 1991), # 37.

[3] *Ibid.*, # 38.

[4] *Ibid.*, # 39.

is the only creature on earth which God willed for itself, cannot fully find himself except through a sincere gift of himself."[5]

In this essay, I wish to reflect on the concept of the gift. The role of this concept in the thought of John Paul II is an indication of its importance. It is not restricted to papal teachings, however. It plays a fundamental role in contemporary thought and culture not so much by its positive presence as by its curious absence. It is not completely absent, but announces its clandestine presence through the category and language of *appropriation*. The whole venture of Marx is based on the project of overcoming alienation by reappropriating the products of man's work and thereby of man himself.[6] The philosophical work of Heidegger centers on the theme of *Eigentlichkeit*. This word is normally translated as "authenticity," a translation which fails to capture Heidegger's own definition of *Eigentlichkeit* as a *"sich zu eigen machen,"*[7] namely, a "making one self one's own."

How does the category of "appropriation" manifest the clandestine presence of the gift? I would suggest here that the very possibility itself of a contingent being appropriating any object whatsoever presupposes that the object in question be a gift. This statement itself presupposes an intuition into the nature of a gift and the implications of a "gift situation." We are dealing with an ultimate datum that is irreducible. It cannot be justified through a derivation from other truths. But it is possible to bring this intuition to clarity by bringing to evidence certain intelligible features of the gift. This essay is a preliminary investigation of some

---

[5] Cf. *The Documents of Vatican II*, Walter M. Abbott, S.J., ed. (New York: America Press, 1966), p. 223.

[6] Cf. Karl Marx, *The Economic and Philosophic Manuscripts of 1844*, Dirk J. Struik, ed. (New York: International Press, 1964). This "early Marx" with his concern for the dehumanization which occurs when the worker is separated from his product is the basis for the "Humanist" form of Marxism, which did not begin until after the discovery of these manuscripts well after the turn of the twentieth century. Central in the early work is the *metaphysical* thesis that work, by its nature, is the externalization of man, his *Entäusserung*. It is through the process of work that man "objectifies" or "externalizes" himself—we might also say, "pro-jects" himself and becomes fully human. It is only under the condition of capitalism that man's *Entfremdung* occurs; i.e., he becomes "estranged" or "alienated" when his self-embodiment in his product is taken away from him by the owners of the means of production.

[7] Cf. Martin Heidegger, *Grundprobleme der Phänomenologie* (Frankfurt am Main: Vittorio Klosterman, 1975), p. 228.

central elements of the phenomenon and reality of a gift and is necessarily restricted in scope. In a preliminary fashion, we can consider these elements as belonging to the concept of the gift. Subsequent phenomenological analysis will have to focus on the question whether these are necessary and intelligible elements of the nature or essence of a gift and the states of affairs attaching to it.

1. We begin with the example of an individual who finds himself struck in the head by some object *thrown* by another. The other inquires why the target of the thrown object didn't express his gratitude. After all, the thrower explains, the object was a gift.

It should be intuitively clear that gratitude cannot be demanded or expected in this situation. A gift would not be thrown. We mean that the addressee would be given an opportunity to *receive* the gift. It is this opportunity, and the intention of providing this opportunity, that distinguishes a giving in the strict sense of the word from an activity that simply has causal consequences.

In our example, the individual hit by the thrown object was simply at the end of a *causal* chain, even if he had, by virtue of excellent reflexes, caught the object before it hit him. The physical activity of reaching out a hand and grasping an object is not yet the act of receiving. It is important to recognize the personal dimension that may or may not be contained in or embodied by physical behavior.

2. A second example will take us a step further in recognizing the unique nature of receiving. Imagine someone sitting at a table on which there are several gift-wrapped packages. Someone passes by, reaches out and takes one of the objects, saying "Thank you." Again, it is intuitively given that gratitude is not in order. The object was not *given* and therefore a gift did not enter into the picture. The behavior of grasping something with the hand is to be distinguished from the phenomenon of receiving, which never occurred in our example. Receiving necessarily presupposes giving as a condition for its possibility. Both are unique acts. Thus, giving may even involve the physical behavior of throwing, but it would be a giving only if it would be a throwing "to" rather than a throwing "at."

We can draw attention to some features of the gift before continuing. First, the gift situation is to be metaphysically distinguished from the merely causal relation. The recipient is not simply metaphysically passive with respect to the donor. And the latter is not simply the agent of a transitive causality. Nor, again, is the recipient reacting. Something more and distinct is present. Second, this "more and distinct" is accounted for by the presence of the *personal* dimension.

It is the metaphysical reality of the personal that differentiates, for example, the causal activity of generation and feeding of the young in animals from the gift character of procreation and nutrition in the human sphere. Again, it is the personal dimension which accounts for an absolute difference between the merely causal relation to the external world through sensation and perception in the animal sphere, and the cognitive receptivity of data, of the world that is given to the human person.

One specific feature of the gift is that it necessarily presupposes the personal dimension on both sides: on the side of the donor and on the side of the recipient. We need to take another step in pursuing the articulation of this specifically personal dimension in the gift.

3. Receptivity is a personal act *sui generis*. It is to be distinguished, as we already noted, from the behavior of grasping with the hand. But this is simply a negative circumscription of the phenomenon. How do we identify it in a positive mode? How would we positively distinguish the activity of grasping a proffered banana by an ape on the one hand from a phenomenally similar activity by a human person on the other hand?

Linguistically, we can make use of the term "appropriate." Receptivity involves appropriation. But it is not equivalent to it. Appropriation means making something "one's own," taking possession of it, becoming the "owner" of what is appropriated. The concept of appropriation is a difficult one. One reason for this is that the analogous term refers to different levels of possible possession, levels determined by the nature of the being which is possessed as well as by the nature of the act involved. Another reason is that this concept involves distinct elements, one of which can be present in something that is not possession even though it is similar to it. Thus, possession implies a certain power and dominion over what is possessed. Yet the exercise of power and dominion can occur when no genuine possession is present. A clear and classical example of this is slavery, in which one being exercises power and dominion over another as if he owned him.

Receiving a gift implies a taking possession of what is offered, of exercising a certain power and dominion over it. How does the mere exercise of power and dominion over something which is not "truly owned" differ from this? In order to bring out the difference, we take the example of a higher order of gift with the "taking possession" implied in it, and contrast it, on the same level, with a mere appropriation which is not a receiving.

Let us take the example of a man and a woman who mutually offer themselves in marriage. The marriage is actualized when there is a mutual acceptance, or receiving. We contrast this with the example of a man who "takes" a woman who never offered herself, indeed, one who resists him. We will not focus at this point on the evident difference with regard to the presence or absence of the free act of the will. Another feature of our example is instructive. Granted that the first example involves the mutually free reception of the other, we note that it also involves the mark of what we shall here call "interiority" or intimacy. In the second example, although the man succeeds in performing the same physical act, he remains "outside" that which he has overpowered and dominated.

It is important to distinguish in what we normally call "appropriation" two distinct but closely related elements. One is the formal aspect of power and dominion. The other is the specific moment of "ownership." The second always presupposes the first, but the first may exist or be attempted without including genuine "ownership," as we saw in the example of the rape. "Taking possession of" or "appropriation" can often linguistically designate the latter instance. It can also do this because in relation to the lower order of being, the element of "interiority" which belongs to true appropriation is less pronounced and evident.

What is the phenomenon of "interiority" or intimacy that is so important in distinguishing true appropriation from the mere exercise of power, ultimately futile, "from outside"? Let us approach it through yet another example. Two men are faced with a locked door. One of them uses an explosive to break the lock. The other uses a surgical tool to gently probe and unlock the mechanism. Both have opened the door. What is the difference? Evidently, the second man was able to enter into the lock, and with a minimal use of force bend it to his will. His skill was grounded in his knowledge of the inner secret of the lock. The first man exercised a causal power "from outside." In the second instance, the causal intervention was minimal. His knowledge of the structure of the lock allowed him to work "from within."

An essential precondition for "appropriation" in the fuller sense of the word is knowledge. In the classical sense, it is the intellection of the object, an *intima rei intus legere*: "a reading into the inner secret of the thing." In a real though analogous sense, the object stands "open" to the one who enters into it and dominates it. As our example suggests, the greater the dominion, the less is the causal alteration or change of the object. The greater the knowledge, the greater the possibility of entering into the being in question. And the greater knowledge permits a greater autonomy to the appropriated object. In a paradoxical sense, the greater the dominion and power over the object, the more is the object allowed to "be itself."

Receptivity, then, involves an appropriation which is a power and dominion over the object through entry into its inner reality. The greater and more complete the appropriation, the less does it disturb or alter the object, the less does it represent a threat of destruction. In this sense, true domination of an object is fundamentally removed from the kind of causal efficacy that occurs in the relations between non-personal beings and their surrounding world.

To the extent that the earth is a gift to man, it categorically differs from the environment of plants and animals. For these, the external world is a threat or it is a "means," in both cases by virtue of its causal effects. Although man is allowed to use the world, he is first called to subdue and dominate it. He can do this authentically only by entering as deeply as possible into its inner secret, and by granting it as much autonomy as possible, even as he uses it. This implies a formal element of co-operation on the part of man with the laws of nature.

As we noted, receptivity involves appropriation as a domination. Yet this phenomenon of dominion through entry into the object does not yet account for that moment of "ownership" that is also implied in appropriation. We must continue our venture.

4. If receptivity is to accomplish the distinct moment of "ownership" that is implied in appropriating, it cannot simply exercise dominion over the object, no matter how intimate. If the object is to be truly received as a gift, the subject must *open* himself. He cannot simply be passive in the face of what "comes toward" him.

Openness is a fundamental category in the metaphysics of the person. It is in virtue of the capacity of the spiritual being to open itself that the person can transcend himself, both in receptivity and spontaneity.[8] In order to grasp the *spiritual* or *personal* nature of transcendence, we can-

---

[8] Cf. Josef Seifert, *Erkenntnis objektiver Wahrheit*, 2nd ed. (München: Universitätsverlag Anton Pustet, 1976), pp. 85ff, for a discussion of the metaphysical meaning of the two basic dimensions of transcendence, receptivity and spontaneity.

not interpret it by analogy with the lower order of beings. In the non-personal universe, beings are capable of exercising a causal activity that affects entities outside the borders of their own being; in other words, beings that are ontologically transcendent. And they are capable of suffering the effects caused by beings that are outside of them. In each case, the relationship is external. If we wished to explain the personal capacity of openness by analogy with the non-personal, we would have to assume that openness somehow always involved a break or rupture in whatever sets the boundaries of our being. Every such "openness" would be a violation or loss of the ontological integrity of our being.

In reality, it is precisely one of the marks of spirituality or personhood that allows us to "open" ourselves without "breaking" or "rupturing" the integrity of our being. Only because we are persons can we "go beyond" ourselves in a way that no material or bodily entity can. So too, because we are persons, can we "take in" and appropriate more truly than is possible in the material order. Thus, openness is a metaphysical act of a being of a higher order than the non-personal.

A *personal* relationship to beings outside of the individual will always involve an act of openness and transcendence. The specific type and kind of openness will depend on the kind of being to which we are open. Thus, the individual must exercise openness in order to reach out beyond himself and receive cognitively the nature or existence of minerals or plants or animals in the external world. As we already noted, this is a relationship which as such excludes causal efficacy, a "working" on the object known. It respects the true autonomy of the object.

At the highest level, a *personal* relationship to another *person* will involve not only the openness of the receiving subject, but also the openness of the other who has to open himself in "self-revelation" so that the other can "enter" and "know." The other can in turn open himself and go beyond himself in an act of self-donation. This gesture of self-donation on the part of another person becomes "completed" only when it is received, when the donor is taken in and comes to belong to the recipient. We cannot go into a more extensive discussion of the implied and related phenomena. At this point, it is enough to point out that a *receptivity* in the full sense of the word implies that something becomes one's own, that in some measure and in some sense it becomes "part of one's being." On the personal level of mutual appropriation and union, the "becoming one" of two persons allows and leaves intact the full autonomy of each person, and indeed, allows for the full actualization of each.

Thus, receptivity implies two distinct but closely related moments. One, it calls for an "entry" into the object and a "grasping," an exercise of dominion and power over it. Such a dominion, as noted, never violates the integrity and autonomy of the object dominated. And two, it involves a "making it one's own," that is, by somehow "taking it into one's being." The various ways in which other beings as well as one's own being can become one's own is a new question.

5. The very fact that man is capable of a receptive relationship to the non-personal things of the earth seems to indicate that if he is truly to receive them, even in knowledge, his relationship to the earth cannot be reduced to a merely causal one. He should not exercise a power over it "from without" which seeks a radical superiority by restructuring and re-creating it. The earth is not simply prime matter, as it were, to be shaped and formed by man alone.

But the very possibility of receiving the non-personal things of the earth by a human person that did not create them is at the same time an indication of their gift character. Even if they are causes and can be used as means or tools, they are also and more primarily *data* for man.

And the possibility of a receptive relationship to other persons, on the one hand, allows an even greater entry into the other person who can also open and reveal himself or herself, but on the other hand, sets up a "barrier" against an entry unless the other gives himself or herself to the recipient who *ought not initiate possession* but only respond to an offer. We are struck here by the awesome mystery that the very existence of other human beings is always and somehow fundamentally a gift for us.

6. The above elements in the concept of a gift would fail to grasp adequately the phenomenon of the gift if we stopped at this point. A fuller grasp of what is meant by receiving, interiority, and ownership depends on several other features. Let us focus on them by correcting, as it were, our previous examples.

Let us now imagine the following situation. A person comes to us with a gift-wrapped package. He does not throw it at us, but gives it to us. We reach out and receive the gift. As we proceed to unwrap it, the package explodes and grievously injures us. Again, manifestly, gratitude is not called for. The apparent gift turned out to be something else. Why? Because it caused us harm.

Another essential element in the concept of the gift is that the gift must constitute some *good for* the recipient. Here again we must qualify.

It is not enough that the recipient is made objectively better or his condition improved. Not only must it be a good, he must know and understand that it is a good and that it is *for him*. Here, we encounter the unique category of a good for the person as opposed to what is simply good. In this context, we need not pursue the significance of the distinct category of the good as benefit to the individual.[9] It is necessary only to further clarify the specific importance of the fact that the gift is *addressed* to another as person not merely as object or terminus of an activity. It throws into relief the importance of the moment and the act of receptivity on the part of the recipient.

An example will throw into relief the importance of this point. A young man needs some money and asks his father for it. The father is aware of the son's need and is willing for him to have the benefit in question. He takes the money from his wallet and then, instead of handing it to his son, looks straight into his eyes and then throws the money on the table. To sharpen the point, we might even say that the father throws it on the floor. Let us say that the son picks it up. He acquires a benefit. It is his and no one else's. The father is the source and the cause of the benefit. Yet we would hardly say that the money is a gift. Something is lacking, or at least not clearly present because it is marred by another feature.

Not infrequently one encounters, as in the above example, the situation where someone wants to make the recipient of his largesse "crawl" for the benefit distributed. Such an individual in fact does want to "do" good. But he is more interested in being the source of the good and in manifesting his superiority and largesse. He clearly recognizes the doing of the good as a condition for his superiority. And he wants the recipient to be conscious of this superiority. He makes him "crawl."

7. The above example manifests the absence of the intention of benevolence which is an integral constituent of the gift. The *intention of benevolence* toward another person, the intention of willing good for

---

[9] Cf. Dietrich von Hildebrand, *Ethics* (Chicago: Franciscan Herald Press, 1972), particularly chap. 3, in which he distinguishes the categories of importance, including the difference between the good "in itself" and the "good for the person." The good for the person is derivative and is grounded either in a good independent of the person or in the nature of the person to which it "addresses itself." This distinction is decisive for ethical theory, since a morality based exclusively on the objective good for the person cannot sustain theoretical justification.

him, is the decisive factor which allows the recipient to be the *addressee* of the act of giving. It is this intention which allows the interpersonal space to be crossed,[10] and for the uniquely personal act of giving to be constituted. The intention of benevolence accounts for the difference between a true gift and the simple will to *cause* something which is an objective benefit to another being, even a person. Thus, for example, a doctor may cause an objective benefit for the patient, he may have clearly intended to create that benefit, and yet he may be completely lacking in benevolence. The patient was never the addressee of the act. Hence the act of doing good never became a personal act for or "toward" the other person. We could also say that the mere act of doing good which is an objective benefit is not *interpersonal* in a strict sense of the word. A fully actual intention of benevolence toward another person necessarily includes, as we shall see immediately below, the giving of oneself. Only then does the other become an addressee as opposed to being a mere object of a causal action.

We can briefly note here another implication of the gift that is addressed to the other by virtue of the intention of benevolence. Although the recipient is in a real metaphysical sense dependent on the donor, and in that sense subordinate to him, the intention of benevolence actualizing itself in a gift never lowers or demeans the recipient.[11] The self-righteous distribution of largesse repels the beneficiary, it intends to create and assert a distance between the "source" of the good and the beneficiary. A

---

[10] Cf. Dietrich von Hildebrand, *Die Metaphysik der Gemeinschaft* (Regensburg: Habbel, 1954), for an analysis of the different ways in which a real crossing of "interpersonal space" occurs in intentional acts, and how some of these acts are decisive not only for a spiritual "touching" of the other, but also for communion and a "becoming one" of two persons.

[11] Cf. John Paul II, Encyclical Letter *Dives in Misericordia* (Boston: St. Paul Editions, 1980), # 6, in which the Pope speaks of God's mercy, whose second name is love: "This love is able to reach down to every prodigal son, to every human misery, and above all to every form of moral misery, to sin. When this happens, the person who is the object of mercy does not feel humiliated, but rather found again and 'restored to value'" He goes on to speak about our prejudices about mercy which are a result of looking at it from the outside: "At times it happens that by following this method of evaluation *we see in mercy* above all *a relationship of inequality* between the one offering it and the one receiving it. And, in consequence, we are quick to deduce that mercy belittles the receiver, that it offends the dignity of man."

genuine will to do good for another person not only allows a true crossing of the interpersonal space, it also intends to draw the recipient toward the donor. Thus, the gift of a superior to someone objectively inferior *raises* the recipient.

8. The above example of the recipient being made to crawl for his
benefit lacks another decisive element in the gift. It lacks the *self-giving
of the donor*, which is necessarily implied in every gift of anything other
than of the donor himself. The father in our example certainly intended
to "do good" for the son, but his gesture was not "toward" the son. *He*
did not *move* toward his son. The failure to stretch out his *hand toward*
the *hand* of the son is a significant and accurate symbolic expression of
the inner content of his act.[12]

We have come to a point where we can more fully circumscribe the
concept of *giving* which was presupposed in the above discussion, but
which remained theoretically undetermined. We saw that for a gift to
exist, the donor cannot simply be the cause or the source of the benefit
constituted by the gift. We noted that the recipient cannot simply be the
objective beneficiary. He must in a real sense be the addressee of the
gift. But this means he must be *given* the gift in a full and strict sense of
the word. Giving as a *personal act*, in contradistinction to the *behavior*
of giving, cannot take place unless it is grounded in a self-giving of the

---

[12] Michelangelo's masterpiece *The Creation of Adam* in the Sistine Chapel is
an extraordinarily sublime, rich, and powerful symbolism of God's self-donation
to man in the act of creation. First, the "hand to hand" situation expresses the
fact that God is not merely the creative cause of Adams' existence, as he was of
pre-Adamic creation. God not only creates Adam, He gives Adam his existence.
Second, at the same time, the whole being of God moves toward Adam. God
gives Himself to Adam. Third, again the "hand to hand" symbolism indicates
that Adam is called to receive the gift of his own existence from God. Fourth, the
gap or slight distance between the hand of God and that of Adam indicates that
God granted Adam freedom and autonomy: as Eccl 15:14 has it, *reliquit Deus
hominem in manu consilii sui*, God left man in the hands of his own counsel.
Thus the almost languid position of the two hands. The theme is not the ineluc-
table power that was operative in creation, but rather a love which expresses
itself in a tender self-donation that refuses to overpower. Fifth, the position of
Adam and his hand indicates not only that he comes forth from God, but also a
movement toward God. Adam not only came from the hand of God, he also
slipped from it in original sin. The position of God's hand is a call and anticipa-
tion of a return. Hence it is also the symbol of a promise of a renewed self-donation in grace and in Christ.

donor. Only when there is a self-giving is the intended recipient *addressed as a person* as opposed to simply being the entity that is objectively benefited.

The significance and the uniquely distinct nature of self-giving comes into particular focus as a phenomenon in the context of, let us say, a mother who receives an incomprehensible scribble from a child, or a very modest gift from a poor friend who apologizes for the insignificance of the gift. Such a woman would surely respond with joy and the comment, "Thank you. It's the thought that counts." What is this "thought" that counts? Is it really a thought? Or is it the act of self-donation that constitutes the valid core of the moment? Again, the significance and distinct reality of self-donation is cast into relief when someone receives a very expensive present, but senses or knows the lack of a self-giving behind the gift. The "thought that counts" is not present, and this can be particularly painful when it concerns someone who should be giving a gift of self. And again, when a young woman is not ready or willing to accept a suitor, she will refuse or be reluctant to accept a gift, especially if it is expensive. Why? Precisely because if she is not ready to accept the suitor, she will not accept the gift which necessarily includes his self-donation.

9. If the moment of self-giving completes and defines the reality of giving on the side of the donor, it also allows us to focus, on the side of the recipient, on another and new essential moment in receptivity which was only implicitly present in the above discussion.

A *personal and active* relation to what is given necessarily includes a *self-possession* on the part of the recipient. This phenomenon is not clearly manifest when we deal with lower order goods which cannot enter, as it were, and become a part of our being. Thus, when we consider such gifts as money, flowers, candy, or some other material goods, or even some material services, in each case, the stress seems to be on "taking possession."

However, when we consider higher order goods which involve a benefit that accrues to the person's being, the situation changes. This difference becomes evident when we consider the receptivity that is involved in the gift of knowledge, or friendship, or above all in the love that another has for us. The higher the gift, the more does it involve and call for the acceptance or taking *possession*, not only of the gift and of the giver, but also *of the recipient by himself*. This mysterious and at the same time intelligible character of the phenomenon can be shown more clearly if we consider the fact that the higher the object in the hierarchy of values and being, the more does the "appropriation" of it involve a *free submission* to its reality.

We already encountered this paradox above in noting that the greater the power and the dominion over an object, the more did it involve an entering into it and allowing it its autonomy. But this means that the recipient must subordinate and *submit*, we can also say *conform*, himself or herself to the "*logos*," to the inner meaning and importance of what is received.

The higher the good of the gift, the more must the recipient actively conform in order to allow the intention of benevolence of the donor to be realized. Turning again to the indispensable example, let us consider an imaginary friend who is a glutton. Apart from the question of the wisdom of offering him a box of candies, we can see that no change in his gluttony is necessary for him to receive the gift and to enjoy it. The fact that he lacks self-possession, that he is possessed by his gluttony, in no way prevents him from appropriating what is given and "making it his own."

Taking a parallel example, let us imagine a young woman who has fallen in love with a man and offers herself in marriage. The man happens to be a lecher, a gambler and a drug addict, the perfect case of someone who lacks self-possession. Even if they go through the public ceremony of marriage and he "takes her as his wife," we can see that she is not "his own," that she cannot belong to him in a way that would correspond to the dignity and importance of the gift of her own being. The reason for this is that he lacks the necessary self-possession.

In order that a gift be properly appropriated and become "one's own," one must first become and be one's own. One must possess one's being in at least two respects. First, one must possess one's being in order to open oneself toward the gift and the giver in general. Only a personal being can open himself in an active self-possession. And second, the appropriation of the object, making it one's own in a receptive act, implies, as already noted, a power and dominion over its inner being. But this in turn calls for a self-submission and a self-conformity which can be performed only if the person possesses his own being, and has active dominion over it.

Here we encounter a paradox, as is so often the case when we deal with the mystery of the personal dimension. One becomes the master only in becoming the servant. So too with one of the most decisive essential marks of the personal being as personal. The capacity of self-possession belongs only to persons. It enters into the "definition" of person as person. But it can become actual only in the performance of its "opposite," namely in the self-submission and self-donation to another.

Genuine receptivity toward the gift calls for an appropriation that is at the same time a subordination to the inner meaning and reality of the gift. Both the active "reaching" out toward the gift as well as the submission by which the gift becomes "one's own" are possible only in the act of self-possession. The moment of self-possession plays a uniquely appropriate role in relation to the self-giving that is implied in every gift. It both actualizes and safeguards the dignity of the person. Whereas nonpersonal entities are "subject" to the laws of nature which determine them, the self-possession of the individual in his submission to the inner meaning of the gift and the giver makes possible his freedom. And it guarantees that freedom. At the same time it is the only proper and fitting response to the gift, as we shall see below.

10. The above discussion allows us to make explicit another fundamental element of the gift. Our imaginary friend will help us again. We give him a priceless gift, a self-portrait of Rembrandt. He thanks us profusely and takes it home. Several weeks later, he is about to change the oil in his car. In order to protect the garage floor, he places the Rembrandt below the oil pan. We catch him in the act and respond with horror. He retorts by saying that the painting is his now and that he can do with it as he pleases. Was it not, after all, given to him for his use, benefit and enjoyment?

Some gifts, indeed, are to be consumed in providing the benefit. Others have an importance which cannot be exhausted or reduced to the function of providing the benefit or enjoyment. They have an autonomous worth and significance. Such is the case with the Rembrandt self-portrait. Our friend is *bound* by this worth and significance, even though not absolutely. Thus, he would be justified in using it to ransom a child, or even in destroying it if that was the condition posed by a kidnapper for the return of the child.

The gift is not only a benefit. It can bind and even bind absolutely and unconditionally. The inner meaning and worth of the gift stand as a *norm which prescribes the proper behavior.*[13] This was already implicit

---

[13] The restrictions of space allow only the mention of other important themes in this relation. Thus, some gifts are unconditional in demanding acceptance,

in our discussion of the requirement that a genuinely receptive appropriation respect the autonomy and the true nature of what is appropriated. It is an integral and essential element of the gift and calls for a thematic *prise de conscience*. It secures our intuition of the nature of the gift against the tendency to reduce it to its *function* of being a benefit for the recipient. And it allows us to introduce another feature of the gift for our final consideration.

11. Every gift when it is accepted binds us normatively to *gratitude*. We abstract here from the affective plenitude that is an essential component of genuine, that is, "heartfelt," gratitude and focus only on its structural moment of *reciprocity*. It is suggested here that every gift, as gift, demands reciprocity. Furthermore, it is suggested that the gift as gift binds the recipient to reciprocity in a moral way.

We have seen that the genuine act of receptivity implies that the subject go out toward the gift and submit himself to the inner meaning of the gift in the act of appropriating it. We have also seen that this "going out" and submitting has a special significance with respect to the personal donor of the gift in his or her self-donation. The acceptance of the gift implies the acceptance of the donor as a gift himself.

But this self-donation to the donor has to become explicit for gratitude to be realized. The submission to the inner meaning of the gift has the form of a self-submission. As such, it is a form of self-donation. Thus, when it is the other person himself or herself that is the gift, the very submission to the person-gift already has the structure of gratitude. There is a self-donation in the acceptance of the person-gift. But it is still a structural part of receptivity. In gratitude, the giving of the self in return must be a distinct act, not merely the structural part of receiving the other person. Nevertheless, it seems that it cannot be a *separate* act. Rather, it must organically grow out of the act of receiving. Indeed, it can only grow organically from the act of receiving. It cannot simply follow by a free decision after the knowledge that one is the beneficiary of a good deed. The self-donation of gratitude is not something that can be initiated one-sidedly or even as a separate response to the act of another. Although it is a free act, and has a structure of spontaneity, by its very nature it seems to be something that is engendered by the act of re-

---

others not. Or, legitimate and objective norms, despite the fact that they bind the individual, can also be considered as a distinct kind of gift to the individual who is bound by them.

ceptivity to a gift.

These final reflections would be the basis for other considerations. One of them would be the question whether any human person can ever even initiate a gift to another, indeed, whether he could ever initiate an act of self-donation to another.[14] We are confronted with the question whether man could ever emerge from solitude, or whether in fact from the very beginning he was ever alone. We seem to be faced with a fundamental form of reciprocity, perhaps we could say *mutuality*, which characterizes the human condition. From the very beginning, it would seem, the very first perception of the other is a perception of the other as gift. But if no man is able to give the first gift, and therefore to initiate his own self-donation, then even though man is a gift to man, he would have to be a gift from a fundamentally Other.

By way of summary and conclusion, we can focus very briefly on some anthropological and theological implications of the above analysis. First, what takes place in the gift situation as such, the receiving and the responding, etc., is not something that occurs merely "in the mind" (if it were merely in the mind, it would not deserve the designation of "metaphysics"). The elements of the gift which we have considered imply a unique and distinct dimension of the metaphysics of the person as person. Second, man's cognitive relation to the world and himself is a fundamentally receptive one. The metaphysical structure of receptivity indicates that in the act of knowledge man subordinates himself to being which is not simply there, but is *given* to him. The very fact that reality is *datum*, given to man, is already an indication that man cannot consider it exclusively as a tool or mere means.

And finally, the recognition that reality, including man, is a *datum* becomes an element in and a basis for a strict philosophical proof for the existence of God, not as "first cause," but as a personal and benevolent omnipotence. John Paul II's intuition, as Karol Wojtyla, into the fact that man is a gift allowed him to come to the explicit cognition, as Pope, that as Creator of man, God already gave Himself to man. He writes that God "*already* as Creator has linked Himself to His creature with a particular love. Love, by its very nature, excludes hatred and ill-will towards the

---

[14] Cf. 1 Jn 4:19, "We love because He first loved us."

one to whom He once gave the gift of Himself."[15] The tradition has always spoken of God as Creator and Father. However, perhaps John Paul II is the first to give that tradition a precision which would allow us to locate God's Fatherhood *already* at the very Creation of man. He writes,

"God, as Christ has revealed Him, does not merely remain closely linked with the world as the creator and as the ultimate source of existence. He is also Father: He is *linked to man,* whom He called into existence in the visible world, *by a bond still more intimate than that of creation.* It is love which not only creates the good but also grants participation in the very life of God: Father, Son and Holy Spirit. For he who loves desires to give himself."[16]

---

[15] *Dives in Misericordia,* # 4, emphasis added. I do not exclude, of course, the action of the Holy Spirit who operates in a special way in the teachings of any Pope.

[16] *Ibid.,* # 7, emphasis added. In my "Man: The Creature of God," in *Creative Love,* John Boyle, ed. (Front Royal: Christendom Press, 1989), pp. 69ff, I argue that only in the case of a created person is existence given as a gift. This implies God's self-donation and hence grounds His Fatherhood in the creative act. The passage from John Paul II quoted above does not, perhaps, literally locate the Fatherhood of God at the creation of man; but the Pope is clearly speaking "already" of creation and his reference to a bond "still more intimate" sets man off against the "rest of creation." *Gaudium et Spes,* # 24, speaks of man as the only creature whom God willed, i.e., loved, for its own sake. And he who loves, as the Pope notes, "desires to give himself." Furthermore, the tradition speaks of the "gift" of life when it speaks of human life. The analysis of the nature of a gift allows us to hold that the very granting of this gift, at creation, allows us to speak of the Creator's self-giving to man, and therefore of His Fatherhood.

THE GOOD AND THE RIGHT

Fritz Wenisch

[This essay is based on a paper presented at the International Academy of Philosophy in Liechtenstein on November 16, 1993, entitled, "Das Rechte und das Gute." It summarizes several key ideas of a larger work on ethics which hopefully will "see the light of day" soon. Also, I would like to thank Stephen D. Schwarz who has made helpful comments on a draft version of this article.]

1. Introduction

a. Clarification of the topic

I do not plan to write about "good" and "right" in general; rather, my topic is limited to the difference and the relationship between what is *morally* good and *morally* right. Also, I will deal only with actions, those unique human acts through which we are able to intervene in the world around us.

Thus, one set of questions to be answered here is, "When are actions morally good, and when are they morally right—and does 'being morally good' always go together with 'being morally right,' and vice versa?"

Both 'good' and 'right' have negative counterparts. I shall use 'evil' and 'wrong' to refer to them. Thus, I also must deal with, "When are actions morally evil, and when are they morally wrong—and does 'being morally evil' always go together with 'being morally wrong,' and vice versa?"

b. A brief explanation of the nature of actions

By way of background, a brief explanation of the nature of actions is to be given. Examples are buying a cup of coffee, throwing a rock at a police officer, helping someone cross the street, mowing the lawn of one's front yard, planting flowers, and starting the engine of one's car.

What do these various instances of conduct have in common such that they are grouped together under the heading of "action"? In response, I offer the following definition (it is rather involved; the reader may wish to return to it after having considered the brief explanations of its parts as given in the subsequent paragraphs): An action is a species of human conduct which involves an observable behavior brought about and sustained by a free decision through which one intends to ensure that, apart from the observable behavior itself, the world outside of one's mind be different from how it would be if the conduct in question would not occur.

The three parts of this definition shall briefly be explained.

The first, that actions involve observable (usually visible or audible) behavior, is included in the definition to distinguish actions from merely internal acts or experiences, such as a purely internal decision to forgive an enemy, or an unexpressed affective response like joy or hatred.[1]

The second part, that in the case of actions the observable behavior is brought about and sustained by an agent's free decision, is included in the definition to distinguish actions from conduct which involves observable behavior not freely engendered. Take, for example, the kneecap reflex. If a person's kneecap is tapped and as a consequence, his or her leg moves, there is clearly an observable behavior on that person's part. This behavior is, however, not freely engendered by him or her; therefore, it is not an action.

The main reason for including the third part—the agent's intending that, apart from the observable behavior itself, the world outside of his or her mind be different from how it would otherwise be—is to distinguish *actions* from *activities* such as taking a walk or dancing. While activities may bring about changes—someone dancing might accidentally knock a table over—they are not engaged in for the sake of these changes, but for their own sakes.

2. The Nature of Moral Goodness and of Moral Evil

I turn next to a brief examination of the nature of moral goodness and moral evil. It shall begin with examples of morally good and morally evil actions.

---

[1] In the latter case, there would usually be no action even if the affective response would express itself in the face or in the conduct of the person, for even though an observable behavior would then be present, most of the time, the second and the third feature of actions, to be discussed below, would be absent.

a. Examples of morally good and morally evil actions

As far as examples of morally good actions are concerned, think about Maximilian Kolbe's sacrifice of his life for a fellow inmate, Francis Gajowniczek, in the Nazi concentration camp Auschwitz. Whenever someone had escaped from this camp, ten persons were randomly selected and locked up in an underground cell without being given water or food until they died. When Francis had been chosen for this cruel fate, Maximilian stepped forward and offered his life for Francis'. The offer was accepted.[2]

Other examples of morally good actions are: You meet an acquaintance who seems depressed, you feel sorry for him, and try to cheer him up. Or you speak out courageously against an injustice about to be committed, even though you are afraid that others will ridicule you for it.

These examples give rise to the questions, "What do they have in common that makes us call them morally good? What distinguishes the positive quality of moral goodness from all other positive qualities which may characterize actions, other types of human conduct, or non-personal beings?"

I turn next to examples of morally evil actions. In his novel, *The Brothers Karamazov*, Dostoyevsky writes about a Russian landlord during the time of serfdom who was a passionate hunter. Once, a serf's child threw a stone at play, and it hit a paw of the landlord's favorite hound. The landlord noticed that the hound was limping. Upon finding out what had happened, he ordered the boy to be locked up all night in a cold shed. The next morning, the villagers were ordered to assemble on a meadow. The child's mother had to stand in front of them. The landowner had the boy brought from the lock-up. He ordered him to undress. Then, he yelled at him, "Run!" The boy obeyed. The landlord told his hunters to unleash his hounds at the boy. The dogs ran after the boy, and tore his little body to pieces.

Here are two more examples of morally evil actions: Someone cruelly tortures a dog; a company president orders hazardous waste dumped on a site the company owns though he knows that this will have disastrous consequences for the health of future generations.

These three examples of morally evil actions raise the counterpart of

---

[2] See Patricia Treece, *A Man for Others: Maximilian Kolbe, Saint of Auschwitz, In the Words of Those Who Knew Him* (San Francisco: Harper & Row, 1982), pp. 170–1.

the questions asked before: "What do they have in common that induces us to call them morally evil? What makes the negative quality of moral evil different from all other negative qualities which may characterize actions, other human conduct, or non-personal things?"

b. Three features of moral evil and of moral goodness[3]

I begin with the questions just formulated.

First, morally evil conduct[4] makes the person engaging in it guilty, second, it makes the agent worthy of blame, and third, feeling guilty is an appropriate consequence of such conduct.

All three apply *only* to morally evil conduct: Nothing but morally evil conduct can make us guilty. Similarly, even though we blame each other for all kinds of things, only morally evil conduct makes us *worthy* of blame—blame for anything else is unjust.[5] Finally, feelings of guilt are an appropriate response only to moral evils existing in one's own person.

This third feature, *feelings* of guilt, differs from the other two features of moral evil in the following way: While both a state of guilt and blameworthiness are inevitable consequences of morally evil conduct, feelings of guilt are not a necessary consequence of morally evil conduct, but only an *appropriate* consequence. They can actually be absent when moral evil (and guilt) is present; furthermore, they can be present in situations in which no moral evil has occurred.

For an example of the first, think of a cold-blooded murderer. Even

---

[3] This part of the paper is deeply indebted to Dietrich von Hildebrand, *Ethics* (Chicago: Franciscan Herald Press, 1972), chap. 15.

[4] Moral evil and moral goodness are not limited to actions, but occur also in other types of human conduct, of which actions are a species, as the definition given earlier indicates. What holds true of the nature of these qualities in the case of actions holds likewise true whenever moral goodness and moral evil occur in other types of conduct. Thus, the explanation of the nature of moral goodness and moral evil given here applies to all instances of conduct capable of acquiring moral qualities, not only to actions. For this reason, I use, under this subheading, the wider expression "conduct" rather than the narrower "action."

[5] Schwarz suggested that there is a sense of "blame" which can rightly be applied to non-moral matters. For the sake of clarity, I propose using in these contexts expressions such as "being at fault" or—even better—"having made a mistake." If Schwarz is right, the same type of ambiguity would apply to "blame" that I point out below with regard to some of the designations of the features characterizing moral goodness.

though his action is morally evil (and makes him guilty), he does not *feel* guilty.

For an example in which feelings of guilt are present even though actual guilt is absent, think of a man who has known up to now only that his mother died when he was still very young. Now, he is told that she died while giving birth to him. It is psychologically understandable that he might feel guilty because of this; but clearly, he is not actually guilty, since what happened was totally beyond his control. This man needs psychological help to overcome his feelings of guilt which are objectively unfounded.

It is, of course, erroneous to consider appropriate guilt feelings experienced in consequence of *actual* guilt merely as a psychological problem. Imagine that I see a psychiatrist, and complain about severe guilt feelings. "Well," he replies, "We will surely get to the bottom of this. Can you recall something from your past which could have caused you to feel in this way—I am thinking of something like an educator who was too severe, or rules which were too rigid, or something else of this nature?" I ask, "Could my guilt feelings be caused by the fact that during the previous month, I killed both my parents?" He answers, horrified, "Is that all?" "No, I also disliked two of my siblings. So I killed them as well."

This psychiatrist should obviously tell me, "Your feelings of guilt are entirely normal. I would worry about you if you did not feel guilty after having acted in that manner. I am not the person to help you. You need a minister, a priest, or a rabbi."

Thus, concerning guilt feelings, the proper response may often have to be, "You feel guilty because you *are* guilty; it is *appropriate* that you feel that way."

To return from this small (but, given today's pop psychology not unimportant) digression: Morally evil conduct is characterized by the fact that it causes the agent to be guilty, that it makes him or her worthy of blame, and that feeling guilty is an appropriate (though not an automatic) consequence.

Next, the characteristics of morally good conduct are to be formulated. I must emphasize right away, though, that some of the terms which I will have to use to characterize moral goodness can also occur in non-moral contexts; they are equivocal terms.

The counterpart to morally evil conduct's bringing about guilt is, in the case of morally good conduct, that it contributes to the agent's righteousness.

The counterpart to blameworthiness of morally evil conduct is the praiseworthiness of morally good conduct.

The counterpart to the feelings of guilt which are an appropriate consequence of morally evil conduct is an experience of inner peace as an appropriate consequence of morally good conduct. Take as an example Florestan as he is introduced in the prison scene of Beethoven's opera *Fidelio*. In spite of the greatest external sufferings which Florestan's unjust imprisonment causes him, he still exclaims: "Sweet consolation in my heart, I have done my duty."[6] It is to be emphasized that, as in the case of "feeling guilty," this feeling of being at peace with oneself is an appropriate, though not a necessary consequence of morally good conduct.

To summarize the main points on the nature of moral goodness and moral evil: Morally good conduct contributes to a person's righteousness, it makes the person worthy of praise, and it *should* be connected with experiencing inner peace; morally evil conduct makes the person engaging in it guilty, it makes the agent blameworthy, and it *should* give rise to feelings of guilt.

3. Moral Restrictions, Demands, and Invitations

What now is the difference between moral goodness and moral rightness, and between moral evil and moral wrongness? To answer these questions, I need to clarify first what I mean by moral restrictions, demands, and invitations.

Imagine that you see a small child walking towards a road with heavy traffic. In this situation, there is a moral *demand* to intervene through an action preventing the child from walking onto the road. Further, imagine that you see a person whom you dislike standing at the edge of a precipice. You experience a strong temptation to push him over the edge. In this situation, you are confronted with a moral *restriction* against giving in to your temptation. Thus, there are moral demands and moral restrictions (henceforth often referred to, for the sake of brevity, simply as "demands" and "restrictions," that is, without the adjective "moral").

---

[6] See Josef Seifert, *Was ist und was motiviert eine sittliche Handlung* (Salzburg: Pustet, 1976), p. 48, footnote 48.

Often, these demands and restrictions are grounded in the nature of the concrete, individual objects which we are able to influence directly through our actions, such as other persons, ourselves, or animals.[7] Concretely and individually existing objects which are able to ground, because of their nature, restrictions and demands, I call "morally significant objects." A morally significant object is, therefore, to be defined as a concretely existing individual object which can be encountered in a situation in which it is the basis of a restriction of a person's liberty to affect it through an action the person may be capable of performing, or in which it issues a moral demand to perform an action affecting it.

Thus, morally significant objects are a first source of moral demands and restrictions. I say "a first source," because besides them, there are other such sources. One of them is a promise. As soon as I promise to omit an action, a restriction against performing it comes into existence; as soon as I promise to perform an action, a demand comes about that I perform it.[8]

Contractual agreements I enter into, commands of a legitimate authority, truth (to lie is not only immoral because it may harm others, but also because of a disrespect for truth which it implies), even the various tasks which one has because of the various situations one enters into during one's life, are sources of demands and restrictions. Here is an example for the last one of these sources: A person's being a parent makes the child a source of demands on the parent which do not issue from someone else's child.

In the case of morally significant objects, there is a third important moral "reality" differing from both the demand and the restriction. I designate it as "moral *invitation*" (again, for the sake of brevity, henceforth often to be referred to without the adjective "moral"). Examples of invitations are provided by most cases in which I could save another person's life only through an action which would risk my own life. Thus, Maximilian Kolbe responded to an invitation, not to a demand.

---

[7] In the previous paragraph, I have used examples of persons. Imagine, however, that you hear a dog howling, and you notice that a heavy door has fallen shut on his tail, thereby trapping him. In this situation, there is clearly a *demand* to help. Similarly, there is a *restriction* against actions inflicting unnecessary pain on animals.

[8] I cannot examine here factors which make a promise invalid, or how cases of conflicting promises are to be solved.

While both demands and invitations involve a call to action, there are the following two differences between them: First, it is morally evil to omit an action which corresponds to a demand one is aware of (such as if I fail to rescue a child from a dangerous situation even though I could easily do so), while it is morally neutral to omit an action corresponding only to an invitation (Maximilian Kolbe's fellow prisoners were subject to the same invitation as he was; they did not respond to it; but certainly, their conduct was not morally evil, but neutral).

Second, an action corresponding to a demand also corresponds to our duty (this is almost a tautology), while a situation in which there is an invitation enables us to perform a morally good action going beyond the call of duty.

4. Moral Evil vs. Moral Wrong; Moral Good vs. Moral Right

a. Moral evils and moral wrongs—the awareness-dependence of the former, and the awareness-independence of the latter

Next, I turn to the question, "What distinguishes a moral evil from a moral wrong?"

Imagine me taking one hundred dollars from you even though I am in no danger of starving to death, and even though also otherwise, there is no emergency situation. Normally, this is a case of a morally evil action—of common theft. I become guilty, worthy of blame, and I should *feel* guilty.

Imagine, however, that a two-year old girl walks to the house next-door, sees several exciting toys lying in the driveway, and takes them back to her own home. It is certainly true that her parents should use the occasion to begin gently teaching her about private property; but it would obviously be absurd to consider her as guilty or worthy of blame. Even though she has performed an action which should not have been done, her action is not morally evil.

Both examples have in common that the agent (I in taking the one hundred dollars, the child in taking the toys) violates a restriction. The difference is, however, that I am conscious of the restriction, while the child is not; furthermore, the lack of knowledge on the part of the child is not her fault—she has simply not yet learned about private property.

Even though the child's action is not morally evil, it remains true, nevertheless, that it violates a restriction. To highlight this morally significant negative property of the action, I designate the action as morally wrong. Thus, a morally wrong action is an action which violates a restriction. As the child's example shows, moral wrongness does not always go hand in hand with moral evil. Whenever a restriction is violated about which the agent does not know, and whenever this lack of awareness is not the agent's fault, the action is morally wrong without being morally evil.[9]

Thus, my theft of the one hundred dollars is both morally wrong (as violating a restriction) *and* morally evil (as making me guilty and worthy of blame). The child's action, however, while being morally wrong (as violating a restriction), is not morally evil (as not making the child guilty).

These examples make clear that an action's being morally wrong presupposes only that the action violates a restriction. Whether or not the action is morally evil depends, however, also on the agent's state of awareness with regard to the restriction. Even though the child violates a restriction, her conduct is not morally evil, since she has no awareness of the restriction violated (and since this lack of awareness is not her fault). Since I am aware of the restriction against taking the one hundred dollars, however, my conduct is morally evil.

In contrast to the last example, it is possible for a conviction that there is a restriction to which an action is contrary to be mistaken. This shows that actions can be morally evil without being morally wrong:

Suppose my friend has won the lottery. He asks me to invite Mr. Smith to the party at which the victory will be celebrated, but not to mention anything to Mr. Miller. I promise to comply with both requests. Since my memory is faulty, however, the next day, I mistakenly believe that I have promised to conceal my friend's winning from Mr. Smith. In spite of my firm and honest (even if mistaken) conviction that I have

---

[9] In the larger manuscript referred to at the beginning of this paper, I explain that an action which causes harm is not morally wrong if the person performing it lives in a society in a state of knowledge such that one cannot reasonably expect the members of this society to know that the action will or may cause this harm. For example, think of a physician three hundred years ago who performed an operation, naturally without sterilizing his instruments. It would obviously be absurd to say that his action was morally wrong because it involved the possibility of great harm—even death—caused by a subsequent infection.

The role which *potential* knowledge of the negative consequences of one's conduct has for the constitution of moral wrongness cannot, however, be discussed in this brief essay.

promised not to tell Mr. Smith anything, I inform him about the entire affair. Objectively, there is, because of my promise, a demand to tell Mr. Smith about the winning; consequently, my action is not morally wrong, since it is not contrary to a restriction. According to my erroneous recollection, however, I believe that the action violates a restriction. Does that not make me guilty? Does it not make me worthy of blame? And is this not an example of an action which is morally evil without being morally wrong?

As explained, it is sufficient for the moral wrongness of an action that the action violates a restriction. It is irrelevant whether or not the agent knows about the restriction. Thus, moral wrongness can be identified as an awareness-independent property of actions.

On the other hand, the presence of a moral evil is, in the following two ways, co-determined by an agent's state of awareness or conviction: First, a lack of awareness of a restriction may, if the agent is not responsible for this lack, have as its consequence that a morally wrong action the agent performs is not simultaneously morally evil; second, an erroneous conviction that an action is contrary to a restriction can have as its consequence that an action which is not morally wrong is morally evil. Moral evil is, in this sense, to be designated as an awareness-dependent property of actions.[10]

b. Moral good and moral right—the awareness-dependence of the former, and the awareness-independence of the latter

I turn now to an explanation of the corresponding difference on the morally positive side, that between moral goodness and moral rightness.

Suppose that I have promised to stay in town one day longer than originally planned in order to help you with an important and difficult problem. A change in circumstances makes it desirable for me to depart as originally scheduled, and I am strongly tempted to break my promise. I keep it, however, for the following two reasons: First, there is a sense of duty, and second, I am genuinely interested in your well-being. If my decision to stay despite the temptation to leave is made in a situation as described, it is morally good, that is, it contributes to my righteousness,

---

[10] It is to be emphasized that moral evil is *really* present in an action even if it violates a restriction which exists only according to the erroneous conviction of a person. A Christian has to admit that a Moslem who drinks wine truly becomes guilty, even if the former thinks that God did not actually forbid the drinking of wine.

makes me worthy of praise, and should be followed by a feeling of being at peace with myself.[11]

Picture now, however, the following different situation: I forgot my promise to stay a day longer. I stay, however, anyway because I intend to try out a new kind of ale about which I have heard, and this fortunate coincidence makes it possible for you to meet me at the time we have agreed on.

The fact that I do not even remember the demand to which my decision to stay objectively corresponds makes it impossible from the outset for my decision to be morally good (that is, to contribute to my righteousness, or to make me worthy of praise). It continues to be the case, however, that my decision corresponds to a demand: I do what I have promised, I stay an additional day. To highlight this morally significant feature, the action is called morally right. Since the first example of an action (where I stayed out of a sense of duty, and out of genuine interest in your well-being) corresponds to the same demand, it is likewise morally right. It is both morally right and morally good. The second action, however, is morally right without being simultaneously morally good. The lack of awareness of the demand to which this action objectively corresponds makes it impossible from the outset for it to be morally good.[12]

Besides actions corresponding to demands, there are also actions corresponding to invitations. These are included in the definition of morally right actions. Thus, Maximilian Kolbe's sacrifice of his life is, though not obligatory, morally right as the term is used here. Accordingly, a morally right action is to be defined as an action which corresponds to a demand or to an invitation.[13]

---

[11] It would be a serious mistake to think that actions corresponding to a person's duty cannot be morally good, in other words, that only actions going beyond the call of duty can be morally good.

[12] It is, of course, not morally evil either.

[13] In everyday language, there is no clear-cut distinction between 'right' and 'good.' (This and what is said below applies, *mutatis mutandis*, to 'wrong' and 'evil'.) The terms can even be used interchangeably. Thus, a part of what I am doing here is to call attention to two different "realities," and then, I stipulate that for one of them, I use the expression "morally right," and for the other, the expression "morally good."

In his insightful article, "The Right and the Good: Two Fundamental Dimensions of Morality," in *Aletheia* 5, 1992, pp. 59–76, Stephen D. Schwarz dis-

It is possible for a person to believe erroneously that an action he or she performs corresponds to a demand. Let me modify my last example once more: After I promised you to stay a day longer, you call me to release me from my promise, telling me that you yourself need to depart a day earlier than you had planned. I forget the phone call, however, and I refrain from departing because I think that staying corresponds to my promise; my sense of duty and my concern for your well-being motivate me to stay. Without any doubt, my decision is *morally good*. Since, however, there is no real but only an imaginary demand, the action is not morally right in the sense in which I have defined the term.[14] This shows that an action can be morally good without being at the same time mor-

---

tinguishes four senses of 'right'. The first is what is *obligatory*. This comes closest to how I define 'morally right'. The two concepts are, however, not identical. My concept of 'morally right' is wider than Schwarz's first meaning of the term, since I include in the category of morally right actions not only those which correspond to a demand (that is, those which are obligatory), but also those which correspond to an invitation. Schwarz's second sense is "what is unobjectionable." This seems to correspond to my category of the morally merely allowed, to be explained later. Schwarz's third sense is, "what is allowed." He explains this through examples such as "to kill an aggressor in self-defense." This could be morally right in the sense in which I use the term, such as if I have a duty to kill the aggressor because of considerations for my family or others whose well-being depend on me, or it could be what I call morally merely allowed, as in cases in which I have a right, but not a duty, to defend myself. Schwarz's fourth sense is that something is right in the sense of, "I have a right to do something," as, for example, in, "I have a right to take back stolen property." This seems to be a sense very different from the other three. In most cases, my category of 'being morally merely allowed' seems to apply to actions falling under this description, though, except for cases in which I have not only a right, but also a duty to act (if, for example, my family's well-being depends on me reclaiming the property). Then, the action would be morally right in my sense of the term.

While I do not wish to deny that in everyday situations, the word 'right' could be applied to any of the four situations Schwarz distinguishes, it seems to me that in the course of a philosophical analysis, it is advantageous to use different expressions for these different senses. At any rate, in the context of this paper, 'morally right' is meant to refer exclusively to actions which correspond to demands or to invitations.

[14] Naturally, it is not morally wrong either. It can, of course, also be morally right in senses other than the one I have adopted here; but then, to respond to what I have just said above, "No, the action *is* morally right," would mean to mistake a verbal dispute for a real one.

ally right.

A chief reason making it possible for the action just used as an example to be morally good is my (erroneous) conviction that there is a demand to which my action corresponds. A chief reason which makes it impossible from the outset for my action to be morally good in the case in which I forgot about my promise is my lack of awareness that my action corresponds to a demand.[15] This shows that the presence or absence of moral goodness is co-determined by the agent's conviction on whether or not moral demands are present. For this reason, moral goodness is to be designated as an awareness-dependent property of actions.

It is, however, sufficient for an action to be morally right that it actually corresponds to a demand or an invitation. It is irrelevant whether or not the agent knows about this correspondence. For this reason, moral rightness is to be designated as an awareness-independent moral property of actions.

There are, therefore, at least two awareness-independent moral properties of actions and of omissions. They are moral rightness and wrongness. There are also at least two awareness-dependent moral properties of actions and omissions. They are moral goodness and moral evil.

c. A difference between how moral evil and moral goodness depend on the agent's awareness

With regard to the awareness-dependent moral properties of actions and omissions, it is to be remarked that moral evil is more immediately awareness-dependent than moral goodness. It suffices to know or to be convinced that an action is contrary to a restriction for the action to be morally evil.

In the case of moral goodness, however, it is *necessary* to be aware or convinced of the fact that an action corresponds to a demand or to an invitation if the action is to be morally good; this awareness or conviction is not *sufficient*, though. Imagine that a woman is in danger of losing her life, and that a man could easily save her. Thus, there is a demand for him to act. Let us also suppose that he knows about the demand, but that

---

[15] This is not to deny that there could be situations in which the action could be morally good because of a factor other than the promise (if for example, my decision is motivated by a desire to help a third party to whom I have not made a promise, and if I act out of sincere concern in that other person's well-being). If, however, no such factors are present, it is impossible for the action to be morally good.

he saves her exclusively because he expects a financial reward. His action does not make him worthy of praise; thus, it is not morally good. On the other hand, the action corresponds to a demand (which causes it to be morally right), and the agent even knows about the demand. Thus, it is clear that the awareness of the demand is not sufficient to make the action morally good.

In this case, the lack of moral goodness of the action is to be explained through the totally self-regarding character of the action. In order to be morally good, an action must, therefore, in addition to the agent's awareness of a demand to which the action corresponds, be characterized by being at least partially non-self-regarding. This requirement can be fulfilled in three ways, which are, of course, not mutually exclusive, but can coexist: First, the agent is genuinely interested in the other person's well-being, second, the agent wishes to make his or her conduct conform to what he or she perceives to be the right thing to do, and third, the agent wishes to bring about an object that is important in itself.[16] A more detailed explanation of these three ways in which an action can be non-self-regarding cannot be given in this context.[17]

d. Moral neutrality and "being morally merely allowed"

As becomes clear from what has been said, we must distinguish the awareness-independent side of actions (moral rightness and wrongness) from their awareness-dependent side (moral goodness and evil). For a complete understanding of these two sides of actions, two further properties are to be highlighted. They come into view if we realize that there are two positive moral properties of actions, moral rightness and moral goodness, and two negative ones, moral wrongness and moral evil. For

---

[16] Thus, the dichotomy between self-regarding and non-self-regarding actions is not the same as that between self-regarding and other-regarding actions. The class of other-regarding actions includes only the first of the three ways in which an action can be non-self-regarding, that of being genuinely interested in another person's well-being. It does not include actions through which the agent aims at conforming his or her conduct to what is the right thing to do; nor does it include actions aiming at a realization of an object that is important in itself.

[17] Also, I cannot explain and justify here the fact that, in the case of the realization of something important in itself, the object realized must, in order to make the moral goodness of the action aiming at its realization possible, also be morally relevant in the sense which von Hildebrand assigns to this term in chap. 19 of his *Ethics*.

this reason, there are also two properties lying between the positive and negative properties. The first one is situated between moral rightness and moral wrongness. I shall call it "morally merely allowed." An action is morally merely allowed if it is neither morally right, nor morally wrong; that is, if it is *in fact* neither contrary to a restriction, nor corresponding to a demand or to an invitation. From what has been stated earlier, it should be clear that the applicability of this description is independent of the state of awareness of the agent. Thus, being morally merely allowed is just as awareness-independent as the two moral properties between which it is situated.[18]

The second of the moral properties which are neither positive nor negative is situated between moral goodness and moral evil. I call it moral neutrality. An action is morally neutral if it is neither morally good, nor morally evil. That moral neutrality, just as the two moral properties between which it is situated, is an awareness-dependent property of actions becomes clear if, once again, we compare my theft of one hundred dollars with the case of the little girl who takes toys from the house next-door. Since I know about the restriction I violate, I become guilty, which means that my action is morally evil. Since the child does not know about the restriction she violates (and since her lack of awareness of the restriction is not her fault), her action is morally neutral.

e. Conformities and discrepancies between the awareness-dependent and the awareness-independent aspects of actions and omissions

Diagramming the moral properties of actions shows that there are nine logically possible combinations between the awareness-independent and the awareness-dependent moral properties of actions.

---

[18] The word 'merely' in "morally merely allowed" is necessary for the following reason: It makes sense, for example, to say that risking one's life to save the life of another person is in some situations morally allowed. In those same situations, risking one's life would, however, also be morally right, since doing so corresponds to an invitation. At this point, however, I wish to speak of actions which are neither contrary to restrictions, nor corresponding to demands or invitations. Therefore, I must choose a term which distinguishes the category spoken about from actions which are morally allowed in the sense just explained. I have chosen "*merely* allowed," whereby the word 'merely' is to express that they are not also morally right.

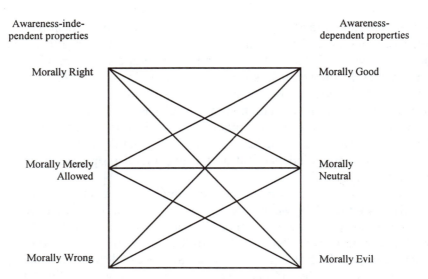

Awareness-inde-
pendent properties

Awareness-
dependent properties

Morally Right

Morally Good

Morally Merely
Allowed

Morally
Neutral

Morally Wrong

Morally Evil

The horizontal lines represent actions the awareness-independent as-pect of which is in conformity with their awareness-dependent aspect. As the diagram shows, there are three logically possible cases of con-formity. They are (1) being morally right and morally good, (2) being morally merely allowed and morally neutral, and (3) being morally wrong and morally evil.

The slanted lines represent actions in which a discrepancy between the awareness-independent and the awareness-dependent properties of actions exists. There are six logically possible cases of discrepancy: (1) Being morally right and morally neutral, (2) being morally right and morally evil, (3) being morally merely allowed and morally good, (4) be-ing morally merely allowed and morally evil, (5) being morally wrong and morally good, and (6) being morally wrong and morally neutral.

A conformity between the two sides of an action exists, for example, if a person acts contrary to a restriction about which he knows (as is the case with my theft of your one hundred dollars). Then, the action is mor-ally wrong and morally evil. Or suppose that a person carries out an ac-tion which is not contrary to a restriction, and which also does not con-form to a demand or to an invitation, and that the agent is conscious of this fact. This action is morally merely allowed and morally neutral. (Example: buying a glass of orange juice.)

A first example of discrepancies is the action of the two-year old girl who takes toys from her next-door neighbor's home. As stated, this action is contrary to a demand about which the girl is, due to no fault on her part, ignorant. Her action is morally wrong, but simultaneously morally neutral. A second example is the case of a woman who does what she has promised even though she does not remember at the time of her action that she has made a promise. Her action corresponds to a demand; however, she is not aware of it. Thus, the action is morally right and morally neutral.

The next task would be to examine for each of the nine possible combinations between the awareness-dependent and awareness-independent aspects, the necessary and sufficient conditions under which it obtains.

In executing this task, it would also have to be realized that up to now, I have only taken *actions* into consideration, not, however, *omissions* of actions. The necessary and sufficient conditions under which an *omission* of an action is morally good, right, wrong, evil, neutral, or morally merely allowed differ from the conditions applying to actions. Thus, a total of eighteen different cases would have to be considered. If and when my larger manuscript on ethics sees the light of day, these investigations will be presented in greater detail.[19]

5. Concluding Remarks

As has been shown, an examination of the moral properties of actions (and of other types of human conduct) is to take account of the difference between their awareness-dependent and their awareness-independent characteristics.

An investigation of this difference is important in its own right. It is, however, also significant in an attempt to argue against moral relativism. As has been shown, whether or not a particular action performed in a given situation is morally good, evil, or neutral depends also on the agent's state of awareness of restrictions, demands, and invitations, while the moral rightness and wrongness of an action does not depend on this awareness. Thus, with regard to the presence or absence of the

---

[19] Also, evidence will be presented there that the two cases of discrepancy appearing most controversial—that between being morally right and morally evil, and that between being morally wrong and morally good—are not only theoretical possibilities, but can actually occur.

awareness-dependent properties of actions, there is a greater relativity to the situation in which a person acts than with regard to the presence or absence of the awareness-independent properties.

Someone leaning towards moral relativism might now be shown that he or she is sensitive to this greater relativity, but mistakenly transfers it to the awareness-independent side of actions.

Arguing this point in detail would, however, be the subject of a different paper.

TWO PERSPECTIVES
ON THE MEANING OF 'GOOD'

W. Norris Clarke, S.J.

It is an interesting fact that in our language (and most modern Western languages, I think), there are two different grammatical ways of using 'good' as an adjective, each of which opens up onto a distinctly different metaphysical perspective. It is worth exploring these two different but related metaphysical horizons hidden implicitly in the very grammar of our language. And the fact that this modest contribution has to do with a reflection on the good, I intend as a personal tribute to the lifelong witness to the good and to value that Balduin Schwarz's own life has always been.

The adjective 'good' can be used first in an attributive position, e.g., "This is good music; this is a good friendship; this is a good man or woman, etc." It can also be used in a predicate position, e.g., "Music is good; friendship is good; humanity is good," etc. One could also rephrase the latter: "It is good that there is music, friendship, etc." The meanings in each case are indeed connected, since we do recognize 'good' as an analogous term. But the meanings in each case are obviously quite different. Let us explore each in turn, and then how they are related.

The Attributive Use of 'Good'

When we use 'good' in the first or attributive way—"This is a good friendship; this is a good man"—we are in what I might call an Aristotelian perspective. 'Good' here means that the entity to which it is attributed has fulfilled its nature, realized the natural potentialities of its nature, and come to a certain state of perfection or fullness. This is the way it should be; it lives up to its promise, to what we expect of it, and so we express our approval by calling it "good," which always connotes in some way the approval of our valuing faculty, our will.

But this approval remains entirely within the limited perspective of the entity's own nature, without any comparison with other beings. It is an affirmation with internal reference only. It is of this perspective that Aristotle has given us a rich metaphysical analysis, in terms of his well-known act/potency doctrine. A "good man" is one who has actualized, brought to actual realization, the natural potentialities already inherent in his nature, waiting to be developed and to be brought to fruition. The realization of the dynamic goal or "final cause" of his nature is well on the way to being attained. The same thing could be expressed in more Platonic terms by saying he has fulfilled or lived up to the Ideal, or ideal archetype, of man in the eternal World of Ideas, although the careful working out of the notion of real, objective potency has not yet been done by Plato.

Both of these metaphysical explanations provide us with a firm support for the grounding of an objective notion of goodness and value within this limited perspective. The affirmation of value here is built on the metaphysics of nature and is not merely the result of arbitrary personal or social opinion or feeling. The same basic Aristotelian analysis is taken over by St. Thomas and many other medieval and modern Christian as well as non-Christian thinkers. In technical Aristotelian terms, the goodness affirmed here belongs to the "accidental" order, since it is possible for a substance to exist without bringing to actuation its natural capacities. This basic act/potency analysis is part of the permanent Aristotelian legacy to the West.

The Predicate Use of 'Good'

The second way of using the adjective 'good', as a predicate ("Friendship is good; music is good; humanity is good . . ."), leads us into a significantly different metaphysical perspective. The context is no longer the limited one of the subject's own nature coming to fulfillment. We are now in the unlimited context of the entire range of being, and we are affirming that the subject in question has its place in the universal order of the good and value, that its very being as a whole is valuable, worthy of approval, in itself. We are equivalently saying, "It is good that *X* should be." Ordinarily, when we speak this way, we do not refer to a particular individual, e.g., "This man is good; that piece of music is good." We tend rather to use the first form mentioned above, e.g., "This is a good man; this is a good piece of music," etc. The predicate form is used primarily to affirm the goodness of a whole kind or level of being, to rate the very nature of the subject in question on the wider scale of be-ing. We can, however, refer to an individual if we wish, by using the form, "It is good that you exist; I am happy that you exist; it is good that we have Beethoven's *Ninth Symphony*"; etc. The metaphysical perspective is the same, the situating of the subject in question in the universal order of the good, in harmony with all the other goods of the universe within the ultimate order of being itself.

The metaphysical explanation of this much broader context is quite different. The previous act/potency analysis in terms of the subject's ful-fillment of its own particular natural potencies will not help us to situate it in the universal and absolute order of the good, where the goodness of its very being, in comparison with all others, is at stake.

Here we must shift to a participation framework. And we must leave Aristotle. He does indeed speak about the order of the good as a kind of universal ordering from lowest to highest; but because of his rejection of Platonic participation, there is no way he can really explain what the in-trinsic common element is in all that is called good. He admits the fact, but has blocked himself off from any further metaphysical explanation, save by extrinsic reference to the highest good, the Prime Mover. For a more adequate metaphysical analysis we must turn to the Platonic—Neo-Platonic participation tradition, especially as taken over by St. Thomas and integrated into a metaphysics of the act of existence (*esse*) as the ultimate source of all perfection.

In Neo-Platonic metaphysics, any particular being or kind of being can be affirmed as good because it participates, according to its own lim-ited mode of being, in the ultimate perfection of the universe, the good from the ultimate Source, the pure, infinite One-Good. Goodness (like unity) is an even more ultimate perfection than being itself, since the lat-ter always connotes some kind of limited intelligible essence within the integrated system of essences.

For St. Thomas, however, goodness itself must be further reduced to the more ultimate perfection of actual existence itself (*esse*), or be-ing in act, of which goodness is one transcendental and inseparable facet, to-gether with unity, truth (intelligibility), and beauty. Something is not a being because it is one and good, as for the Platonic tradition; rather, something is good because it participates in actual being, possesses an act of existence in some degree, as received ultimately from the Supreme Being, the pure, subsistent Act of Existence, which is also by this very fact the ultimate pure subsistent Goodness. The goodness affirmed of something in this perspective refers, therefore, not just to the accidental fulfillment of the subject's own potentialities, but to its very substantial being itself.[1]

It is important to note that for St. Thomas, only actually existing beings can be good; possibles, ideas, etc., are not yet in themselves good, but only master plans, guiding models, or exemplars for what *could* become actual goods once they entered the order of actual existence. Just as a possible being is a coherent intelligibility that could become a real being if brought into being by an existing cause, so a possible good is an intelligibility that could become an actual good if realized in an existing being. Aquinas differs sharply here from various post-Kantian thinkers, like Max Scheler, for whom the Good, Value, is a separate ontological realm of its own, independent, it seems, both of our ideas about it and of its instantiations in existing being. The root of all these positions, it seems to me, is the original Kantian split between the order of intelligibility and the order of real being. Since the real in itself is not intelligible for us, the realm of the intelligible is severed from its original rooting in being itself, and becomes a distinct realm for our minds; so too goodness and beauty, flowing from intelligibility, become distinct realms of their own for us, detached from being itself, as Josef Pieper has brilliantly shown.[2]

To affirm, therefore, that something is good in this absolute perspective is to situate it in its place in the universal hierarchy of all goods as a participant, according to its own nature or essence, in the ultimate perfection of existential being itself. It also means, implicitly, to situate it as an image of God, a created and limited participation in the ultimate goodness of the one who said, "I am who am." Only such a universal perspective can be an adequate grounding for moral vision.

The Relationship between the Two Perspectives

What is the relationship between the two perspectives we have just outlined, the good as relative to the nature of this particular subject, and the good as belonging to the universal order of the good? Which one has priority over the other? Clearly it must be the second which has primacy;

---

[1] St. Thomas, *Summa Theologica*, I, Q. 6, a. 3.

[2] Josef Pieper, *The Truth of All Things*, esp. chap. 1; reprinted in *Living the Truth* (San Francisco, 1989).

the absolute perspective grounds the relative. For when we say, e.g., "This is a good friendship," we are affirming explicitly that this friendship is realizing or fulfilling well the nature of friendship, what a friendship ought to be. But are we not also implicitly affirming two more things? (1) That this nature or kind of thing itself is something good in virtue of its participation in the universal value of being, i.e., "Friendship itself is good," and also (2) that the fulfillment of its nature is itself something good, i.e., "It is good to fulfill a nature."

Thus, it turns out that the attributive use of 'good', its relative meaning, is actually a derivative of its predicate use, its absolute meaning, and builds upon it. For unless we somehow recognized that the fulfillment of a nature is itself something good, something valuable, deserving our approval, better than its non-fulfillment in the universal order of good, unless this fulfillment is itself a new accidental participation in the value of being itself, we would have no good reason to give our approval to it—which we are always doing whenever we call something good.

And so it appears that the relative order of the good ("This is a good *X*") is really an expansion or development of the absolute order of the goodness of being itself. For it is in the nature of every finite being to expand, to reach out toward the fullness of being beyond, to participate in it insofar as the potentialities of its nature allow, and therefore to expand its own participation in the good as richly as it can. To be a finite being is to be on a journey towards the fullest possible participation in the absolute good, the value of being itself. And so to be "a good human being" means to be well along the way to achieving this expansive fullness. The order of the accidental or relative good is really only the flowering of the order of substantial good. "Every substance," St. Thomas says, "exists for the sake of its operation,"[3] and again even more clearly: "Each and every thing shows forth that it exists for the sake of its operation; indeed operation is the ultimate perfection of each thing."[4]

It is important to note, however, as this text clearly indicates, that, when we speak of this relative or accidental meaning of good, applied to a created being to indicate the fulfillment, in whole or in part, of its natural drive to the full perfection of its nature, "accidental" should not be taken to mean unimportant. The absolute meaning of good, as belonging to a being because of its very existence and indicating its place in the hi-

---

[3] *Summa Theologica*, I, Q. 105, a. 5.
[4] *Summa contra gentiles*, bk. 3, chap. 113.

erarchy of being, does indeed have priority in the order of foundation or ground, as substance always does over its accidents. But in the order of its own perfection, of achieving the end for which it is ordered by its nature, the accidental order of its movement toward the achieving of this end takes priority over the substantial or absolute dimension. Without it, the substantial being itself remains radically incomplete, frustrated in the purpose of its existence—unless, of course, if it is a sub-personal being, it can be used by some other being as a means for its own fulfillment. But for a human person, for example, whether he ends his life in heaven or hell is, in the metaphysical order, an "accident"; but which one it is determines whether the person's whole existence is a radical success or a radical failure. So in the last analysis the absolute and the relative dimensions of goodness are complementary and inseparable for the full intelligibility of any created being. And each takes priority in its own order. Only God transcends the distinction, since his very being is already the ultimate fullness of all perfection. But even in the created order we can still join the two together by saying that it is good, a good thing in the absolute order of being itself, that each being achieve as far as possible the fulfillment of its own nature, participate as fully as its nature allows in the plenitude of being as good.

What is it that enables us to weave together the two orders of goodness and thus recognize their relationship and form the analogous concept of *good* to apply to both? It is our faculty of the good, our spiritual will, rooted in the intellect, which reaches out to the entire unlimited order of being presented to it by the intellect, to love and approve it, and thus, by informing our intellectual consciousness, enables the latter to declare that being in all its manifestations is "good." It is one of our essential roles as human beings to be "the spokesmen of being" as both true and good, echoing, in fact, the great creative affirmation of God Himself, who both creatively knows and loves all that is.

Such, it seems to me, is the wonderfully rich texture of our most ordinary, everyday language, which constantly makes use of this richly analogous term 'good', playing back and forth without always being aware of it between these two metaphysical perspectives, the relative and the absolute. And every meaningful use of the term 'good' finally opens up, in some way, onto the ultimate all-embracing hierarchical order of being itself, in its many modes of higher and lower participation in the ultimate Good, the subsistent Act of Being itself, that is the Source of all being and goodness.

IN DEFENSE OF OBJECTIVE VALUES AND MORALITY

VALUES AND EDUCATION

Mark Roberts

It is not uncommon for many teachers and educators to maintain that the educational process should be value-free. This is often defended by the thesis that all values are relative, and therefore, students have the right to form their own set of values. No set of values should be imposed upon them, as this would presume that the imposed set of values was the correct set or better than any set the students formed on their own. Yet, under a value relativism, no set of values can be correct or better than another set since all values are relative; or instead, there is no way to know which set is correct or incorrect.

A value-free educational system is impossible to achieve, however, and any attempt to do so can only lead to numerous and diverse problems in the quality of education. Values necessarily pervade education and are by no means limited to the place of moral values in education and the development of moral virtue in students. Values are present in the goals of education, in curriculum design, and in the choices made regarding what is to be taught in each course. Therefore, value judgments, that is, judgments about what has positive or negative value or what lacks value, must be made whenever one determines the goals of education, designs a curriculum, or selects the contents of a particular course.

For example, educators and politicians declare that one problem in American education is that our schools are not producing a sufficient number of mathematicians and scientists. This obviously threatens the prosperity of our society which is one goal of education. We need scientific study in order to have machines to create images of the heart through the use of sound waves, or lasers to fill cavities without anesthesia. Yet, what it means for our society to prosper cannot be understood without introducing the concept of value. If human beings have no positive value, filling cavities without pain is no achievement. An abortion pill, though it is a technological accomplishment, accounts for a greater prosperity within a society only under the view that abortions are not morally evil. Indeed, how can the prosperity of society be a goal of education if the various forms of human community, such as the family, have no positive value?

Another example of the place of values in education is found when a school board decides that students should have a course in algebra, but not in the history of soap operas; or a course in sex education, but not on the influence of Christianity on Western Civilization. These decisions necessarily involve value judgments, for even if they are made solely on the basis of what students will need in life or what benefits society, value judgments are made in determining what it means to live well in society, what it is to be a good citizen, and what is beneficial or harmful to society. This also presupposes that society itself has a positive value. Moreover, if a course is included in a curriculum based upon what students will need in life, this implies that without this course students might be less happy in life. Yet, the future happiness of students must then be something which one judges to be of value which again presupposes the value of human beings.

Consider another area of education where value judgments are involved. Value judgments are involved if in designing a history course, one decides that the life of Martin Luther King or Susan B. Anthony should be studied, but not the life of Nathan Forrest or Alexander Stevens. Judgments involving aesthetic values must be made in designing a literature curriculum. Since not all poems or stories can be read, certain poems or stories must be judged, by some value criterion, to be better than others when they are selected for inclusion within a course.

Moral values are also presupposed in education. Students must respect each other and their teachers, and teachers must respect their students. Without the values involved in honesty, perseverance, patience, and especially self-esteem and reverence, it is impossible for students to be properly educated.

These brief examples should make it quite plain that education cannot be value-free. Indeed, the view that education should be value-free itself presupposes the value judgment that a value-free educational system is better than one in which values are incorporated. Moreover, the view that values should not be imposed upon students and that students have the right and freedom to form their own set of values is itself a value judgment which is imposed upon students, since they are educated by a system designed according to this thesis. This thesis also presupposes that human freedom has a positive value and that the rights of human beings should be respected.

Although the preceding remarks about the place of values in education are admittedly sketchy, it is not unreasonable to surmise that, when teachers attempt to make the classroom value-free, there will be devastating consequences in education and also within society itself. If one instead adopts the view that all values are relative and incorporates this theory of value within education, there will also be negative consequences, although it is not clear that educators recognize that this will occur and that it might, in fact, be the source of many of the problems they have. For example, it is inconsistent for teachers to complain that students do not respect them, while also maintaining that all values are relative. If all values are relative, including the value of persons, how is it wrong for students to be disrespectful, and why should teachers be respected? Indeed, is it even possible to respect someone if the value of a person is relative?

Teachers also complain about the poor reading and writing skills of their students. Yet, many of them also maintain that aesthetic values are relative and so believe that it cannot be true that "Elegy in a Country Churchyard" by Thomas Gray is in itself a much finer poem than "Trees" by Joyce Kilmer; or that *Oliver Twist* is in itself a marvelous novel. Nevertheless, teachers will make the value judgment that their students have inferior writing skills and poor reading comprehension. Not only are they in this respect inconsistent, but they fail to realize that one main reason why their students do not read and write well is that they are often not reading fine, well-written works of literature. (This is one problem with the adage that it is not important what students read, but simply that they read.)

Moreover, literature is one way in which students should develop and sharpen their ability to perceive values in the world around them. For instance, a gifted novelist can describe various qualities of an object or event through the use of appropriate adjectives and adverbs that refer to values. A mountain might be described as awesome or a person's action as admirable. In order to know the meaning of these adjectives, the reader must himself be conscious of the values they refer to, although he may first become aware of these values through the novelist's absorbing and penetrating description of the literary objects which bear them. Through reading certain literary works, a person can come to appreciate the difference between calling something awesome as opposed to majestic, or respectable as opposed to admirable.

The preceding remarks make it plain that the place of values in the formal education of youth is a topic of enormous complexity. For this reason, it is impossible to examine here the various ways in which values shape the quality of education. Rather, this paper will concentrate upon one problem in education which many teachers and parents might believe at first is not directly related to the issue of the place of values in learning, but which, on the contrary, is perhaps the most significant and fundamental way in which values form the foundation of education.

Many students are bored with school and learning. They lack what many educators call a love of learning. This is not confined to any particular grade or subject, nor is it confined only to students who do not apply themselves. Students might seriously study the material presented to them although they do not find it very interesting. Consider a particular imaginary situation typical of the problem just mentioned. Nick is fifteen years old and in the tenth grade. He is required to take biology which he finds moderately difficult, but not impossible as long as he studies the material. He does not like biology, however. He does not find it interesting and is bored by it.

Nick's biology teacher, Mrs. O'Rourke, suspects that Nick is bored although he usually pays attention in class. Finally, one day when Nick is especially bored, he interrupts the class and says, "Mrs. O'Rourke, why do we have to study biology? What is so important about biology?" It is crucial to recognize that if Nick asks these questions, he is bored and uninterested in biology class. A student who enjoys biology does not ask questions like this. Mrs. O'Rourke recognizes this, for she understands that the gist of Nick's question is his desire to know what is interesting about biology. Naturally, she wants Nick to enjoy biology and to be interested in it, so she does not reply (at least not at first) "Nick, I don't have time for this. Just pay attention to what I am saying and be quiet." No, she will attempt to answer Nick's query and will direct her answers to his question. In other words, she hopes that her answers will somehow enable Nick to enjoy biology. She does not want Nick merely to buckle down and seriously study biology. She instead wishes to engender in him a love of learning. Yet, does Mrs. O'Rourke fully understand exactly what it is about biology that enables it to be an object of interest and to engender the enjoyment many people feel when they study it? Consider three of the typical ways teachers attempt to answer questions similar to the one Nick has asked Mrs. O'Rourke.

Mrs. O'Rourke might first explain to Nick that biology is needed for the prosperity of his society since scientists use it. It is used in medicine, agriculture, oceanography, and so on. This is true, of course, and biology is important for this reason. Let us further assume that Nick is concerned about the prosperity of his society. Mrs. O'Rourke overlooks the simple fact, however, that nearly all people are interested in their society's prosperity, although they are not interested in studying those things which are needed to bring it about. Someone can be interested in toilets that flush and pipes that do not leak without being interested in studying plumbing. Someone might want laser machines that will painlessly fill cavities without the need for Novocain, without also having an interest in studying dentistry or engineering. The point is that Nick is probably interested in having many of the gadgets and conveniences found in a technologically advanced society, but this is quite consistent with his complete disinterest in studying those subjects used to invent them.

A second answer Mrs. O'Rourke might give Nick is that he will need biology in life. Yet, is this really true? Without question we need some knowledge of the physical life of plants and animals to get along in life, but it is very questionable whether we need most of the knowledge found in tenth grade biology. Most people will admit that they forgot most of what they learned in high school biology class.

Suppose we assume, however, that Nick will need biology in life. Mrs. O'Rourke overlooks the point that a person can recognize that he will need the knowledge of a certain subject in life and study it for this reason, but still not enjoy it. Examples might include a knowledge of typing, computers, mathematics, automobile repair, insurance, geography or a foreign language.

Thus, if Mrs. O'Rourke convinces Nick that he will need biology in life, Nick will not suddenly be delighted with biology. She wrongly presumes by her answer that Nick is bored with biology because he did not know that he will need it in life.

Lastly, let's consider another typical answer Mrs. O'Rourke might give Nick. She might tell him that he will need biology in his career. The first problem she might encounter is that Nick might have picked a career that does not require a knowledge of biology; for example, accounting, insurance, or merchandising. Mrs. O'Rourke might then resort to the tactic of telling Nick that his mind needs to be broadened; otherwise he would be unable to converse or interact well with other people. The implausibility of this answer is surpassed only by the fact that some students accept it; as if when people get together they talk about biology, or knowing biology will make one popular or likable.

Suppose we assume, however, that biology is relevant to Nick's career since he wants to be a paramedic. This leaves us with two possible situations. First, if he is not enthusiastic about becoming a paramedic, then he will not be interested in biology and enjoy studying it simply because he is informed that he will need it in his career. This might, in fact, dissuade him from becoming a paramedic. Second, if he is enthusiastic about becoming a paramedic, he would probably not find biology boring to begin with. Of course, a person who is very excited about a particular career still might not enjoy studying something he needs to know for that career. Biology and the biological knowledge used by paramedics are similar enough, though, that Nick probably enjoys biology if he is enthusiastic about becoming a paramedic. Thus, in the latter case, Nick would not have been bored with biology to begin with.

There are additional problems with the answers Mrs. O'Rourke offers Nick. Notice that all three answers propose some end or goal of education, and therefore, present education merely as a means to these ends. For this reason, Mrs. O'Rourke overlooks several difficulties with the strategy she proposes.

First, if any of her answers did motivate Nick to be interested in biology, his interest would be merely utilitarian; that is, it would be that of a means to an end. This presupposes that Nick have an interest in one or more of these ends, and if he does not, her answers are ineffective; for the importance of a means is a function of the importance of the end; and so an interest in the means presupposes some interest in the end.

Second, if any of her answers did motivate Nick to be interested in biology, his interest is quite compatible with a dislike of biology. An interest in something which is viewed as a means to an end need not be enjoyed. A person might study accounting and tax law in order to save money on his income taxes, but he need not enjoy such study. He has an interest in it as a means to saving money, and he will enjoy saving money; but he need not enjoy studying what is needed to realize the savings. Thus, utilitarian interest is consistent with a dislike of the means one has an interest in.

Third, as previously mentioned, a person can have an interest in an end without even a utilitarian interest in the means. This is why Nick might be interested in his society's technological advancement, without having an interest in the means necessary to bring it about.

In summary, Mrs. O'Rourke's answers need not engender in Nick any interest in biology, but even if they did, the interest would be merely utilitarian and would not be a love of learning.

This same point can be made by approaching the issue from a different angle. Suppose that Nick enjoyed biology so much that he wanted to be a biologist. How effective are Mrs. O'Rourke's answers in explaining Nick's interest and motivation? His motivation cannot be explained by stating that biology is relevant to his career, since the question concerns precisely why he chose the career that he did.

Is it realistic to suppose that Nick's interest in biology stems from a concern with the technological advancement of his society? One difficulty with this supposition is that there are numerous disciplines that are relevant to the technological progress of a society. Thus, an interest in the technological advancement of society cannot explain why he chose biology rather than some other relevant area.

It is for this same reason that monetary reward cannot explain Nick's desire to become a biologist; for there are innumerable careers as lucrative or more lucrative than biology.

One might remark that Nick just likes biology, or is interested in it, that is, that he has a love of learning. It should be obvious, however, that his love of learning is not explained by the kinds of answers Mrs. O'Rourke gave when we supposed that Nick was bored with biology. Her answers cannot engender a love of learning in Nick; for if he had a love of learning, he would not be motivated by the kind of interest suggested by Mrs. O'Rourke's answers. The fundamental reason for this is that what is viewed merely as a means to an end is in that respect not loved. Just as someone who loves another person does not view that person merely as a means to an end, someone who loves learning does not in that respect treat learning merely as a means to an end. This is what is overlooked in the contemporary educational climate: a love of learning presupposes that learning and education cannot be merely means to certain ends. A love of learning will not be engendered by an educational climate in which education is stressed primarily as a way to "get ahead," or an opportunity for one's financial advancement. The latter can produce only the interest one has in a means to an end. A desire to marry a person merely because the person is rich is an interest in that person, but it is hardly love. Therefore, the utilitarian nature of Mrs. O'Rourke's answers need not motivate Nick to be interested in learning, but even if they did, the interest would be utilitarian, and the latter is not a genuine love of learning.

There are perhaps educators who would agree with the previous remarks, but they probably do not realize that the possibility of a genuine
love of learning introduces within the classroom not just the realm of
values, but values which cannot be relative and are instead intrinsic. To
develop this topic further, a number of observations must be made concerning the nature of value.[1]

Some objects are important or have a value because of the particular
effect they have on a person. For example, objects can be positively or
negatively important because they have the capacity to cause pleasure or
pain. Certain foods, for instance, have a positive value because some
people enjoy their taste. It is the capacity of these foods to cause pleasure when they are eaten which accounts for the positive value they have.
If these foods ceased to cause pleasure in anyone who ate them, then
they would lose this particular value.

Yet, because their positive value, what might be called the "value of
the pleasurable," results from a particular effect these foods have on certain persons, their positive value is relational. It is not a value these
foods have in themselves, but a value which is dependent upon the particular pleasurable effect these foods have on a person. Thus, these foods
have the value of the pleasurable, but they have this value in relation to
the persons in whom they cause pleasure. These foods do not have this
value intrinsically; that is, they do not have this value in themselves.

These same foods, of course, might not be enjoyed by other people.
They might find these same foods unpleasant. In this case, these foods
would have the value of the displeasurable, again, not intrinsically, but
in relation to the people in whom they caused displeasure. Thus, the
same foods might simultaneously have the positive value of the pleasurable and the negative value of the displeasurable because these foods do
not have these two values intrinsically. Rather, because these foods have
these two values as a result of whether they cause pleasure or displeasure, they have these two values in relation to two different groups of persons.

It is worth noting that even if every person enjoyed a certain food,
the food would still have the value of the pleasurable *in relation* to all
people. Its value would not in this instance become intrinsic simply be-

---

[1] In the analysis of values which follows, I must express my debt to the
views of Dietrich von Hildebrand, although some of my points and my terminol-
ogy deviates from his.

cause there was no variation. The value is relational because of its dependence upon a specific relation between the object and a person; not because the object's value might vary from one person to another.

These same foods can have another type of value which also depends upon the particular effect they have on persons. Foods can be beneficial or harmful to the person who eats them. Thus, they can have the value of the beneficial because they have a beneficial effect on certain persons. For this reason, these foods, again, would not have this value in themselves, intrinsically; they would have the positive value of the beneficial in relation to the persons in whom they had a beneficial effect.

It is, of course, also true that other people might be allergic to these foods. In this case, these foods would have the value of the harmful in relation to these other people. Moreover, as is too often the case, a certain food can have the value of the pleasurable and the value of the harmful, or the value of the beneficial but also the value of the displeasurable.

It is crucial to recognize that objects which have these types of values have them as a result of a relation to certain persons and the particular type of effect these objects have on these persons. It is in this way that a value is relative inasmuch as the predication of one of these values to an object requires a reference to a person or group of persons. It is incomplete to assert, "Lobster has the value of the pleasurable," since lobster cannot have this value intrinsically, but only with reference to one or more persons who experience pleasure when they eat lobster. Thus, the proposition would have to be expressed in the form, "Lobster has the value of the pleasurable in relation to Smith and Jones." If a certain activity, such as smoking, is harmful for everyone, then it is still incomplete to assert, "Smoking is harmful"; one should add, "for everyone." The harmfulness of smoking is still relative and not intrinsic even if it is harmful for all people.

The preceding remarks acknowledge then that certain values are relative, since these values are dependent upon a relation between one or more persons and the objects which have these values. These values can certainly motivate us; for example, we eat certain foods because they are pleasurable, and avoid others because we find them unpleasant. We also eat certain foods because they are beneficial, and avoid others because they are harmful. Yet, when we are motivated by a relative value, a value dependent upon a relation between the object and ourselves, our interest in the object stems from our interest in the effect the object has on us, that effect which accounts for the object's value. For example, if lobster has the value of the pleasurable in relation to Smith, and Smith takes an interest in lobster for this reason, Smith is interested in the lobster because of the pleasure he receives from eating it. To put it simply: Smith eats the lobster because of an interest in his own pleasure. He acts with an interest in himself, an interest in some personal advantage. This results necessarily from the fact that the value of the lobster in this instance depends upon whether Smith feels pleasure when he eats it. Since the lobster has the value of the pleasurable in relation to Smith, Smith must be acting with an interest in himself if this value motivates his interest in the lobster. In this instance, Smith must approach the lobster with an interest in his own pleasure, since the lobster has the value of the pleasurable precisely in relation to Smith and not intrinsically.

This example illustrates a central principle concerning relative values which is unfortunately overlooked by those people who assert that all values are relative. If all values are relative, persons can care only for themselves and must always act only with an interest in themselves, with regard to some personal benefit; for their interest in the object cannot exceed their interest in the particular effect which accounts for the object's value. Alternatively, if, in certain instances, persons can care for someone or something else, if they can act with an interest not in themselves, but simply in someone or something else, then the value of the object which motivates their actions cannot result from a relationship to themselves. The value of the object would have to be intrinsic; it would have to be a value the object has because of what it is.

Two important clarifications should be made. First, it is important not to equate intrinsic values with ends. This is an exceedingly complex topic, and it will have to suffice to point out that something which is desired can be an end without in that respect having intrinsic value. To desire chocolate for the pleasure it provides shows that pleasure can be the end of an action without the value of the chocolate being intrinsic.

Second, it is crucial to recognize that this issue of relative and intrinsic values centers upon the question of interest, not on the question of whether or not certain actions have some effect. If a man marries a woman merely because she is rich, then his interest is merely in the beneficial effects he intends to receive through the marriage. If he instead genuinely loves her and marries her, he will still receive the same benefits, but his interest was not in these benefits. The question of motivation is not settled, then, by the question of whether or not there are benefits, but rather by the question of whether or not the interest is in the benefits.

Are there instances in education in which someone has a non-utilitarian interest in an object?

People of all ages have a fascination with dinosaurs. Children are especially interested in them, as are college students, for among the most popular courses at many colleges and universities are the courses on dinosaurs. Yet, compare the interest children and college students have in dinosaurs with the three ends of education mentioned by Mrs. O'Rourke in her response to Nick's query. The interest children and college students have in dinosaurs clearly does not stem from an interest in the prosperity of their society. One would also be hard-pressed to explain how they can use their knowledge of dinosaurs later in life. Moreover, children who are too young to have seriously picked a career cannot explain their interest in dinosaurs by the relevancy such knowledge has for a career. Indeed, the college students who are interested in dinosaurs are hardly limited to those who wish to become paleontologists. Since their interest cannot be explained by an interest they have in one or more of the ends of education, what, then, engenders the interest children and college students have in dinosaurs? (This question can be extended to the interest they often have in nature in general: in animals, insects, numbers, the sky and the stars, etc.)

What should also be stressed is that the interest children and college students have in dinosaurs is not an interest in some personal benefit. They do not act with an interest in themselves, but with an interest in knowing something about dinosaurs. Yet, they do not view the knowledge of dinosaurs from the point of view of how it can be applied or what they can do with it. They do not have a utilitarian interest, but instead what has traditionally been described as an interest in knowledge for its own sake. This is precisely what a love of learning is. To love a person or some thing is to care about that person or that thing and to act for its sake. Should this be so surprising? Is this also not, in fact, a type of interest paleontologists, mathematicians, sociologists, philosophers, etc., do have themselves? Have they not also a love of learning? How reasonable is it to believe that the interest scientists and philosophers have in their disciplines is identical to the reasons Mrs. O'Rourke offered to Nick?

The reply might be given that scientific and philosophical knowledge has a use and application, and does benefit, in diverse ways, the scientists and philosophers themselves. Moreover, although children and college students may not realize it, their pursuit of knowledge does benefit themselves and society. This is all true. Nevertheless, it exposes a critical misunderstanding of the present issue, a misunderstanding previously mentioned. The question is not whether there *is* some benefit or effect of their interest, but whether their interest is *in* some benefit or effect.

Therefore, when people pursue knowledge for its own sake, it does not follow that there is no personal benefit involved, or some benefit to society. It is rather a question of their motives, not of the mere effect of their pursuit. Thus, children's interest in dinosaurs may have some benefit for them, but an examination of their interest in dinosaurs reveals that their interest is not in this benefit, but simply in the knowledge about dinosaurs.

Similarly, the claim that scientists and philosophers also pursue knowledge for its own sake is not refuted by showing that such knowledge has a use, and that acquiring such knowledge has certain personal benefits for them or society. It would be refuted only if one could show that scientists and philosophers, in their pursuit of scientific and philosophical knowledge, are always interested only in themselves or in the effect of their study upon society. Yet, are not their long hours of experimentation and study instead simply a development of that simple pursuit of knowledge a child has, and which they themselves have now, and probably also have had as children?

Perhaps one problem is that the pursuit of knowledge for its own sake is not the romantic or quixotic notion many people might take it to be. It may be as simple as a child's interest in learning about dinosaurs without a consideration of how it will benefit him; or as simple as a person's interest in raising objections to some of the theses which have been put forth in this article. The person's desire to expose the falsity he believes has been asserted is an interest in truth for its own sake, and is hardly reducible merely to an interest in some personal benefit, which in all likelihood has not entered his mind.

Yet, as previously argued, it is possible to take an interest in an object for its own sake only if its value is intrinsic. Thus, it is only possible to pursue knowledge for its own sake if knowledge has an intrinsic value. Without it, a love of learning is not possible; for to love learning is to care about it, and this is not possible if knowledge does not have an intrinsic value. Accordingly, not only must values have a place in education, but only by recognizing the intrinsic value of knowledge can one avoid the further deterioration of the educational system brought about by the view that education is only a means to some end. In this way, students can at least partially overcome the complete self-centeredness fostered by the latter view. For what is love without self-donation, and what is the love of learning, except the sacrifice of oneself for the sake of something higher?

A Refutation of Moral Relativism

Peter Kreeft

I. Purpose

The essence of living in a free society is to live freely. Just as "a good society is one that makes it easy to be good" (Peter Maurin), so a free society is one that makes it easy to be free.

To be free and to live freely is to live spiritually. Only spirit is free. Matter is not.

To live spiritually is to live morally. The two essential properties of spirit that distinguish it from matter are intellect and will, the capacity for knowledge and morality, the ideals of truth and goodness.

The most radical threat to living morally today is the loss of moral principles. Moral practice has always been difficult for fallen humanity, but at least there has always been the lighthouse of moral principles, no matter how stormy the sea of moral practice got. Today for the majority of our mind-molders, in formal or informal (media) education, the light is gone. Morality is a fog of feelings. As Chesterton said, "Morality is always dreadfully complicated—to a man who has lost his principles."

Principles mean moral absolutes, unchanging rocks beneath the changing waves of feelings and practice. Moral relativism is the philosophy that denies moral absolutes. That philosophy is the Prime Suspect, Public Enemy Number One; that is, the philosophy that has put out the light in the minds of our teachers, then their students, and eventually, if not reversed, our whole civilization.

Therefore the purpose of this essay is not just to present a strong case against moral relativism, or arguments against it, or good reasons for rejecting it, but to *refute* it: to unmask it, to strip it naked, to humiliate it, to shame it, to give it the Texas-sized *whuppin'* it deserves.

II. Definitions

We should begin with the most necessary part: a definition of moral relativism. Moral relativism usually includes three claims: that morality is (1) changeable, (2) subjective, and (3) individual; that it is relative to (1) changing times ("You can't turn back the clock"), (2) what we subjectively think or feel ("There is nothing good or bad, but thinking makes it so"), and (3) individuals ("Different strokes for different folks").

III. Importance

How important is this issue? After all, it's just philosophy, and philosophy is just "ideas."

But "ideas have consequences." Sometimes these consequences are as momentous as a Holocaust, or a Hiroshima. Sometimes even more momentous.

Philosophy is just thought. But "sow a thought, reap an act; sow an act, reap a habit; sow a habit, reap a character; sow a character, reap a destiny." This is as true for societies as it is for individuals.

How important is the issue? The issue of moral relativism is merely the single most important issue of our age. No society in human history has ever survived without rejecting the philosophy we are about to refute. There has never been a society of relativists. Therefore our society will either (a) disprove one of the most universally established laws of all history, or (b) repent of its relativism and survive, or (c) persist in its relativism and perish.

How important is the issue? C. S. Lewis says (in "The Poison of Subjectivism") that relativism "will certainly damn our souls and end our species." Please remember that Oxonians are not given to exaggeration.

Why "damn our souls"? Because Lewis, as a Christian, does not disagree with the fundamental teaching of Christ (and all the prophets in his Jewish tradition) that salvation presupposes repentance, and repentance presupposes an objectively real moral law. Moral relativism eliminates that law, thus repentance, thus salvation.

Why "end our species" and not just modern Western civilization? Because the entire human species is becoming increasingly westernized—a kind of cultural vampirism, with all non-Western cultures as its victims, the global metastasizing of a malignant moral cancer.

It is ironic that America, the primary source of relativism in the world today, is by far the West's most religious nation. For (to extend our analogy) religion is to relativism what Dr. Van Helsing is to Count Dracula. Within America, the strongest opposition to relativism resides in the churches. Yet—a still further irony—according to the most recent polls, Catholics are exactly as relativistic, both in belief and behavior, as non-Catholics; 62% of Evangelicals disbelieve in any absolute or unchanging truths; and Jews are significantly *more* relativistic (and more secular) than Gentiles. Only Muslims, Orthodox Jews, the Eastern Orthodox, and Fundamentalists seem to be resisting the culture, but not by converting it but by withdrawing from it.

When Pat Buchanan told us, in 1992, that we were in a "culture war," nearly everyone laughed, sneered, or barked at him. Today, nearly everyone knows he was right. And the "culture war" is most centrally about this issue.

IV. Arguments for Relativism Refuted

The arguments *for* moral relativism should be examined first, and refuted, to clear the way for the arguments against it. First we refute each of the arguments for relativism (Section IV), then we refute relativism itself (Section V).

First argument

In practice, psychological "becauses" (subjective, personal motives) are a more powerful source of moral relativism than logical "becauses" (objective, logical arguments). What is the main motive for preferring relativism? Probably the fear that an absolute moral law would make us unhappy and guilty, so we call moral absolutism "unloving" or "uncompassionate."

Turned into an argument, it looks like this: good morality has good consequences, bad morality has bad consequences. Feelings of unhappiness and guilt are bad consequences, while feelings of happiness and self-esteem are good consequences. Moral absolutism produces the bad feelings of guilt and unhappiness, while moral relativism produces the good feelings of self-esteem and happiness. Therefore moral absolutism is bad and moral relativism is good.

Response

(a) The answer to this argument is, first of all, that absolute moral law is there not to minimize but to maximize people's happiness, and therefore is maximally loving and compassionate—like labels, or road maps. You're hardly happy if you eat poison or drive off a cliff.

(b) What about guilt? Removing moral absolutes does indeed remove guilt, and guilt obviously does not make you happy in the short run. But guilt, like physical pain, may be necessary to avoid greater unhappiness in the long run—if it is realistic, that is, in tune with reality. The question is: Does reality include objective moral laws? Guilt is an experience as pointless as paranoia if there is no real moral law, but as proper as pain if there is, and for a similar reason: to prevent harm. Guilt is a warning in the soul analogous to pain as a warning in the body.

(c) The argument has a question-begging assumption: that feelings are the standard for judging morality, whereas the claim of traditional morality is exactly the opposite: that morality is the standard for judging feelings.

(d) If the argument from self-esteem vs. guilt is correct, it follows that, if rapists, cannibals, or tyrants feels self-esteem, they are better persons than if they feel guilty.

Second argument

A second argument for relativism seems impregnable because it is based on an indisputable fact. The claim is that anthropologists and sociologists have discovered moral relativism to be an empirical fact. Different cultures and societies (and different individuals) do in fact have very different moral values. In Eskimo culture, killing old people is right; in pre-Kevorkian America, it's wrong. In contemporary America, fornication is right; in Christian cultures, it's wrong. And so forth.

Descartes notes, in the *Discourse on Method*, that there is no idea so strange that some philosopher has not seriously taught it. Similarly, there is no practice so strange that some society has not legitimized it (e.g., genocide, cannibalism) or forbidden it (e.g., entering a temple with a hat on—or without one).

So anyone who thinks values are not relative to cultures is simply ignorant of facts.

Response

(a) To see the logical fallacy in this apparently impregnable argument, we need to look at its unspoken assumption, which is that moral rightness is a matter of obedience to cultural values; that it is right to obey your culture's values. Only if we combine *that* hidden premise with the overt premise that values differ with cultures, do we get the conclusion that moral rightness differs with cultures, that what is wrong in one culture is right in another. But surely this hidden premise begs the question. It presupposes the moral relativism it is supposed to prove. The absolutist *denies* that it is always right to obey your culture's values. He has a trans-cultural standard by which he can criticize a whole culture's values. That is why he can be a progressive and a radical, while the relativist can only be a status quo conservative, having no higher standard than his culture ("my country right or wrong"). Only massive media "Big Lie" propaganda could have so confused people's minds that they spontaneously think the opposite. In fact it is only the believer in the old-fashioned Natural Moral Law who can be a social radical and progressive. He alone can say to a Hitler: "You and your whole social order are wrong, and wicked, and deserve to be destroyed." The relativist can only say: "Different strokes for different folks, and I happen to hate your strokes and prefer mine, that's all."

(b) A second logical weakness of the argument about cultural relativism is its equivocation on the term "values." The absolutist distinguishes subjective opinions about values from objectively true values, just as he distinguishes subjective opinions about God, or life after death, or happiness, or numbers, or beauty (just to take five other non-empirical things) from the objective truth about these things. It may be difficult (or even impossible) to prove, or to attain certainty about, or even to know, these things; but that does not mean they are unreal. Even if these things cannot be known, it does not follow that they are unreal. Even if they cannot be known with certainty, it does not follow that they cannot be known by "right opinion." Even if they cannot be proved, it does not follow that they cannot be known with certainty. And even if they cannot be proved by the scientific method, it does not follow that they cannot be proved at all.

The equivocation in the cultural relativist's argument is between "value opinions" and "values." Different cultures may have different *opinions* about what is morally valuable, just as they may have different opinions about what happens after death; but this no more entails the conclusion that what is right in one culture is wrong in another, than different opinions about life after death entails the conclusion that different things happen after death depending on cultural beliefs. Just because I think there is no eternal Hell does not prove there is none, and that I will not go there. If it did, the simple and infallible way to escape Hell would be simply to stop believing in it! Similarly, just because a good Nazi *thinks* genocide is right does not prove it is. Unless, of course, "there is nothing good or bad but thinking makes it so"—but this is the relativist's *conclusion*. It cannot also be his premise without begging the question.

(c) There is still another error in the cultural relativist's argument. (It seems that just about everything that can possibly go wrong with an argument goes wrong with this one!) The argument from "facts" doesn't even have its facts right. Cultures do *not* in fact differ totally about values, even if the term "values" is taken to mean merely "value opinions." No culture ever existed which believed and taught what Nietzsche called for: a "transvaluation of all values." There have been differences in emphasis, and areas of moral blindness—e.g., our ancestors valued courage more than compassion, while we value compassion more than courage— but there has never been anything like the relativism of opinions about values that the relativist teaches as history. Just imagine what that would be like: a society where justice, honesty, courage, wisdom, hope, and self-control are deemed evil; and unrestricted selfishness, cowardice, folly, betrayal, addiction, and despair are deemed good! Such a society is never found on earth. If it exists anywhere, it is only in Hell (and its colonies). Only Satan (and his worshippers) say "Evil, be thou my good!"

There are important disagreements about values between cultures, but beneath the disagreement about lesser values lies agreement about more basic ones. Or else, beneath disagreements about applying values to situations (e.g., should we have capital punishment?) lies agreement about values (e.g., murder is evil, since human life is good). Moral disagreement, between cultures as well as individuals, would be impossible unless there were some moral agreement, some common premises.

Moral values are to positive laws what concepts are to words. When you visit a strange country, you experience an initial shock: the language seems totally different. But then, beneath the different words, you find common concepts, and this alone makes translation from one language to another possible. Analogously, beneath different social laws we find common human moral laws, similar morals beneath different mores. The moral agreement among Moses, Buddha, Confucius, Lao Tzu, Socrates, Solomon, Jesus, Cicero, Muhammad, Zoroaster, and Hammurabi is far greater than their moral differences. Only an ideologue could fudge that fact.

Third argument

A third argument for relativism is similar to the second, but is more psychological than anthropological. This argument is also supposedly based on a scientifically verifiable fact: the fact that society conditions values in us. If we had been brought up in a Hindu society, we would have had Hindu values. The origin of values thus seems to be human minds themselves—parents and teachers—rather than something objective to human minds. And what comes from human subjects is, of course, subjective, like the rules of baseball, even though they may be public and universally agreed to.

Response

(a) This argument, like the previous one, also confuses values with value-opinions. Perhaps society conditions value-opinions in us, but that does not mean society conditions values in us—unless it is claimed that values are nothing but value-opinions, which is precisely the point at issue, the conclusion, in which case the argument begs the question.

(b) There is also a false assumption in this argument: that whatever we learn from society is subjective. This is not true. We learn the rules of baseball from society, but we also learn the rules of multiplication from society. The rules of baseball are subjective (man-made), but the rules of multiplication are not. (The language systems in which we express the rules are, of course, man-made.) The mind creates, rather than discovers, the rules of baseball; the mind discovers, rather than creates, the rules of multiplication. So the fact that we learn x from our society does not prove that x is subjective.

(c) The expressed premise is also not wholly true. Not all value-opinions are the result of our social conditioning. If they were, then there would be no nonconformity to society based on moral values, only rebellions of force rather than of principle. But in fact there are many principled nonconformists. *They* did not derive their values wholly from their society, since they disagree with their society about values. The existence of nonconformists shows the presence of some trans-social origin of values.

Fourth argument

A fourth argument is that moral relativism guarantees "freedom," while absolutism threatens it. People today often wonder how they can be truly free if they are not free to create their own values. Indeed, our

Supreme Court has declared that we have a "fundamental right . . . to define the meaning of existence." (This is either the most fundamental of all rights, if it is right, or the most fundamental of all follies, if it is wrong; either the wisest or the stupidest thing the Court has ever written.)

Response

(a) The most effective reply to this argument is often an *ad hominem*. Say to the person who demands the right to be free to create his own values that you too demand that right, and that the value system you choose to create is one in which his opinions have no weight at all, or one in which you are God and rightly demand total obedience. He will quickly protest, in the name of truth and justice, thus showing that he really does believe in those two objective values after all. If he does not do this, and protests merely in the name of his alternative value system which he has freely created, then his protest against your selfishness and megalomania is no better than your protest against his justice and truth. Then the "argument" comes down to brute force. And this is hardly a situation that guarantees "freedom"!

(b) Freedom cannot create values because freedom presupposes values. Why does freedom presuppose values? First, because the relativist's argument that relativism guarantees freedom has to assume that freedom is really valuable—thus assuming at least one objective value. Second, if freedom is really good, it must be freedom from something really bad—thus assuming some objective good and bad. Third, the advocate of freedom will almost always insist that freedom be granted to all, not just some, thus presupposing the real value of equality, or the Golden Rule.

(c) The simplest refutation of the argument about freedom is experiential. Experience teaches us that we are free to create alternative *mores*, like socially acceptable rules for speech, clothing, eating and driving; but it also teaches us that we are *not* free to create alternative *morals*, like making murder, rape or treason right, or charity and justice wrong. We can no more create a new moral value than we can create a new color, or a new arithmetic, or a new universe.

And if we could, they would no longer be moral values, just arbitrarily invented rules of a game. We would not feel bound in conscience by them, or guilty when we transgressed them. If we were free to create "thou shalt murder" *or* "thou shalt not murder," as we are free to create "thou shalt play nine innings" or "thou shalt play six innings," we would no more feel guilty about murder than about playing six innings. As a matter of fact, we all do feel *bound* by some fundamental moral values, like justice and the Golden Rule. We experience our freedom of will to choose to obey or disobey them, but we also experience our lack of freedom to change them into their opposites, e.g., to "creatively" make hate good or love evil. Try it: you just can't do it. All you can do is to refuse the whole moral order; you cannot make another. You can choose, or desire, to hate, but you cannot experience a moral obligation to hate.

Except, perhaps, the radically immoral few, the Marquis de Sades and Jeffrey Dahmers. Is *that* the state of consciousness advocated by the relativist with his demand for "freedom to create your own values"? If so, the advocate deserves something rather more infantile than an argument; he deserves a spanking.

Fifth argument

A similar argument, equally common today, is that moral relativism is "tolerant" while absolutism is "intolerant." Tolerance is one of the few non-controversial values today; nearly everyone in our society accepts it. So it is a powerful motivator for any theory or practice that can claim it. What of relativism's claim to tolerance?

Response

(a) First, let us be clear what we mean by tolerance. It is a quality of *people*, not of *ideas*. Ideas can be confused, or fuzzy, or ill-defined, but this does not make them tolerant, any more than clarity or exactness makes them intolerant. If a carpenter tolerates three sixteenths of an inch deviation from plumb, he is three time more tolerant than one who tolerates only one sixteenth of an inch, but no less clear. One may tolerate no dissent from his fuzzy and ill-defined views, while another may tolerate much dissent from his clearly defined views.

(b) The relativist's claim is that absolutism—belief in universal, objective, unchanging moral laws—fosters intolerance of alternative views. But this has not been so in the sciences. The sciences have certainly benefited and progressed remarkably because of tolerance of diverse and "heretical" views. Yet science is not about "subjective truths" but objective truths. Therefore objectivism does not necessarily cause intolerance.

(c) The relativist may argue that absolutes are hard and unyielding, and therefore the defender of them will tend to be like them; but this is another *non sequitur*. One may teach hard facts in a soft way, or soft opinions in a hard way.

(d) The simplest refutation of the "tolerance" argument is its very premise: it assumes that tolerance is really, objectively, universally, absolutely good.

If the relativist replies that he is not presupposing the objective value of tolerance, then he is demanding the imposition of his subjective personal preference for tolerance; and that is surely more intolerant than the appeal to a universal, objective, impersonal moral law.

If no moral values are absolute, neither is tolerance. The absolutist can take tolerance far more seriously than the relativist. It is absolutism, not relativism, that fosters tolerance.

(e) And it is relativism that fosters intolerance. *Why not* be intolerant? Only because tolerance feels better? Or because it is the popular consensus? Suppose it no longer feels better? Suppose it ceases to be popular? The relativist can appeal to no moral law as a dam against intolerance. We need such a dam because societies, like individuals, are fickle. What else will deter a humane and humanistic Germany from turning to an inhumane Nazi philosophy of racial superiority, or a now-tolerant America from turning to a future intolerance against any group it decides to disenfranchise? It is unborn babies today, it may be born babies tomorrow; homophobes today, homosexuals tomorrow. The same absolutism that homosexuals fear because it is not tolerant of their behavior is their only secure protection against intolerance of their persons.

(f) Examination of the essential meaning of the concept of tolerance reveals a presupposition of moral objectivism. For we do not tolerate goods, we tolerate evils, in order to prevent worse evils. A patient will tolerate the nausea brought on by chemotherapy in order to prevent death by cancer, and a society will tolerate bad things like smoking in order to preserve good things like privacy and freedom.

(g) The advocate of tolerance faces a dilemma, especially when it comes to cross-cultural tolerance. Most cultures throughout history have *not* put a high value on tolerance. Some have thought it a moral weakness. Should we tolerate this intolerance? If so, if we *should* tolerate intolerance, then the tolerant subjectivist had better stop bad-mouthing the Spanish Inquisition.

If not, why not? Because tolerance is really a good, and the Inquisition really an evil? In that case, we are presupposing a universal and objective trans-cultural value.

Because our consensus is for tolerance? But history's consensus is against it. Why impose ours? Is this not culturally intolerant?

(h) Finally, there is a logical *non sequitur* in the relativist's argument. Even if the belief in absolute moral values *did* cause intolerance, it does not follow that such values do not exist. The belief that the cop on the beat is sleeping may cause a mugger to be intolerant to his victims, but it does not follow that the cop is not asleep.

Thus, there are no less than eight weaknesses in the "tolerance" argument for relativism.

Sixth argument

A sixth argument for relativism stems from the apparent relativity of situations. Situations are so diverse and complex that it seems unreasonable and unrealistic to hold to universal moral norms. The cliché "the exception proves the rule" seems to show that popular opinion recognizes no exceptionless rules. Even killing can be good—if war is necessary for peace. Theft can be good—if you steal a weapon from a madman. Lying can be good—when you're a Dutchman lying to the Nazis about where the Jews are hiding.

The argument is essentially this: morality is determined by situations, and situations are relative; therefore, morality is relative.

A closely related argument can be considered together with this one: that morality is relative because it is determined by *motive*. We all blame a man for *trying* to murder another, even though the deed is not successfully accomplished, simply because his motive is bad; but we do not hold a man morally guilty of murder for *accidentally* killing another (e.g., by giving a sugary candy to a child he has no way of knowing is seriously diabetic).

This argument is essentially that morality is determined by motive, and motive is subjective, therefore morality is subjective.

Both the situationist and the motivationist conclude against moral absolutes: the situationist because he finds all morality relative to the situation, the motivationist because he finds all morality relative to the motive.

Response

We reply with a common sense distinction. Morality is indeed *conditioned*, or *partly* determined, by both situations and motives; but it is not *wholly* determined by situations or motives. Traditional, common sense morality involves three "moral determinants," three factors that influence whether a specific act is morally good or bad: the nature of the act itself (what you do), the situation (when, where and how you do it), and the motive (why you do it).

It is true that doing the right thing in the wrong situation or for the wrong motive is not good. Making love to your wife is a good deed, but doing so when it is medically dangerous is not. The deed is good but the situation is not. Giving money to the poor is a good deed, but doing it just to show off is not. The deed is good but the motive is not.

However, there must first *be* a deed before it can be qualified by subjective motives and/or relative situations; and this is surely a morally relevant factor too.

A good life is a work of art, like a good story. A good work of art requires *all* its essential elements to be good. A good story must have a good plot, good characterization, *and* a good theme. A good life requires that you do the right thing (the act itself) for the right reason (the motive) *and* in the right way (the situation).

Furthermore, situations, though relative, are objective, not subjective. And motives, though subjective, come under moral absolutes; they can be recognized as intrinsically and universally good or evil. Goodwill is always good; the will to harm is always evil. So even situationism is an *objective* morality; and even motivationism, or subjectivism, is a *universal* morality. Even if situationism were true, it would still be *objectively* right to kill or lie sometimes (e.g., to Nazis). And even if subjectivism were true, it would be a *universal* moral obligation to be subjectively sincere, well-intentioned, and true to your own private conscience.

(Indeed, we find that the vast majority of Americans who say they no longer believe in any moral absolutes still do believe in that one. Have you ever met someone who really believed it was good to deliberately disobey his own conscience, or evil to obey it? They may have abandoned any *objective* moral absolutes, but not this remaining subjective moral absolute.)

Furthermore, subjective motives are naturally connected with objective deeds. There are some deeds (like rape) that are incompatible with good motives, and some motives (like love) that naturally produce good deeds (like philanthropy).

Just as motives presuppose deeds and are not isolable from deeds, so is it with situations. The fact that the same principles must be applied differently to different situations *presupposes* the validity of those principles rather than undermining them or eliminating them.

Moral absolutists need not be absolutistic about applications to situations. But flexible applications of a standard presuppose a rigid standard. If the standard is as flexible as the situation, it is no standard. If the yardstick with which you (flexibly) measure the length of a twisting alligator is as twisting as the alligator, you cannot measure with it. Yardsticks *need* to be rigid.

And moral absolutists need not be "judgmental" about motives, only about deeds. When Jesus said "Judge not," he surely meant "Do not claim to judge hearts and motives, which only God can know" rather than "Do not claim to judge deeds, do not morally discriminate bullying from defending, killing from healing, robbery from charity."

In fact the moral absolutist alone, and not the relativist, can condemn "judgmentalism" (of motive), just as he alone can condemn intolerance. The relativist condemns only moral absolutism.

V. The Arguments for Absolutism

Merely refuting all the arguments for relativism does not refute relativism itself, of course. We need positive arguments for absolutism as well. Here are six.

1. The pragmatic argument from consequences

If the relativist argues against absolutism from its supposed consequences of intolerance, we can argue against relativism from its real consequences. Consequences are at least a relevant indicator; they are clues. Good morality should have good consequences, and bad morality bad ones.

It is very obvious that the main consequence of moral relativism is the removal of moral deterrence. The consequences of "Do The Right Thing" are—doing the right thing; and the consequences of "If It Feels Good, Do It" are—doing whatever feels good. It takes no Ph.D. to see this. In fact, it takes a Ph.D. to *miss it. All* immoral deeds and attitudes (with the possible exception of envy) feel good; that's the main reason we do them. If sin didn't seem like fun, most of us would be saints.

No saint has ever been a moral relativist. That is the consequentialist refutation of relativism.

The same goes for societies. Compare the stability, longevity, and happiness of societies founded on the principles of moral relativists like Mussolini and Mao Tse-tung with societies founded on the principles of moral absolutists like Moses and Confucius. A society of moral relativists usually lasts only one generation. Hitler's "Thousand-Year Reich" is a good example.

By the way, the following quotation from Mussolini should be sent to the U.S. Supreme Court, the ACLU, the NTA, Hollywood, and network TV executives:

> Everything I have said and done in these last years is relativism by intuition. . . . If relativism signifies contempt for fixed categories and men who claim to be the bearers of an objective, immortal truth . . . then there is nothing more relativistic than Fascistic attitudes and activity. . . . From the fact that all ideologies are of equal value, that all ideologies are mere fictions, the modern relativist infers that everybody has the right to create for himself his own ideology and to attempt to enforce it with all the energy of which he is capable.[1]

2. The argument from consensus

The argument from consensus, or "common consent," can only be probable, but it is massive, and it should appeal to egalitarians who argue against absolutism because they think it is connected with snobbery. It is exactly the opposite. Absolutism is *traditional* morality, and tradition is egalitarianism extended into history. Chesterton called it "the democracy of the dead": the extension of the franchise to that most powerless of classes, those disenfranchised, not by accident of birth, but by accident of death. Tradition counters the small and arrogant oligarchy of the living, those who just happen to be walking around the planet today.

To be a relativist, you must be a snob, at least on this centrally important issue, for you stand in a tiny minority, almost totally concentrated in one civilization, the modern West (i.e., white, democratic, industrialized, urbanized, university-educated, secularized, apostate, post-Christian society). And you must believe that nearly all human beings in history have tried to order their lives by an illusion, a fantasy, right at life's center.

Even in societies like ours that are dominated by relativistic "experts," popular opinion tends to moral absolutism. Like Communists, relativists often pretend to be "the party of the people" while in fact scorning the people's philosophy. In fact, for a generation now a minority of relativistic elitists who have gained the power of the media have been relentlessly imposing their elitist relativism on popular opinion by

---

[1] Benito Mussolini, *Diuturna*, pp. 374–77. Quoted in Helmut Kuhn, *Freedom Forgotten and Remembered* (Chapel Hill, NC: University of North Carolina Press, 1943), pp. 17–18.

accusing popular opinion (i.e., traditional morality) of elitism!

But an argument from consent or consensus can only be probable. As the medieval philosophers well knew, "the argument from (human) authority is the weakest of all arguments." An indication of the success of the modern elitists is the fact that most people today are shocked by that statement. They have been taught that the Middle Ages, being religious, were authoritarian while modern "Enlightenment" civilization is rational—whereas the truth is almost exactly the opposite. Medieval theologians and philosophers were rational to a fault, while modern philosophy since the Enlightenment has attacked reason in a dozen different ways, and preferred the authority of the passions, pragmatism, politics, or power.

3. The argument from moral experience

The argument from moral experience is probably the simplest and strongest argument for moral absolutism. In fact it is so strong that it seems like an unnatural strain to put it into the form of an argument at all. It is more like primary data.

The first and foundational moral experience is always absolutistic. Only later in the life of the individual or society does sophistication sometimes suggest moral relativism. Every one of us remembers from early childhood experience what it feels like to be morally obligated, to "bump up against" an unyielding moral wall. This memory is enshrined in our words "ought," "should," "right," and "wrong."

Moral absolutism is based on experience. For instance: Last night you promised your friend you would help him at eight o'clock this morning—let's say he has to move his furniture before noon. But you were up till three A.M., and when the alarm rings at seven, you are very tired. You experience two things: the desire to sleep, and the obligation to get up. The two are generically different. You experience no obligation to sleep, and no desire to get up. You are moved in one way by your own desire for sleep, and you are moved in a very different way by what you think you ought to do. Your feelings appear "from the inside out," so to speak, while your conscience appears "from the outside in." Within you is the desire to sleep, and this may move you to the external deed of shutting off the alarm and creeping back to bed. But if instead you get up to fulfill your promise to your friend, it will be because you chose to respond to a very different kind of thing: the perceived moral quality of the deed of fulfilling your promise, as opposed to the perceived moral quality of refusing to fulfill it. What you perceive as right, or obligatory, (getting up) *pulls* you from without, from itself, from its own nature. The desires you feel as attractive (going back to sleep) *push* you from within, from yourself, from your own nature. The moral obligation moves you as an end, as a final cause, from above and ahead, so to speak; the desire moves you as a source, as an efficient cause, from below, from behind.

All these are primary data, fundamental moral experiences. It can be denied, but only as some strange philosophy might deny the reality immediately perceived by our senses. Moral relativism is to moral experience what the teaching of Christian Science is to the experience of pain, sickness, and death. It tells us they are illusions to be overcome by faith. Moral absolutism is empirical; moral relativism is a dogma of faith.

This basic moral experience exists not only privately and individually, but also on every important group level, like widening circles made by a stone dropped in a lake: friends, families, neighborhoods, the nation, the world, and world history. On all of these levels there is desire (e.g., for territorial gain) and there is conscience (e.g., keeping treaties). The second (the moral) is not reducible to the first (the non-moral). Moral experience does not come to us in relativistic garb. We get moral absolutism from moral experience; we get moral relativism from relativistic philosophers. The argument here is simply that moral absolutism alone is true to its data.

4. The ad hominem argument

Even the relativist reacts with a moral protest when treated immorally. The man who appeals to the relativistic principle of "I gotta be me" to justify breaking his promise of fidelity to his own wife, whom he wants to leave for another woman, will then break his fidelity to that principle when his new wife uses it to justify leaving him for another man. This is not exceptional but typical. It looks like the origin of relativism is more personal than philosophical, more in the hypocrisy than in the hypothesis.

The contradiction between theory and practice is evident even in the relativist's act of teaching relativism. Why do relativists teach and write? To convince the world that relativism is right and absolutism wrong? Really right and really wrong? If so, then there is a real right and a real wrong. If not, then there is nothing wrong with being an absolutist and nothing right with being a relativist. So why do relativists write and teach?

Really, from all the effort they have put into preaching their gospel of delivering humanity from the false and foolish repressions of absolutism, one would have thought that they believed this gospel was true, and teaching it was really good!

5. The argument from moral arguing

A very obvious argument, used by C. S. Lewis at the very beginning of *Mere Christianity*, is based on the observation that people *quarrel*. They do not merely *fight*, but *argue* about right and wrong. This is to act as if they believed in objectively real and universally binding moral principles. If nothing but subjective desires and passions were involved, it would be merely a contest of strength between competing persons or between competing passions within a person (if I am hungrier than I am tired, I will eat; if I am more tired than hungry, I will sleep first). But we say things like, "That isn't fair," or "What right do you have to that?" If relativism were true, moral argument would be as stupid as arguing about feelings: "I feel great." "No! *I* feel terrible."

6. The argument from moral language

A variation of the above argument is the observation that the moral language that everyone uses every day—language that praises, blames, counsels, or commands—would be strictly meaningless if relativism were true. We do not praise or blame non-moral agents like machines. When the Coke machine "steals" our money without delivering a Coke, we do not argue with it, call it a sinner, or command it to obey good morality. We kick it.

But moral language *is* meaningful, not meaningless. We all know that. We know how to use it, and we do. Relativism cannot explain this fact.

VI. The Cause and Cure of Relativism

The real source of moral relativism is not any of these arguments, not any argument at all, not any piece of reasoning. Neither philosophy nor science nor logic nor common sense nor experience have refuted traditional moral absolutism. Not reason but the abdication of reason is the source of moral relativism. Relativism is not rational, it is rationalization; it is not the conclusion of a rational argument, but the rationalization of a prior passion, the repudiation of the principle that passions must be evaluated by reason and controlled by will. As Plato and Aristotle pointed out, self-control is not just one of the cardinal virtues but a necessary ingredient in every one. This classical assumption is almost the definition of civilization; but the romanticists, existentialists, Freudians and others have convinced many people in our society that it is repressive, unhealthy, and "inauthentic." If we embrace the opposite principle, and let passion govern reason rather than reason governing passion, there is little hope for morality—or for civilization.

Sexual passion is obviously the strongest and most attractive of the passions. It is therefore also the most addictive, and the most blinding. So there could hardly be a more powerful undermining of our moral knowledge and our moral life than the sexual revolution. Already, the demand for sexual "freedom" has overridden one of nature's strongest instincts, motherhood. A million and a half mothers a year in America alone now pay hired killers who are called healers, or physicians, to kill their own unborn daughters and sons. How could this happen? Only because abortion is driven by sexual motives. For abortion is backup birth control, and birth control is the demand to have sex without having babies.

Divorce is a second example of the power of the sexual revolution to undermine basic moral principles. Suppose there were some other practice, not connected with sex, which resulted in (1) betraying the person you claimed to love the most, the person you had pledged your life to, betraying your solemn promise to her or him; and thereby (2) abusing the children you had procreated and promised to protect, scarring their souls more deeply than anything else except direct violent physical abuse, making it far more difficult for them ever to attain happy lives or marriages; and thereby (3) harming, undermining, and perhaps destroying your society's future. Would not such a thing be universally condemned? Yet that is what divorce usually is, and it is almost universally accepted. Betrayal is universally condemned—unless it is sexual. Justice, honesty, not doing others harm, all these moral principles are affirmed—unless they interfere with sex. The rest of traditional morality is still very widely believed and taught, even in TV sitcoms, soap operas, and movies. The driving force of moral relativism seems to be almost always exclusively sexual.

Why this should be and what we should do about it are two further questions. Those two questions demand much more time and thought than we have available here and now. If you want a very short guess at an answer to both, here is the best I can do.

A secularist has only one substitute left for God, only one experience in a desacralized world that still gives him something like the mystical, self-transcending thrill, the standing-outside-the-self, the ecstasy that God designed all souls to have forever, and to demand until they have it. Unless he is a surfer, that experience has to be sex.

We are designed for more than happiness. We are designed for joy. Aquinas writes, with simple logic: "Man cannot live without joy. That is why one deprived of spiritual joys must go over to carnal pleasures."

Drugs and alcohol are attractive because they claim to feed the same need. They lack the ontological goodness of sex, but they provide the same mystical thrill: the transcendence of reason and self-consciousness and responsibility. This is not meant as moral condemnation but psychological analysis. In fact, though this may sound shocking, I think the addict is closer to the deepest truth than the mere moralist. He is looking for the very best thing in some of the very worst places. His demand for a state in which he transcends moral responsibility is very wrong, but it is also very right: wrong immediately, right ultimately. For we are designed for something beyond moral responsibility, something in which morality will be transformed: mystical union with God. Sex is a sign and tiny appetizer of that. Moral absolutists must never forget that morality, though absolute, is not ultimate, not our summum bonum. Sinai is not the Promised Land; Jerusalem is. And in the New Jerusalem what finally happens, as the last chapter of human history according to divine revelation, is a wedding, between the Lamb and His Bride. Deprived of this real Jerusalem, we buy into Babylon. If we do not worship God, we worship idols, for we are by nature worshippers.

Finally, what is the cure? It must be stronger medicine than philosophy. I can give you only three words in answer to the last, most practical question of all—what we should do about it, what is the cure. And they are totally unoriginal. For they are not my philosophical arguments but God's Biblical demands: repent, fast, and pray. I know of no other answer, and I can think of nothing that can save this civilization except saints.

Be one.

Utilitarianism as Destructive of Justice: Cicero and the Roman Jurists

Wolfgang Waldstein

[The following paper was read at an international symposium held at the International Academy of Philosophy in Irving (Texas) on March 3, 1982. In the meantime, the Academy has been moved to the Principality of Liechtenstein (Europe).[*]]

In a discussion concerning questions of modern philosophical ideas, it might seem to be rather out of place to deal with authors and thinkers who wrote about two thousand years ago. On the other hand, it is certainly true that any truth discovered at any time in history is, if it is a truth, still true. And therefore, Cicero himself was justified in saying that history, which is often regarded as a support for relativism, in fact provides us with the light of truth (*historia vero . . . lux veritatis*[1]). In this sense, I will try to contribute some historical experiences which might be helpful for a discussion of modern problems, because I am convinced that they represent *natural* truths. Even though they were found under circumstances in some respects very different from those of our times, there are also many respects in which these circumstances coincide.

Before I turn to the thinking of Cicero and the Roman jurists, however, I consider it necessary to discuss at least briefly some essential points of utilitarianism itself.

Next, I will try to show why especially Cicero explicitly, and the Roman jurists more implicitly, thought utilitarianism to be destructive of justice.

---

[*] A version of this paper was published in *Orbis Iuris Romani*, vol. 2 (1996). That version contains updated information on the legal situation with regard to euthanasia in Holland and Australia. The version contained here is printed with permission.

[1] Cicero, *De Oratore*, 2, 36.

I. Some Essential Points of Utilitarianism

Utilitarianism is "most generally . . . described as the doctrine which states that the rightness or wrongness of actions is determined by the goodness and badness of their consequences."[2]

This view concerning moral actions is, however, not limited to the ethical question of what we ought to do, but is also extended to the epistemological question of truth in general. Karl Popper, for instance, pointed out rightly that the "*classical* conception of truth ('true—corresponding with reality')" is "in contrast . . . with the utilitarian conception ('true—in a certain respect useful')."[3]

This more general view is, of course, applied in different utilitarian theories in different ways, "according to which we get various species of utilitarianism," which Smart lists as, "act and rule utilitarianism," "egoistic and universalistic utilitarianism," "hedonistic and ideal utilitarianism," and finally, "normative and descriptive utilitarianism."[4]

It is clear that these different understandings of utilitarianism give rise to very different answers to the question as to which consequences of an action should be regarded as good and which ones as bad, or which view concerning the question of truth should be called useful and which one should not be called useful. This makes evident that one cannot hope for more rationality, or for results that are more demonstrable, if one transfers the question of truth from the content of a statement to its utility, and the question of the rightness or wrongness of an action to the question of what good or bad consequences follow from it. Not only do all the difficulties in answering the primary questions of truth or goodness in itself arise again on the new level, because one is forced to find criteria by which the consequences can be said to be good or at least useful; in addition, completely new and rationally fairly insolvable questions arise. Some of them can perhaps be clarified by some pertinent examples.

Though Smart, whom I have quoted above, is himself a utilitarian, he brings up some very good examples which, as he rightly thinks, make

---

[2] J. J. C. Smart, "Utilitarianism," in *The Encyclopedia of Philosophy*, P. Edwards, ed. (New York: Macmillan, 1976), vol. 8, p. 206.

[3] Karl R. Popper, *Objective Knowledge: An Evolutionary Approach*, Revised edition 1981, p. 367.

[4] Smart, "Utilitarianism," pp. 206 ff.

it "fairly easy to show that both act utilitarianism and rule utilitarianism are inconsistent with our usual ideas about ethics, or what can be called the common moral consciousness."[5] Referring to rule utilitarianism, he says:

> For example, a riot involving hundreds of deaths may be averted only by punishing some innocent scapegoat and calling it punishment. Given certain empirical assumptions, which may perhaps not in fact be true, but which in a certain sort of society might be true, it is hard to see how a rule utilitarian could object to such a practice of punishing the innocent in these circumstances, and yet most people would regard such a practice as unjust. They would hold that a practice of sometimes punishing the innocent would be wrong, despite the fact that in certain circumstances its consequences would be good or that the consequences of any alternative practice would be bad.

Smart thinks that "in the world as it is, the rule utilitarian will," of course, not "be in favour of a practice of punishing the innocent, but it can be shown that in a certain sort of world he would have to be."[6]

As a matter of fact, it can be shown, however, that Smart's assumption is not at all merely hypothetical. There are numerous historical examples of such situations. Perhaps the most famous one can be found in the gospel of St. John. John reports the well-known statement of the high priest Caiaphas concerning the question of what actions should be taken against Christ in order to stop his growing influence. The chief priests and Pharisees are reported to have "gathered together in a council" in which it was recognized that "this man is working many signs." And they further said, "If we let him go on like this, all will believe him, and the Romans will come and take away both our sanctuary and our nation."[7] The possible consequence envisioned can in any utilitarian sense be regarded as very bad for the Jewish people. The extermination of an entire nation is certainly much worse than a riot involving hundreds of deaths.

I will now not deal with any of the theological implications of the following statement of Caiaphas; rather, I will only consider its immediate meaning with respect to a utilitarian view. He said to the council:

---

[5] *Ibid.*, p. 208.
[6] *Ibid,*, pp. 208–9.
[7] Jn 11:47 f.

"You know nothing at all; nor do you realize that it is expedient for us to have one man die for the people, instead of the whole nation perishing."[8] And that plainly utilitarian statement led to the result that "from that day forth their plan was to put him to death."[9] The unjust trial and the most cruel crucifixion followed from this utilitarian view.

Possibly, one could argue now that a unique good was brought about precisely by Christ's death, a good which would never have come about without this event: the good of salvation, with all its enormous and innumerable good consequences. But these are not the consequences which utilitarians could have in mind. The utilitarian view was only concerned with the future fate of the people and the country involved. And precisely in this respect, the view failed to be correct. The actual consequences of the event were not the ones Caiaphas had spoken about. The act was not able to prevent Jerusalem from being destroyed, and almost the entire nation from perishing. As the arguments in the trial show, the Roman governor himself had to be threatened with getting entangled into a conflict with the emperor if he would not give in and let a man be killed whom he himself had found to be innocent. So the possible bad consequences turned out, in fact, to be only a *pretext* for an action which they were claimed to justify. Besides, in fact, there is no way in which all possible consequences of a certain action could be predicted, while at the same time, the action is supposed to derive the quality "good" from these very consequences. Moreover, saying that only the immediate consequences are to be taken into account and not the more remote ones is certainly not in the least more rational than asking from the outset whether the act itself was right or wrong. No possible consequences could bestow, in any meaningful way, the quality "right" upon the unjust trial, the mendacious dealings, and finally, the condemnation of an innocent person to death (and what a cruel death besides!).

Nowadays, there are similar considerations in many countries on other levels. The quality of life, for example, is regarded as a good for which one is entitled to strive. And in many respects, it certainly is. Is now every action which somehow promotes the quality of life, understood as a higher standard of living with more pleasure and leisure and less burdens and troubles, an action which could, by this good consequence, become right? It is a fairly widespread view that killing an un-

---

[8] Jn 11:49 f.
[9] Jn 11:53.

born child, for example, is right if it is done for the sake of preventing trouble for the mother, and therefore promoting the quality of her life. But there are serious problems concerning the possible consequences. At the time of the abortion, one could predict only with some reasonable probability that the mother might be able to avoid some imminent trouble she can think of by having her child aborted, and thereby somehow promoting her quality of life.[10] But it is well known that many other unexpected troubles can arise of which the mother did not think at all. Furthermore, the consequences of such actions will, in all likelihood, not at all result in a promotion of the quality of life. That we are not merely imagining things can be gleaned from the following prediction gleaned from demographic statistics: As soon as those who are now in a position of enjoying their quality of life grow older and are no longer able to work themselves, the burden of earning money in order to be able to pay for social welfare will fall on fewer working people than it does now. That could make the burden quite unbearable, so that people will begin thinking about means of getting rid of this unbearable burden. So it might follow that the pursuit of the quality of life will incline them to kill those whom they find to be burdensome, including those who thought it good to kill unborn children for the sake of their own quality of life. Euthanasia is in fact the logical consequence of admitting abortion as a means to promote the quality of life. Therefore, it is already openly discussed in many countries, especially in Europe and in the United States.

The whole problem of how the so-called good consequences of promoting a "quality of life" are supposed to make the action of abortion right cannot be investigated here. But one thing is certain, namely that the possible consequences of actions of that nature are so complex and so little predictable that, even if the immediate consequences seem to be good, possible bad consequences can never be excluded, and are in fact very likely to follow. And besides, by what criteria can any consequence be regarded as good? The answer cannot lead beyond replies to the question, "What actions are good *in themselves*?" And because one cannot know all possible consequences anyway, it is much more reasonable to look at the actions themselves, which one can know, than at conse-

---

[10] For the general question, see Stephen Schwarz, *The Moral Question of Abortion* (Chicago: Loyola Press [currently distributed by Sophia Institute Press], 1990).

quences which one cannot know.

Against this background I will now turn to some relevant findings of ancient authors.

II. The Thinking of Cicero and the Roman Jurists Concerning Utility and Justice

It is obvious that I can show only a few aspects here which can be gathered from the relevant texts.

It is a fact that utility played a very important role in the thinking of both Cicero and the Roman jurists. Many legal provisions are said to have been introduced for the sake of the *utilitas publica*, the common utility or expediency. The term *bonum commune*, the common good, which is closely related to the common utility, is, as far as I can see, used for the first time by Seneca in his *De Clementia*, where he says that man as a social animal is born for the common good (*sociale animal communi bono genitum*).[11] This does not, however, imply that the goodness or justness of laws or of persons themselves was measured by their aptitude to promote or serve the common utility. On the contrary, it can be seen from many texts that only what is in itself just and good was thought to be also apt to serve the common good. In this sense, Cicero says in *De Officiis* 3, 31, as the passage is translated by Miller in the Leob Classical Library edition, that "Nature's law itself . . . protects and conserves human interests."[12] From another passage, it becomes quite clear that there cannot be any common utility or good at the cost of sacrificing the personal utility or expediency of single members of the society, although some exceptions under certain circumstances are admitted, which are, however, themselves thought to be founded in natural law, and which I cannot discuss here.[13] But the important passage from *De Inventione* 2, 160 f. reads as follows:

"Justice is a habit of mind which gives every man his" due[14] "while

---

[11] Seneca, *De Clementia*, 1, 3, 2.

[12] The Latin text says, "*lex ipsa naturae . . . utilitatem hominum conservat et continet.*"

[13] An example is, in the words of Art. 51 of the *Charter of the United Nations*, "the inherent right of individual or collective self-defense," which can already be found in a passage from the Roman jurist Ulpian (died A.D. 223) in Justinian's *Digest* 43, 16, 1, 27, and in other passages.

[14] H. M. Hubbel, *The Loeb Classical Library*, translates *dignitatem* with

preserving the common advantage." Its origin (*initium*) "proceeds from nature, then certain rules of conduct became customary by reason of their advantage; later still both the principles" (rather, "the norms") "that proceeded from nature; and those that had been approved by custom received the support of" the obligation "and the fear of the law. The law of nature is that which is not born of opinion (*quod non opinio genuit*), but implanted in us by a kind of innate instinct."[15]

Before Cicero enters into the discussion of justice itself, he deals with other views such as those of the Old Academy; or the Stoics, of whom he thinks that they agree with him; or the hedonists, of whom he says that they "practice self-indulgence," "are slaves of their own bodies, and test the desirability or undesirability of everything on the basis of pleasure and pain"; or of the New Academy of Cicero's time, of which he says that "it contributes nothing but confusion to all these problems." These different views cause him to say of his own principles: "Of course I cannot expect that they will be universally accepted, for that is impossible; but I do look for the approval of all who" saw (deduced, *duxerunt*[16])

> . . . that everything which is right and honourable is to be desired for its own sake, and that nothing whatever is to be accounted a good unless it is praiseworthy in itself, or at least that nothing should be considered a great good unless it can rightly be praised for its own sake.[17]

And in his *De Officiis*, he says in connection with the problem of the search for truth and man's capability to grasp the truth: "Thus we come to understand that what is true, simple, and genuine appeals most strongly to a man's nature."[18] After discussing some further elements peculiar to man, he adds in the sense of the passage quoted before:

"desert," which, of course, is correct, but there are other texts which make clear that "due" is the more general meaning.

[15] "*Sed quaedam in natura vis insevit,*" referring rather to a natural sense or "intelligence common to us all," as will become clear from another text. The translation by H. M. Hubbell of Yale University is, it seems to me, in many respects not quite correct.

[16] Loeb: "believe"; not correct.

[17] Cicero, *De Legibus*, 1, 37 ff.

[18] The Latin reads, *id esse naturae hominis aptissimum*, which rather means, "is most fitting to human nature."

It is from these elements that is forged and fashioned that moral goodness which is the subject of this inquiry—something that, even though it be not generally ennobled, is still worthy of all honour; and by its own nature, we correctly maintain, it merits praise, even though it be praised by none.[19]

Immediately prior to beginning his discussion of justice itself, he also makes the following point which is especially important for our question. He says (and I think it is necessary to quote at least the main part of the rather long passage):

Furthermore, those of us who are not influenced by virtue itself to be good men, but by some consideration of utility and profit, are merely shrewd, not good. For to what length will that man go in the dark who fears nothing but a witness and a judge? What will he do if, in some desolate spot, he meets a helpless man, unattended, whom he can rob of a fortune? Our virtuous man, who is just and good by nature, will talk with such a person, help him, and guide him on his way; but the other, who does nothing for another's sake, and measures every act by the standard of his own advantage—it is clear enough, I think, what he will do! If, however, the latter does deny that he would kill the man and rob him of his money, he will not deny it because he regards it as a naturally wicked thing to do, but because he is afraid that his crime may become known—that is, that he might get into trouble. Oh, what a motive, that might well bring a blush of shame to the cheek, not merely of the philosopher, but even of the simple rustic![20]

Thus Cicero. Since his time, the sense of shame, generally speaking, seems to have suffered quite a setback. Under the influence of positivism, one tends to think that at least the justice of what had been enacted by majority votes cannot be measured by any objective criteria. Concerning these questions, Cicero now becomes especially explicit. In *De Legibus* 1, 42 ff., he first says:

. . . [T]he most foolish notion of all is the belief that everything is just which is found in the customs or laws of nations. Would that be true, even if these laws had been enacted by tyrants?

---

[19] Cicero, *De Officiis*, 1, 13–14.
[20] Cicero, *De Legibus*, 1, 41.

He then notes examples of tyranny,[21] and goes on to show that justice can exist only if there is one law which "binds all human society."

In this connection, he then formulates a statement which is especially important for the relation between justice and utility. He says:

> But if justice is conformity to written laws and national customs, and if, as the same persons claim, everything is to be tested by the standard of utility, then anyone who thinks it will be profitable to him will, if he is able, disregard and violate the laws. It follows that Justice (*iustitia*) does not exist at all if it does not exist in Nature, and if that form of it which is based on utility can be overthrown by that very utility itself.[22]

From this, it becomes evident that Cicero does not see utility in itself as a criterion by which a law could be understood to be good. On the contrary, if that were the decisive criterion, justice simply would cease to exist. This becomes still more evident from the following passages which I would like to quote at least in their most important parts. Cicero goes on to say:

> For Justice is one; it binds all human society, and is based on one Law, which is right reason applied to command and prohibition. Whoever knows not this Law, whether it has been recorded in writing anywhere or not, is without Justice.[23]

After further remarks, all of which are very important to refute relativistic ideas of justice, he continues:

> But if the principles of Justice [he says *iura*, which means the legal order as a whole, including justice] were founded on the decrees of peoples, the edicts of princes, or the decisions of judges, then Justice would sanction robbery and adultery and forgery of wills, in case these acts were approved by the votes or decrees of the populace. But if so great a power belongs to the decisions and decrees of fools, that the laws of Nature can be changed by their votes, then why do they not ordain that what is bad and baneful, shall be considered good and

---

[21] As examples, he mentions "the well-known Thirty" at Athens and a Roman law proposal "to the effect that a dictator might put to death with impunity any citizen he wished, even without trial." The dictator meant is Sulla.

[22] Cicero, *De Legibus*, 1, 42 at the end.

[23] *Ibid.*, 1, 42.

salutary? Or, if a law can make Justice out of Injustice, can it not also make good out of bad? But in fact we can perceive the difference between good laws and bad by referring them to no other standard than Nature; indeed, it is not merely Justice and Injustice which are distinguished by Nature, but also and without exception things which are honourable and dishonourable. For since an intelligence common to us all makes things known to us and formulated them in our minds, honourable actions are ascribed by us to virtue, and dishonourable actions to vice; and only a madman would conclude that these judgments are matters of opinion, and not fixed by Nature.[24]

As far as we know, Cicero was working on his *De Legibus* (the "Laws") in the last years before his assassination in 43 B.C.

These statements were accepted, and I think rightly so, by many great thinkers throughout the centuries as evidence for the existence of a natural truth which can be grasped by human intelligence, provided that man honestly investigates it. Precisely for this reason, the Fathers of the Church, in particular St. Augustine (and later on St. Thomas Aquinas), were able to incorporate these elements of natural truth into their own teaching. They did so because they found by their own investigation that much of what had been said already was true. Because it was true, it had been accepted. And if it is true, it will never cease to be true, even if a unanimous vote of a people should decide the contrary.

There are, of course, objective difficulties with grasping these truths. These difficulties may seem to justify the view that statements about justice really are matters of opinion. Cicero himself was aware of these difficulties, and therefore also dealt with them. He rightly saw that the main argument for this view lies in the fact that one can find very different concepts of justice under different circumstances. The passage concerning these problems is remarkable, and reads as follows:

> But we are confused by the variety of men's beliefs and by their disagreements, and because this same variation is not found in the senses, we think that Nature has made these accurate, and say that those things about which different people have different opinions and the same people not always identical opinions are unreal (*ficta*). However, this is far from being the case. For our senses are not perverted by parent, nurse, teacher, poet, or the stage, nor led astray by popular feeling; but against our minds all sorts of plots are constantly being

---

[24] *Ibid.*, 1, 43 ff.

laid, either by those whom I have just mentioned, who, taking possession of them while still tender and unformed, color and bend them as
they wish, or else by that enemy which lurks deep within us, entwined
in our every sense—that counterfeit of good, which is, however, the
mother of all evils—pleasure. Corrupted by her allurements, we fail to
discern clearly what things are by Nature good, because the same se-
ductiveness and itching does not attend to them.[25]

This is a remarkable statement indeed, extremely important for the theory of knowledge. But are the senses really as reliable as Cicero thinks?
The famous Viennese Professor of Psychology Victor Frankl once said
that if each of several people had to draw a picture of a certain house,
the pictures would all differ, one from the other. Would that prove that
the house itself does not exist at all, but only the different pictures? No
one would claim that. But in the realm of nonsensory facts, one does
argue like this, and this is obviously not justified.

It now could be shown on the basis of the entire heritage of Roman
jurisprudence, as far as it has been preserved, especially by Justinian's
codification, that the entire aim of Roman jurists was to find just decisions for given cases, decisions which were just in themselves.[26] The
famous jurist Celsus, who lived in the first part of the second century
A.D., defines the term *ius*, which means "right" and "law," as "the art of
the good and the just" (*ars boni et aequi*).[27] And Ulpian, who lived in the
third century A.D., adds the following statement:

Of this art we may deservedly be called priests; we cherish [*colimus*]
justice and profess the knowledge of the good and just, separating the
just from the unjust, discriminating between the permitted and the
forbidden, desiring to make men good, not only by the fear of penal-
ties, but also by the incentives of reward, affecting, if I mistake not, a
true and not simulated philosophy.[28]

Ulpian was one of the greatest Roman jurists, and not a Christian
writer. The statement concerning true philosophy goes against all kinds
of sophistry and in general against all kinds of philosophy not dealing

---

[25] *Ibid.*, 1, 47.

[26] For more details see Waldstein, "Justice in Roman Law," in *Internationale
Festschrift für Alfred Verdross zum 80. Geburtstag* (München, 1971), p. 549 ff.

[27] *Digest* 1, 1, 1 pr.

[28] *Digest* 1, 1, 1, 1.

with the things themselves. And even if Roman jurists often saw that some norm had been introduced for the sake of common utility, it is equally clear from their whole attitude towards justice that this utility in itself could not be the criterion by which justice as such could be measured. They used their capacity to grasp what is just in itself, as did Cicero and all other great thinkers, such as Plato, Aristotle, and many others. This enabled them to find, step by step, so many elements of a just and in itself clearly intelligible order that the numerous individual decisions cumulatively resulted in a system of law, very much admired, which later on was even regarded as being simply the written natural law. If they would have looked for good consequences according to utility rather than for decisions which could be grasped to be just in themselves, then the really good consequences of their work would never have come about, and the entire history of Europe and also of other countries would have been different.[29] What we still have as elements of a just order is mainly based on Roman law. Therefore, I think that these historical experiences can contribute insights into truths which are helpful for an understanding of the entire question of justice, especially if they are considered in greater detail than I was able to present them here.

In any case, I am very happy that the ideal of philosophizing about "things themselves," cherished by Balduin Schwarz, in whose honor this paper is written, and by many of his students and friends, coincides with the Roman jurists' striving for "true philosophy," as well as that of the greatest philosophical thinkers of ancient Greece and Rome. Only "true philosophy" can serve also in the future the true common good, and promote "a more human way of life . . . even in this earthly society."[30]

---

[29] Cf. also T. Honoré, *Tribonian* (London, 1978), p. 255.

[30] Cf. Vatican II, *Dogmatic Constitution on the Church*, art. 40 at the end.

THE RIGHTS OF THE HUMAN PERSON

Thompson M. Faller

One of the most newsworthy and attention-getting issues of our day concerns the rights of the human person. It is not that previous ages ignored this problem. In fact, even philosophers of the golden age and of the Middle Ages treated the matter of rights, although most of the latter did so principally in relationship to duties, and with regard to a person's membership in some group such as a guild. But beginning with the dawning of the Age of Reason, increasing philosophical attention has been given to questions concerning the nature of rights and the criteria for them; to the point that a major concern and a milestone of the twentieth century has certainly been that particular topic.

The early part of the twentieth century witnessed the issue of the right to vote for women in the United States. This has been followed by the civil rights marches, as well as the activities of Black Americans, South Africans, and numerous other ethnic groups around the world; by the questions relating to employment, housing, and various forms of reputed discrimination, questions raised concerning such groups as homosexual men and women; and by other major movements, such as feminism. On the international level, there has been the pressing need to deal with the basic rights of human beings especially as these rights are violated by less than benevolent governments, by the ravages of war, and sometimes the forces of nature itself. There are also such widely debated rights issues as the right to life, the rights of patients in hospitals, and children's rights.

Scholars also are increasingly dealing with the question of rights. Consequently, a plethora of works has appeared in bookstores and in journals. Examples are Morton Winston's *The Philosophy of Human Rights*,[1] Judith Jarvis Thompson's *The Realm of Rights*,[2] and articles

---

[1] Morton E. Winston, *The Philosophy of Human Rights* (Belmont, CA: Wadsworth Publishing Company, 1989).

[2] Judith Jarvis Thompson, *The Realm of Rights* (Cambridge, MA: Harvard University Press, 1990).

such as, "The Nature and Value of Rights" by Joel Feinberg,[3] and "Human Rights and the General Welfare" by Davis Lyons.[4]

Even though the notion of rights has received such wide-spread attention, there still appears to be considerable confusion as to its meaning, especially in the expression, 'human rights'. For example, the *United Nations Universal Declaration of Human Rights*, while claiming in its title to deal with the subject of rights, does not treat of the actuality of rights, but with a set of desired goals which would assist in the development of a human society. Thus, it becomes apparent why a correct understanding of the reality of rights is so vital. This article is intended to be another attempt to clarify specifically the concepts pertinent for the *datum* of human rights.

While some members of society may claim a lack of understanding of what a human being is when dealing with right-to-life questions, there is generally no major stumbling block for most people with regard to either defining or at least recognizing what a human being is. Therefore, the focus of our attention will not be a metaphysical, sociological, or psychological study of what it means to be human, but rather a philosophical analysis of the issue of *rights* themselves, and principally as attributed to humans.

The word 'right' used in the legal sense is frequently taken to mean only a well-founded claim upheld by law, as is done in "The Foundations of a Theory of Rights" by Paul Vinogradoff;[5] or a power, notably the power to act or achieve something, as is proposed by Baruch Spinoza.[6] These interpretations of rights usually refer to something the state confers upon its citizenry. For example, we enjoy the rights and privileges a particular country offers, such as the privilege of voting, because we are citizens of that country. Rights of this kind may actually be called legal rights, since they are based on civil law, and are subject to the contingent will and the legislating of a civil authority or lawmaker. Legal rights, therefore, are not constant; rather, they can emerge, change, or

---

[3] Joel Feinberg, "The Nature and Value of Rights," in *The Journal of Value Inquiry* 4 (1970), pp. 243–251.

[4] David Lyons, "Human Rights and the General Welfare" in *Philosophy and Public Affairs*, 6, no. 2 (Winter 1977).

[5] Paul Vinogradoff, "The Foundations of a Theory of Rights" in *Collected Papers* (Oxford, 1928), vol. 2, chap. 20, pp. 367–380.

[6] A. G. Wernham (trans. and ed.), *Benedict De Spinoza: The Political Works* (London, 1958).

even vanish at the whim of legislator or society.

Philosophically speaking, however, there are also inherent or natural rights. These rights are legitimate and inviolable powers vested in, not conferred upon, a person; powers on account of which he or she can claim something as due to or belonging to him or her. These rights spring from a source other than society; they can be said to pre-exist a society. They relate to the dignity of the individual within a society, not to the social community itself. Since these inherent powers are a part of a moral person, they can be called "*moral* powers." They are designated as "powers" because they *allow* its possessor to perform some action as opposed to *obliging* him or her to do so. That is, a right so understood implies neither what persons must do nor what they ought to do, but rather what they *may* do if they so choose. The powers in question have been called "legitimate." This is to show that the person may act or not act in a given way so that neither the act nor its omission would be wrong or evil. To call rights "inviolable," as has been done above, is not to say that they are unlimited. Every right has limitations which, when ignored, cause infringement upon the rights of others. Still, this inviolable power does carry with it true security from any undue interference, and thus protects one in what is one's own.

In addition to their character as moral powers, such rights are closely associated with law, for if a person has a right to do, to demand, or to possess something, others are obliged not to interfere with the exercise of that right. But since this obligation of non-interference can arise only from law, which is the source of all moral obligations, the law itself can be called a right. Likewise, a law commands or forbids a person to do something, or to abstain from doing it; it entitles people by virtue of a moral power to lay hold of certain things and to hold them against the claims of all others. The basis of every right, therefore, lies in some law, and without laws there would be no rights.

Since rights spring from laws, we can assert that there are as many kinds of rights as there are kinds of law. The following are some of the rights directly and indirectly referred to in most discussions on the subject:

1) There are the legal or civil rights, which are based on civil law, or depend on the contingent legislation of a lawmaker.

2) Rights can also be designated private or public. Private rights have to do with private law, and relate to the individual good, i.e., a fulfillment of one's respective end; public rights have to do with public

law, and relate to the common good or end. (Ius publicum quoad rem publicam spectat, ius privatum quoad singulorum utilitatem spectat.)[7]

3) When we actually possess something, our right is said to be real. If we have acquired a title to something but do not yet possess it, then our right is called potential.

4) Likewise, our rights may be divided into juridical rights, which are strictly imposed by law, and non-juridical rights, which do not stem from law, but are enforced by law. The former are frequently called perfect because they are necessary for the moral order, that is, morally required for the individual or social good; while the latter are labeled as imperfect rights because they merely pertain to what is fitting.

5) Finally, there are natural rights, which flow from what is called the natural law, since they relate to the nature of the beings possessing them. It is these natural rights which are of the greatest interest to us, for the following reasons: First of all, it is concerning these rights that the largest amount of discussion occurs. Secondly, as stated by Jacques Maritain in *The Rights of Man and Natural Law*, even our civic or political rights depend indirectly upon the natural law, "not merely because in a general manner the regulations of human law fulfill an aim of natural law by completing that which natural law leaves undetermined, but also because the manner in which this completion takes place corresponds, in the case of political rights, to an aspiration inscribed in man's nature."[8]

To comprehend more fully what is meant by a natural right and its relationship to the natural law, we must begin by looking at human actions, and, more pointedly, at the purposes of such actions. We need not have many purposes for a fulfillment of our nature. On the other hand, there are some actions whose purposes imply responsibility, that is, we are morally bound to satisfy the ends of these actions. These ends, which are the foundation of responsibility and which are rooted in our human nature, are called existential ends.

It must be noted that by its very nature, such a responsibility absolutely precludes any interference with a realization of its purpose. A responsibility of this sort is automatically suspended if it is prevented by some external force from being met. As a result, anyone capable of as-

---

[7] Sohm, *Institutionen, Geschichte und System des römischen Privatrechts*, 16th ed. (1919), p. 25.

[8] Jacques Maritain, *The Rights of Man and Natural Law* (New York: Charles Scribner's Sons, 1945), p. 83.

suming responsibilities must honor the claim for respect inherent in the very nature of these responsibilities. From this, we can conclude that these existential ends, when establishing a human being's natural responsibilities, also imply that a title corresponds to them, a title which other persons ought not obstruct. These titles are called rights. Thus, it can be stated that the origin of natural rights is found in the natural law, which encompasses the existential ends of human beings both as individuals and as the unified members of a society which forms a common good.

In the sphere of a theology which regards God as the Creator of all, this Supreme Being often has been regarded as the ultimate source of rights. This stems from the fact that this Being imbues human nature with its natural law, as well as with existential ends, thereby assigning responsibilities to human nature, and thus giving rise to the rights associated with those existential ends. Such a theistically oriented position, however, does not detract from the view of "law-based rights," since actually God would only be the author of the laws from which the rights follow. Even in the civic arena, the polity is not regarded as the origin of the right, but only the drafter of the law which recognizes or bestows the right.

Although it is unnecessary, if not impossible, to discuss here all of the innumerable other proposed origins of law from which the concepts of rights may be ascertained, it might be beneficial to note the very comprehensive work *Social Ethics* by Josef Messner. That volume presents a lengthy list of applicable concepts, including: 1. the social contract; 2. the social "institution": institutional theory; 3. the autonomy of the individual: rationalist, Kantian school; 4. the will of the people: liberalist school; 5. the folk spirit: historical school; 6. social experience: empiricist and evolutionary school; 7. individual utility: individualist-utilitarian school; 8. effective command: positivist and analytical school; 9. coercive power: physical force school; 10. the "mode of production in material life": the dialectical-materialist school; 11. social utility: socialist-utilitarian school; 12. social functions: collectivist schools; 13. the utility of the people: national-socialist school; 14. the objective spirit: idealist, Hegelian and Neo-Hegelian schools; 15. the initial legal hypothesis: pure theory of law; 16. law identical with its actual effects: the sociological school; and 17. the sense of justice: subjectivist school.[9]

Returning to a consideration of the essence of law as the genesis of rights, we find, as previously stated, that in the Scholastic tradition, law is an order of society, an order with a function traced back to the existential ends inherent in the nature of a human being and even of society itself. Through law, titles to a certain kind of behavior are granted, and these are enforceable. Each of the individual titles is the basis of a particular right. So, once again, we see that a right is a power to claim something, or to possess it, or to act regarding it, without any outside interference. The exercise of these rights may be impeded, but that does not annul them. They are inviolable. This was the circumstance, for example, with the American slaves, who could not exercise their natural human rights, but still had them. Thus, the rights which we enjoy allow for the ability to act independently of any outside force in fulfilling the responsibilities stemming from our human nature and, more specifically, our existential ends.

In spite of the fact that these existential ends and their corresponding responsibilities are found in each individual human being, it must be noted that, because they are derived from human nature itself, and, more specifically, from the laws governing that nature, they are the same for all human beings; that is, they have both an individual and a universal aspect. Thus, we are able to see not only why we have the ability to control the pursuits of these ends in ourselves, but also why we have the obligation not to interfere with the pursuit of these ends in others. This two-fold concept further indicates that our rights are essentially limited, since they are not able to exceed the particular ends to which they apply, but also are restricted by the respect demanded from each person for the rights of everyone else. Our natural rights, then, are actually a realm of power which allows for self-determination in the fulfillment of our existential ends; they are derived from an order which corresponds to these human existential ends. This order is law itself.

It can be definitively stated, therefore, that, because I am a human being, I possess certain rights which are based on my human nature, and which consequently are mine in a special sense. As a person who enjoys control of myself and of my actions, I am not merely a means to an end, but an end in itself, which must be respected as such. The natural law

---

[9] J. Messner, (J. J. Doherty, trans.), *Social Ethics: Natural Law in the Modern World* (St. Louis: B. Herder Book Co., 1949), p. 150.

which governs my nature and the attainment of its existential ends as-sures me that I possess certain rights. The very fact that I am a human being as well as the dignity which is accorded to that nature guarantee me a proper respect and the status of a subject of rights.

Because of our responsibility to perform actions necessary for meeting our existential ends, our right to fulfill that destiny, and, conse-quently, our right to what is necessary to achieve that goal, we are able to recognize the correlation which exists between the notion of right and that of moral obligation. Both of them are based on the freedom which beings such as ourselves enjoy.

A further indication of the mutuality between the notion of right and of moral obligation is that law has a moral nature, since it is rooted in the existential ends of human beings. And the highest moral principle, socially speaking, the ordering of our social relations in accordance with human existential ends, is nothing other than the natural law as it applies to our life in society, and the order to these ends projected onto our common human existence. Our everyday experiences are sufficient to firmly establish the truth of this principle. Included in this supreme moral principle are general principles such as, "render to everyone his or her due," "superiors must be obeyed," "evildoers must be punished," "contracts must be fulfilled," which pertain to the correct ordering of our social relations and represent the fundamental rights common to all hu-man beings, the power of command of the legislative authority, the right to enforce the order of law, and the rights springing from contracts within the national or international community.

As part of the natural law, these principles inhere in our moral con-sciousness, and include the components characteristic of law: specifi-cally, as we have previously stated, that it is morally wrong to infringe upon the rights of others, and also that, when enjoying any particular rights, we can expect and even demand from others that they respect our rights. Therefore, from the nature of these principles, there is no denying that there is a power of control inherent in every right.

It is imperative to note that from a consideration of the natural law, which relates primarily to the social order, only general principles emerge as opposed to specific codes of law; a *schema* for some eternal legal system. Nevertheless, guidelines for uncomplicated situations and basic principles for preserving the social order do come forth.

In treating this particular realm of the natural law and the specific rights pertaining to it, we have dealt with what could be called the natural juristic law as distinct from the natural law in general. Thus, the minimum of morality required for a proper ordering of society is, as in the proper ordering of our individual lives, law.

Messner drew three particular consequences from the fact that a part of the natural law pertains to jurisprudence and the social order of humans. They are:

> 1. No real law can exist in contradiction to natural moral law. By its substance a right contradicts the natural law if the end on which it pretends to be based is intrinsically incompatible with natural existential ends of man. 2. Different from such intrinsically void pretensions to rights is the abuse of intrinsically genuine rights. This abuse consists in the exercise of a right for some purpose contrary to its intrinsic end, or in some other way in contradiction to natural law. Such abuse does not abrogate a right; but its exercise may be restricted so far as it infringes the rights of others. 3. Rights in the sphere of law are, therefore, also something different from what is spoken of as the 'rights of God' in relation of the Creator to the created. They constitute an essentially different kind of control. St. Thomas (*Summa Theologica*, II-II, Q. 58, a. 2) leaves no doubt about this when he restricts law to the human social sphere, referring to Cicero's *De Officiis* (1, 7), where Cicero says: "Justitia ea ratio est, qua societas hominum inter ipsos, et vitae communitas continetur. (The object of justice is to keep men together in society and mutual intercourse.)"[10]

Any study of natural rights rooted in our human existential ends with the accompanying responsibility for the realization of these goals must include the fact that these rights are essentially both inalienable and inviolable. To propose that these natural rights are inviolable means that they are secured against any violation and are not capable of being annulled. Thus, each of us has the duty to protect these rights. Calling them inalienable is to specify that they may not be given up. Even Thomas Hobbes conceded that certain rights are inalienable, since the ultimate responsibility for them could not be delegated to anyone else, not even to the sovereign. He maintained that it is to assure our possession of these rights that we enter into the social contract with each other in the first place. If those rights were alienable, that is, if they could be renounced, then we would revert back to our natural stage, which he calls "solitary,

---

[10] *Ibid.*, pp. 157–158.

poor, nasty, brutish and short."[11]

From the analysis of these two characteristics of natural rights, we can further ascertain the relationships in which these rights stand to the element of duty, These are that rights are united with the duties bound up with their respective ends, and that the rights of each person impose on everyone else the duty of respecting them.

These concepts jointly lead to the conclusion that the correct idea of the rights of the human person is tied to the idea of the natural law. It is that particular law which delineates our basic duties and which establishes the binding force of all law that in turn allots to us our most basic rights. As Maritain so aptly said when speaking about what the great thinkers of antiquity called "the unwritten law":

> I am taking it for granted that you . . . admit that man is a being gifted with intelligence and who, as such, acts with an understanding of what he is doing, and therefore with the power to determine for himself the ends which he pursues. On the other hand, possessed of a nature, being constituted in a given, determinate fashion, man obviously possesses ends which correspond to his natural constitution and which are the same for all—as all pianos, for instance, whatever their particular type and in whatever spot they may be, have as their end the production of certain attuned sounds. If they don't produce these sounds they must be tuned, or discarded as worthless. But since man is endowed with intelligence and determines his own ends, it is up to him to put himself in tune with the ends necessarily demanded by his nature. This means that there is, by the very virtue of human nature, **an order or a disposition which human reason can discover and according to which the human will must act in order to attune itself to the necessary ends of the human being. The unwritten law, or natural law, is nothing more than that.**[12]

This doctrine of "natural rights," that is, of rights based on our human nature and, therefore, of rights to which we believe to have a special claim, has been part of our human history for thousands of years. Beginning with the ancient Greek philosophers—and even poets, such as Sophocles in his *Antigone*, references, even if veiled, to these rights may be noted when the natural law is taken up. Especially in political philosophy, there has been an extensive tradition which supports the idea

---

[11] Thomas Hobbes, *Leviathan*, i, 13. Michael Oakeshott, ed. (Oxford, 1946).
[12] Maritain, *Rights*, p. 61.

that there are some rights that all humans possess equally because these rights are rooted in the very being of humans, i.e., in human nature. John Locke, for example, wrote *Essays on the Law of Nature*; and even in his political writings, he speaks of natural rights, and includes the rights to life, liberty and property. During the political unrest of the eighteenth century, this same theory of natural law with its component of natural rights played an important role, as anyone familiar with the American Revolution, for example, and the *Declaration of Independence of the United States of America* can attest to.

If the features of this natural rights doctrine were examined, we would find some variations as they are listed at various times and places throughout its history. However, a number of basic properties common to all times can also be identified. These include the fact that every person has some rights which apply everywhere and under all circumstances, that a person is entitled to these rights irrespective of any social or governmental positions regarding them, and that these rights may not be personally relinquished or abandoned. Writers of the seventeenth and eighteenth centuries added two further traits: that all human beings participate in the same nature and experience the same needs, and that some particular rights are apprehended in the mere process of coming to understand our basic human nature.[13]

A list of some special natural rights reflecting these qualities can be found in the writings of philosophers such as John Locke, who joined with Thomas Hobbes in declaring the rights to life, liberty (to do anything as long as there was no rule or moral reason against it), and property (such things as make life worth living) to be the fundamental, inalienable rights of all human beings.[14]

In the contemporary period, there has been a further emphasis on the social aspect of these rights, and it has even been said that today, human rights are the corollary of the notion of social justice (Stanley I. Benn).[15] A positive side to this new thrust is that it allows the issue of human rights to be more recognized by society itself as essential to the development of the human person. However, these "Human Rights" or

---

[13] Harold Titus and Morris Keeton, *Ethics for Today,* 5th edition (New York: D. Van Nostrand Company, 1973), p. 255.

[14] John Locke, *Two Treatises on Government,* Peter Laslett, ed. (Cambridge, 1960).

[15] Stanley I. Benn and R. S. Peters, *Principles of Political Thought* (New York, 1964).

"Rights of Man," as they are referred to in various texts, are now regarded as belonging only partially to the natural law itself as previously developed, since some of these rights are derived also from the application of the natural law to the development of the total realization of human life, which includes a social and political dimension.

A list of some of the currently recognized human rights would include:[16]

a) The right to life; that is, we are entitled to preserve our life. This is a fundamental condition for the fulfillment of our existential ends. Without this basic right, no other rights would exist, since there would be no place for them to reside if we did not possess physical existence in the first place.

b) The right to the inviolability of the person. There is nothing which can more readily be called our own than the right to our body with all of its faculties. These are what enable us to realize our goals.

c) The right to physical and mental health. Life can hardly be worth living if one does not enjoy good health. Thus, society should recognize this need and provide for medical care necessary for each person, to the extent reasonably possible.[17]

d) The right to freedom of expression. To limit a person's freedom of speech and thereby his or her freedom of opinion is considered to violate both the natural existential ends and the social ends of that person.

e) The right to our good name. To be unjustly deprived of a good reputation is to cut us off from a society which is critical to our growth and development as human beings.

f) The right to do what we consider morally required of us, and the right not to do what we consider morally prohibited to us. Society may not ask us to act contrary to our conscience so far as the voice of conscience is clear and in accordance with natural law. This particular right is regarded as guaranteed by the natural law, and even when our conscience is in error, its freedom may not be impaired, but only constrained conditionally, that is, acting according to it may be prevented only if otherwise there would be an infringement on the definite rights of others, whether of individuals or of the community.

g) The right to select what one wants to do in life, that is, to choose

---

[16] Cf. Titus, *Ethics*, pp. 258–260; Messner, *Ethics*, pp. 222–226.

[17] Titus, *Ethics*, p. 258.

the form of employment which one pursues. Naturally, certain social and economic restrictions are applicable to this right, but in general, persons should be able to use their given talents for their individual good and for the good of society.

h) The right to develop one's personality. Since education and knowledge appear to be almost indispensable for the realization of other rights, this particular right includes a right to the education needed for meeting the challenges to self-preservation and creative achievement which today's complex world presents. Closely related to this concept is the recognized right—affiliated with duty—of parents to provide for the general education of their children, as well as to determine their religious and moral education.

i) The right to control our own material goods. This right allows us to use those goods to which we have personal entitlement, and even disposing of them.

j) The right to work. Access to the means of livelihood is tied to our self-preservation. As humans, we are also entitled to a wage sufficient for the proper maintenance of our being, and to the working conditions necessary for the development of that being. This right has been elaborated on by Harold Titus and Morris Keeton:

> Emphasis on the right to work and receive a living wage was not so necessary in an agricultural civilization. With the development of a complex, industrial civilization, however, access to the means of livelihood is often beyond the control of the individual. Since the forces affecting a man's opportunity to earn are social, society must assume the responsibility and must recognize the human right to a means of livelihood. Because under ordinary conditions man can live only by means of work, to refuse him work is to deprive him of the opportunity to develop his personality. When work cannot be provided, it would appear that society is obligated to share with the individual the goods and services produced. In numerous forms of relief and in the principles of unemployment insurance, society is coming to recognize this fact.[18]

We could also include as an accompanying aspect of this right that we be freed of work sufficiently in order to have time for recreation and leisure so as to develop our personality more fully.

---

[18] *Ibid.*

k) The right to associate with whomever we please. It is acknowledged that we are social beings and thus dependent on our associations with others for the development of our very being. No one should interfere with us when we join with other persons for religious, social, intellectual, economic, or recreational purposes, as long as the circumstances involved are compatible with the rights of others and the common good. This is a natural right springing from the social nature of all human beings by which we are dependent upon social cooperation for the development of ourselves.

l) The right to have some say in the governance of the society in which the person lives. This right does not demand a particular form of government, but simply that, whatever the form, the person have some share in controlling the social conditions under which he or she lives.

m) The right to worship. This is closely related to the right of conscience, and allows a person to worship God in whatever form he or she chooses and according to the dictates of his or her conscience, or not to worship at all. It guarantees that no one else may interfere with the exercise of this right in any way.

n) The right to choose those whom we love. This includes the right to select the partner with whom we enter into unions such as marriage without interference or hindrance from our society.

o) The right to express and fulfill the transcendental aspects of our very being such as goodness, beauty, and truth. This means that we are entitled to share in the cultural heritage of our human race, and that the values expressed in these three aspirations of our being belong to all individuals.

The above list contains many different kinds of rights. The important differences between the various types have been illustrated well by Maritain in his *The Rights of Man and Natural Law*,[19] and can in summary form be listed as follows:

A. The Rights of the *Human Person*

B. The Rights of the *Civic Person*

C. The Rights of the *Working Person*

While undoubtedly, many other rights could be listed which spring from both our individual, natural, existential ends and our social nature, the above list should suffice to illustrate what is generally meant by "The Rights of the Human Person." Serious reflection on this topic would

---

[19] Maritain, *Rights*, pp. 73–111.

seem to be adequate for admitting these rights, and possibly even for making the existence of them generally and specifically a self-evident truth. If such reflection is not adequate, then it is hoped that in light of what has been written here, one would join one's voice to those philosophers and other serious thinkers throughout the ages who, as previously noted, have recognized these rights relating to our human nature.

EXISTENTIAL
PERSPECTIVES

MORAL VALUES IN A WORLD WITHOUT GOD

Ronald Tacelli, S.J.

You may have read about a mass murderer. He killed at least seventeen young men; then he mutilated their corpses and ate parts of them. Many remains, like grisly souvenirs, he kept strewn through his apartment. When the police finally tracked him down, even the most hardened could scarcely endure what they found there. The level of horror passed beyond the threshold of comprehension; it was, they said, "too awful" to take in.

Imagine yourself for a moment in that apartment. Look around at the carnage, the gnawed and decomposing remains. "Dear God!" you might think. "This is monstrous beyond belief! This should never have happened!" But now suppose that the "Dear God" you invoked does not exist: that there is nothing—No One—to address when you say "Dear God!" Just the expression of an overpowering emotion. In that case and in such a world, what reason is there to believe that this horror surrounding you should never have happened; what reason to believe that there really—truly—objectively—are some actions that ought never to be done? This is the question I seek to answer.

When unbelievers are giving a candid account of their world view, they often go to great pains to emphasize the purposeless and pitiless character of the process of our coming-to-be. Here, for example, is Bertrand Russell:

> That man is the product of causes which had no prevision of the end they were achieving; that his origin, his growth, his hopes and fears, his loves and his beliefs, are but the outcome of accidental collocations of atoms; that no fire, no heroism, no intensity of thought and feeling, can preserve an individual life beyond the grave; that all the labors of the ages, all the devotion, all the inspiration, all the noonday brightness of human genius, are destined to extinction in the vast death of the solar system, and that the whole temple of man's achievement must inevitably be buried beneath the debris of a universe in ruins—all these things, if not quite beyond dispute, are yet so nearly certain that no philosophy

that rejects them can hope to stand. . . . How, in such an alien and inhuman world, can so powerless a creature as man preserve his aspirations untarnished? A strange mystery it is that nature, omnipotent but blind, in the revolutions of her secular hurryings through the abysses of space, has brought forth at last a child, subject still to her power, but gifted with sight, with knowledge of good and evil, with the capacity of judging all the works of his unthinking mother.[1]

Russell calls it a mystery that nature, our blind, unthinking mother, has brought forth children gifted with knowledge of good and evil. But, given his unsparingly grim account of our origin and final destiny, it seems even more mysterious that there can exist a "good" and "evil" of which nature's children can have knowledge. For nature as such possesses no moral goodness and does not act for any ends. Things simply happen. So when Russell exhorts us to "live constantly in the vision of the good,"[2] we might feel puzzled. What exactly is the good he urges us to see, and where could we possibly find it? He instructs us to slay "the eagerness, the greed of untamed desire";[3] to shed "over every daily task the light of love";[4] to lighten the "sorrows [of our fellow men] by the balm of sympathy, to give them the pure joy of never-tiring affection, to strengthen failing courage, to instill faith in hours of despair."[5] But this litany of Russell's wishes and desires cannot tell us whether he or anyone else *ought* to desire them; whether it would really be *wrong*—and not merely tasteless or unpleasant—for people to act on desires very different from his own.

Consider, for example, the words of another writer who set about, as Russell did, to describe our place in a godless universe.

No earthly creature is expressly formed by Nature, none deliberately made by her; all are the result of her laws and her workings, in such sort that, in a world constituted like ours, there had necessarily to be such creatures as we find here; very different creatures probably inhabit other globes, the myriads of globes wherewith space is freighted. But these creatures are [in themselves] neither good nor beautiful, precious nor created; they are the froth, they are the result

---

[1] From Bertrand Russell, "A Free Man's Worship," in *Why I Am Not a Christian*, ed. Paul Edwards (New York: Simon and Schuster, 1957), p. 107.

[2] *Ibid.*, p. 110.

[3] *Ibid.*, p. 112.

[4] *Ibid.*, p. 115.

[5] *Ibid.*

of [that blind mother's] unthinking operations, they are like vapors which rise up from the liquid in a caldron that is rarefied by heat, whose action drives out the particles of air this liquid contains. The steam is not created, it is resultative, it is heterogeneous, it derives its existence from a foreign element and has in itself no intrinsic value; its being or not has no adverse effect upon the element it emanates from; to this element it adds nothing, owes nothing, this element owes nothing to it. . . . Let Nature become subject to other laws, these creatures resulting from the present laws will exist no more under these different ones, but Nature will nonetheless still exist.

These words contain striking similarities to Russell's—most striking of all, perhaps: the image of nature as a blind, unthinking mother. But their author was Donatien-Alphonse-François de Sade, better known simply as the Marquis de Sade, and he wrote them as part of an elaborate justification for murder.[6]

Here then is a paradox. What is essentially one and the same view of our place in the universe has provoked two very different responses. Russell urges us to be sympathetic; Sade encourages us to indulge our cruelest desires. Does our blind mother really sanction the one and condemn the other?

Or put it another way: Is there any place for objective moral values in the world these authors describe? This does not mean that someone who believes in such a world is a bad or wicked person. But it does mean that if we adopt this belief, we might not be able to say what a bad or wicked person really is; whether there really are some sorts of actions that a good person—any good person, every good person—ought never to do.

Read over once again the words of Sade and Russell. It seems that so-called moral "goods" and "evils" can be rooted in nothing deeper than the desires of the human will. And yet each desire is rooted in the purposeless motions of the matter that produced it. How then could one desire be objectively more or less moral than another? Given this vision of our origin and destiny, it is very hard—in fact, I think, impossible—to see how it could be.

That is why ethical subjectivism seems to fit so nicely with atheist

---

[6] The passage is from *Juliette*, trans. Austryn Wainhouse (New York: Grove Press, 1968), pp. 766–7. The words, "that blind mother" (Sade's descriptive phrase for "Nature"), occur in the paragraph immediately preceding the one quoted; hence the square brackets.

materialism—with the view that the universe and the human beings within it were not made for any moral purpose. Human beings *do have* certain purposes, of course; for they feel certain needs; and so they find certain things desirable—in other words, they *do have* certain desires. What *ought* to be is what satisfies those desires, fulfills those needs. Can desires or needs themselves be judged? Yes—but only by other desires and needs. Or so at least it seems in the sort of world Russell and Sade have described. The mass murderer, for example, was fulfilling his desires. I and many others find what he did horrible, repulsive. This means that we find his acts of killing *undesirable:* that we are *repulsed* by them. And we have in effect served notice on such behavior in our laws and social institutions. So we will prevent him from further satisfying his desires by satisfying *our desire* to punish him.

Notice: if Russell and Sade are correct, we can offer neither that killer nor ourselves a *moral* critique of his actions; we can say nothing about the way he *really ought* to behave. Our critique is grounded in collective desire. Its power is the (inward) strength of those desires and the (outward) strength of the collectivity imposing them. We say to the killer, "Those other things you desire (like freedom, or perhaps life itself) will be taken from you because you have acted on *this* desire and done these horrible things." And we say to numberless others (and perhaps to some dimly apprehended darkness within ourselves), "If *you* do such things as these, some other things you very much desire will be taken from you. So *choose.*"

Now this may be an *effective* injunction; but is it a *moral* one? It seems rather an appeal to desire, and a promise that those with power will use it to enforce their will and prevent others from enforcing theirs.

Thus, if ethical subjectivism really does follow from a denial that God exists, we seem to have an answer to our initial question—namely: No; there is no sort of act that is objectively monstrous in a world without God; no sort of act that a truly good person ought never to do.

But that might seem too drastic. You might object that we can *recognize* certain things as noble (e.g., the life of St. Francis) and other things as base and degrading (e.g., slavery). There are certain goods that all human beings recognize as contributing to their flourishing as *human* beings—i.e., as beings having a certain kind of nature. Surely, belief in God need not enter into the apprehension of these goods as genuine goods. And therefore, *whether or not God exists,* we can still rationally hold that certain things ought and other things ought not to be done. There is no need to bring God into the picture at all.

But is this really so? You may *in fact* recognize that St. Francis' life was truly noble, and also *in fact* deny that God exists. The point here is not that atheists are incapable of recognizing moral nobility; but that such recognition is *incompatible* with a consistent atheist world view.[7]

For suppose, as you say, you are the product of a nature blind to purpose. You have been born among beings who have purposes and who value certain things as "good," as "desirable," and who see certain sorts of actions as "bad," or "wicked." You find that you desire approval from some of these beings. And therefore you model your own life on the kind of life you believe they would approve of—the kind of life that is "good" and "noble" and "worthwhile. " That desire to win approval is a genuine desire; and in desiring approval you can come actually to desire the things that win it. But look deeply within yourself; you may find other less highly regarded desires existing there. And I ask you: Why should you not follow them? Against what standard of judgment do you tell me, "No—these desires ought not to be followed"? Is it merely your desire to keep the approval of conventional society? But this is a way of affirming the conclusion you claim to be rejecting. If you deny ethical subjectivism, you need to point to some *objective* moral standard.

In your objection, you spoke of human nature. Is this the objective standard of moral measure? But I ask you: *Whose* human nature? Yours? You, after all, are a being of a certain kind; and suppose that part of the kind of being you are is one who takes pleasure in what I and others say ought never to be done. But you do desire these things; they seem to be an expression of your concrete nature—of the kind of being you really are;

---

[7] Cf. John Finnis ("Beyond the Encyclical [*Veritatis Splendor*]," *The Tablet*, 8, January 1994, pp. 9–10): "Judaeo-Christian revelation annihilated all the strange gods, and with them everything beyond the human which channelled and restrained human desires. The natural world lost its old sacredness. The only holy reality remaining was the one God. Nothing else, apart from man, determined meanings and values which man could recognize and had to respect. As God's image, man shared his dignity, and man's innate grasp upon the principles of right and wrong was confirmed as participation in God's wisdom and love. . . . From this world-view, subtract God. What remains? Man—but no longer in God's image. Man's natural grasp on the principles of right and wrong—but not as a participation in anything, since there is nothing beyond man in which those principles could be a participation. The value of the things which fulfill human beings—but only insofar as this value might satisfy *this or that person's or group's desire*" (emphasis added).

the kind of being our "blind mother" has produced. So why are they morally wrong?

You may answer, "It isn't merely the *fact* that I desire something that places it within the moral standard grounded in human nature; certain sorts of action violate the very meaning of living a *human* life. Real goods are goods to all beings sharing this nature. And so, for example, to say that there is nothing wrong with depriving someone else of life means that there is equally nothing wrong with someone else depriving *you* of life. But this would make communal existence impossible, and we need some community in order to live. Therefore some sort of actions are obviously inconsistent with living a flourishing *human* life."

But all of this assumes that you *ought* to want and value community; that you *should not* desire what is ultimately inconsistent with your having friends whom you can trust and who can trust you. It assumes that you *ought* to respect the desires of other human beings and believe that they have as much a "right" to fundamental goods as you do—and that you ought therefore to respect those rights. But this begs the question. Are there really any rights for you to respect? You know you have these desires; and you know that if others have them, they might try to do to you what you would like to do to them. To some, the resulting situation seems bleak: the only "community" it would ultimately allow for is the kind established by gangsters and criminals—a convenient (but ultimately unstable) partnership to further a common interest.[8] But so what? Who is to say that Nature has not implanted in some of us desires that will lead in the end to death and destruction? For in the end, we are all dead.

The real—but unacknowledged—force of the objection is *theological*. We look upon human nature as having been created for a certain end that ought to be pursued. And in that case, it makes sense to distinguish among desires, and to look at all humans as if they were characters in a story or drama—or better, a project or adventure; one that includes the entire species within the hope of high destiny. But on an atheist view this seems absurd.

---

[8] Cf. J. L. Mackie, *Ethics: Inventing Right and Wrong* (NY: Penguin Books, 1977), pp. 10–11: "[P]erhaps the truest teachers of moral philosophy are the outlaws and thieves who . . . keep faith and rules of justice with one another, but practice these as rules of convenience without which they cannot hold together, with no pretence of receiving them as innate laws of nature." Could Mackie not also have included terrorists, hit men, and child pornographers among these best of teachers?

Kai Nielsen, who has written extensively in defense of ethics without God, has recently endorsed something called "reflective equilibrium."[9] He means that human beings *in fact* have come to a kind of consensus that certain things are "bad" and other things are "good." It need not have been that way; but in fact it is. And so without dragging God or crypto-theological notions like a "nature" created by God into our picture of the world, we can rationally agree that certain things ought and others ought not to be done.

[A]ll we can finally do, for those [moral] judgments that are not dependent on factual claims, is to say that we have reflected carefully on them, taken the matter to heart, and when we do these are the judgments to which we feel committed.

This would be unsettling indeed if there were not a very considerable *de facto* consensus quite world wide. People will dispute about just who are innocent and who are not, but, all the same, there will be no society in which people take it to be tolerable that innocent children can be tortured just for the fun of it or that friends can break trust easily or treat their promises lightly or randomly kill people on a whim. These are all obvious things but they do show, whatever their logical status, that there is a wide cross-cultural consensus about such actions. When we can also show that these considered judgments are not in conflict with anything we factually know or have good grounds for believing, then their acceptability is further enhanced. Where this is so we do not have to rely on a brute *de facto consensus.*[10]

But I wonder: How many people did Nielsen consult about moral consensus? And how many does it take before an "is" becomes an "ought"? *Of course* many people agree that certain things are "good" and others are "bad." But the moral beliefs of the vast majority of human beings have roots in many things, among them religious beliefs—beliefs about the origin and destiny of our species. And we can experience the force of an "ought," of a moral imperative, even when we have forgotten the soil from which it sprang. But when people forget or come to disbelieve or even disdain religion, their moral lives do begin to change. There is no doubt, for example, that when people lost religious faith and joined the Communist

---

[9] The phrase is John Rawls'. Cf. his *A Theory of Justice* (Cambridge, Mass: Harvard University Press, 1971), pp. 20, 41–51, 120, 432.

[10] From Kai Nielsen, *Ethics Without God* (New York: Prometheus Books, 1990 [revised ed.]), p. 22.

or Nazi parties, they did things they could never have done, had their faith remained intact. We judge that what they did was monstrous. But we can do that only if there are standards to which we appeal and which *they ought to have observed*. And it seems pitifully contrived to say that most other people in fact disapprove of such behavior—feel commitment to a standard that condemns it. For we want to know whether those who feel no such commitment really *ought* to. Nielsen sees that he cannot appeal to "nature"; this, he says, is a way of smuggling God into our picture of the world. And in this, he is surely right.[11]

We are so used to moral discourse that we seldom take time to notice how odd it is.[12] There are things in nature that happen, and some of these are the activities of human beings. But of some of these, we say that they "ought" to happen. We treat them as having an intrinsic value: a quality that other kinds of things do not have. But why is that? Acts of will and actions willed are events within nature. They are and they happen, like other events. But about these, we speak as if they do or do not measure up to a standard. That standard is rooted within what constitutes a human being. And since human beings are part of the being of nature, we naturally speak as if that standard is rooted in nature; as if values are part of the very constitution or fabric of being.[13] The notion of "end" or "purpose" of human striving is inseparable from morality. And so the notion of a purposive nature is involved in our reflection on the moral life. But a purpose that

---

[11] Cf. also Paul Edwards, *The Logic of Moral Discourse* (New York: The Free Press, 1955), p. 241: "[U]nless [a person] first rejects God in all his forms, whether in the form of Jehovah or in the form of 'laws which are independent of my likings and dislikings'. . . or in the form of the non-natural quality called 'good', he will not even begin to try [to rid himself of deep-seated fears and guilt-feelings]."

[12] This thought (and much else besides), I owe to George Mavrodes' "Religion and the Queerness of Morality" (cf. William L. Rowe and William J. Wainwright [eds.], *Philosophy of Religion: Selected Readings* [3rd ed. Fort Worth: Harcourt Brace College Publishers, 1998], pp. 197–207). My thinking on morality and religion has also been influenced by William Lane Craig (cf. his *Reasonable Faith* [Wheaton, IL: Crossway Books, 1994], pp. 51–75). and J. P. Moreland (cf. his and Kai Nielsen's published debate *Does God Exist?* [Nashville: Thomas Nelson Publishers, 1990], esp. pp. 97–135).

[13] Cf. Mavrodes (*ibid.*, p. 203): "[W]hat we have in Kant['s moral argument for God's existence] is the recognition that there cannot be, in any 'reasonable' way, a moral demand upon me, unless reality itself is committed to morality in some deep way."

includes within it the ideal destiny and form of life of all human beings is most naturally thought of in terms of a "plan." And a plan involves a mind that conceives it.

That is why theism is so congruent with the notion that there are objective rights and wrongs.[14] Morality is something that belongs intimately—inseparably, I believe—to will and desire. And so we naturally think of our obligations and duties—the goods we ought to pursue, the evils we ought to avoid—as grounded ultimately in a creative will: a will that made the kind of world in which our natures can develop; and made our natures such that they ought to develop in certain ways: ways which lead to our finding fulfillment in such a world. When people say that a human will really ought to strive after x, y, or z, and really ought to avoid a, b, and c, they are assuming a picture of the world radically at odds with atheist materialism. If they profess atheism, they are oblivious to the way in which their moral rhetoric has become unhinged from the sort of world in which real moral norms must be rooted. They may believe that a secular morality is one purified of needless superstition. In fact, however, they are robbing morality of its true rational ground; denying to the "ought" they profess the only context able to contain it and allow it to survive.

And if God is denied—what will the practical effects be? It does not follow that people will suddenly sink into lives of boundless brutality. Society, at least for a while, will probably get on pretty much as before. No one can say for sure what a world without God will look like. But we can see in our own time where the denial of God has led us: a widespread sense of despair, a general cheapening or devaluing of human life, an unwillingness to sacrifice. People still keep bits and pieces of the old morality, faded notions of moral norms, like mementos, in their hearts. But the feeling that it is all meaningless, that keeping the wolf at bay is ultimately pointless and hopeless, seems to have taken hold—and seems likely to grow stronger with the passing of time. But even in the fullness of that possible time, the old morality will surely not have died. Even then, in a moment of devastation and horror, there will surely be some still able to

---

[14] Dietrich von Hildebrand has penetrated to the heart of this issue. Cf. *Christian Ethics* (New York: David McKay Company, Inc., 1953), p. 163: "[E]ven though . . . [moral] values can be grasped without referring to God, objectively God is definitely presupposed by them." The deep meaning of experienced value has been brought to light with brilliance and sensitivity by Balduin Schwarz. Cf. especially: "The Healing Power of Gratitude," printed in this volume, beginning on p. 11.

look around them and mean it when they say, "Dear God! This should never have happened!" They will be the lucky ones.[15]

---

[15] I want to thank those who made comments on earlier drafts of this paper: Kelly James Clark, Michael Pakaluk, Stephen D. Schwarz, and Sharon Yannaccone.

THE CONCEPT OF ETERNITY

Ronda Chervin

Balduin Schwarz has been many things to me: mentor in the process of my conversion to the Catholic faith, godfather at my baptism, and spiritual guide. He was also one of my professors of philosophy at Fordham University. Of the electives Dr. Schwarz taught with such fervor and profundity, one of my favorites was the philosophy of time. It awakened in me an abiding interest in the subjects of time and eternity. This paper will demonstrate why I consider the meaning of eternity to be worth probing.

To give you, the reader, a foretaste of what might be at stake from the standpoint of the existential and spiritual, consider your own future eternity. Do you imagine that it will consist in:

ONE: Living on forever and ever, moment by moment, in "the new heaven and the new earth," with the grace to experience to the highest degree any joy that you now have on earth without any admixture of frustration and sorrow? Or,

TWO: Rapt unity with God in timeless bliss?

I had always thought of eternity as Eternity Two. When my son died, I began to understand why Eternity One could be a strong image, and to wonder how One and Two could be combined.

Regardless of which image of eternity you would pick, the deeper question is, of course, "Which concept is the true one?" Or could both be true in some way hard to imagine, but required by correct metaphysical analysis?

Two Concepts of Eternity

The word 'eternity' is common in ordinary language. It appears in contexts as diverse as these:

"It took us an eternity to get to the airport."

"She looked into my eyes, and it seemed as if time stopped completely and we were in eternity."

"Before you make important choices, ask, 'What does this mean for eternity?'"

Does the word 'eternity' mean precisely the same thing in each of these three sentences? I think not.

That the word 'eternity' must have more than one meaning is also clear from philosophical and theological usage. There are at least two different conceptual meanings of 'eternity', reflecting the two conceptions of our own eternal life that we considered a moment ago:

Eternity ONE: *Foreverness*. Everlasting time, continuing forever and ever.

Eternity TWO: *Timelessness*. Being entire and all at once without any successiveness. The complete absence of time.

Both concepts of eternity presuppose some idea of the nature of time, including different types of time, such as clock time, psychological time (subjective experiences of the passage of time), "natural" time, cyclical time, linear time, duration, and temporality.

A famous definition of time is that of Aristotle. For Aristotle, "time is the measure of motion" (*Physics*, bk. iv). But other formulations, such as those to be found in Augustine (*Confessions*, bk. xi) or, more recently, Bergson, are concerned not with measure, but with the extension of the mind or with an uninterrupted flow of duration.

As Bergson showed so well in his philosophical analysis of clock-time and linear time vs. duration, our tendency to think of time in a spatial way, due to our use of clocks, can lead to many distortions. An example of such a misunderstanding might be the way a young person thinks of eternity, namely, not as a "now" that co-exists with linear time, but rather as a big chunk of solid time at the end of the line. If I have a long way to walk along the line of time before I come to death and to the chunk of solid time named eternity, it will naturally seem that eternity, in the sense of timelessness, Eternity Two, is far away. Yet actually, the timeless "now" of God is co-present with every moment of linear time.

A Third Concept

Are there really only two categories, time and eternity? Maybe not. We find in Thomas Aquinas a seeming hybrid, *aeveternty*. According to Thomas, there are purely temporal beings which begin and end in time, such as rocks and cats and dogs. Then, there is the eternal, non-temporal being of God. In between, we find those entities which begin in time but have no end, such as angels and human souls. Does this differentiation mean that only God is ever timeless, or is there some way in which human creatures participate in timelessness once in heaven? That is what we will seek to determine.

Scripture

What does Scripture tell us? Is the Biblical concept of the eternal univocal? Most often, we find the idea of the eternal as everlasting *foreverness*, Eternity One; not *timelessness*, Eternity Two. The word that is translated from Hebrew as "everlasting" comes from the image of the East where the sun rises unfailingly, forever and ever, "world without end."

Passages such as, "Blessed be they that dwell in Thy house, O Lord; they shall praise Thee forever and ever" (Ps 83:5), convey the image of *foreverness*, of everlasting time, or what we have called Eternity One. The famous Pauline description of eternal life as "beholding the glory of the Lord, changed into his likeness from one degree of glory to another" (2 Cor 3:18) certainly doesn't sound like timelessness, since there is to be growth from one state of being into another, literally ad infinitum.

Yet the image of eternity as *timelessness*, Eternity Two, is suggested by such passages as "Be still and know that I am God" (Ps 46:10). Being still is a way of avoiding being pulled along by the exigencies of time, and this is a way of getting closer to God who is "always the self-same" (Ps 101:28). "This is eternity that they may know Thee, the only true God" (Jn 27:3), and "we know that when He shall appear, we shall be like unto Him, because we shall see Him as He is" (1 Jn 3:2), point to an eternity that is the knowing of a timeless being: God. Or, "He that shall overcome, I will make him a pillar in the temple of My God; and he shall go out no more" (Rev 3:12) might be suggestive of a timeless unchanging state as our permanent way of being in the next life.

Eternity One and Eternity Two in the Writings of Philosophers

Given the lack of any immediate clarity about whether the concept 'eternity' is to be understood as *foreverness* or as *timelessness*, let us now consider what has been written about eternity by some of the most significant philosophers who have written about this subject.

There is no question that Plato thought of eternity as timelessness. If "time is the moving image of eternity," as depicted in the *Timaeus*, it follows that eternity is motionless and not merely a longer succession of time. For Aristotle, as for Plato, the world itself is eternal, but only in the sense of everlasting, having no beginning and no end. Aristotle's Unmoved Mover is eternal, in the sense of timelessness; but the status of the human soul is ambiguous as to whether it will gain foreverness, not to mention timelessness.

The philosophy of time and eternity of Plotinus is a direct challenge to that of Aristotle. Objecting to the Aristotelian formulation that "time is the measure of motion," Plotinus insists that time is directly derived from eternity. It is not so much a moving image as a mimicry of eternal timelessness.

"We must not muddle together Being and Non-Being, time and eternity, not even everlasting time with the eternal; we cannot make laps and stages of an absolute unity" (*First Ennead*, v, 7). The soul participates in eternity not through temporal action but through untemporal contemplation. Time derives from the overflow of the All-Soul, the Third of Plotinus' Divine Triad. Although the human soul is usually preoccupied with temporal concerns, it is immortal because it can know eternal pure forms. What can possess the eternal must be eternal (*Fourth Ennead*, vii, 8). Eternal here is clearly identified with timelessness, Eternity Two.

In the Christian philosophy of St. Augustine, we find reference to the timeless eternity of God. Time only comes to be with creation (*Confessions*, xi, 30). The soul goes on beyond the death of the body. It seems to be eternal mainly in the sense of foreverness, since it will be joined eventually to the body which means movement and change (*City of God*, xiii, 20). Even if a creature had existed forever, it would not be co-eternal with God, for God is unchangeable, and the creature is always changeable (*City of God*, xii, 16).

Yet it appears that the soul, in the philosophy of Augustine, does come close to the eternal in the sense of timelessness, since in heaven the blessed will "see God without intermission" (*City of God*, xxii, 29), and will see all things in God with God ever present (*City of God*, xxii). On the one hand, Augustine asserts that we will participate in the unchangeable immortality of God in heaven (*City of God*, xii, 20). Yet he realizes that it is very difficult for our human minds to grasp how such a participation is possible: "In the eternal nothing passes, but the whole is present, whereas no time is all at once present. . . . Who shall hold the heart of man, that it may stand still, and see how eternity, ever still-standing . . . utters the times past and to come?" (*Confessions*, xi, 11.)

It is Boethius who gives us one of the most incisive descriptions of Eternity Two, timelessness, "the whole, perfect and simultaneous possession of endless life" (*Consolation*, v, 6). "The now that flows away makes time, the now that stands still makes eternity" (*De Trinitate*, iv).

Following Boethius, Thomas teaches that time equals the changing instant, and eternity the enduring instant. God alone is wholly unchanging. Thomas removes many difficulties by pointing out: "As God although incorporeal, is named in Scripture metaphorically by corporeal names, so eternity, though simultaneously whole, is called by names implying time and succession" (foreverness).

For Thomas, only God is eternal in the sense of Eternity Two, timelessness, but other creatures can share in eternity. There are two parts to the definition of eternity:

1. Not having a beginning nor an end, which corresponds to Eternity One, *foreverness*.

2. Being entire and all at once without any successiveness, which is Eternity Two, *timelessness* (see *S.T.*, I-I, 10, 1).

Only the second part is eternity proper. In heaven we will still have successive affections and acts of understanding (Eternity One, *foreverness* with changes), but our vision of glory will be unchanging! (See *S.T.*, I-I, 10, 5, ad 1.) In hell there is no true eternity, only everlasting time (see *S.T.*, I-I, 10, 3, ad 2).

In the *Summa contra Gentiles* (61), it is explained that the vision of God involves a supernatural gift above our natural capacities; "whatsoever is seen in it is seen all at once and at a glance. That this vision takes place is a kind of participation of eternity." With respect to what is above, the intellectual soul is caught up in the timelessness of its object, God, while with respect to lower being, it is itself temporal, the intellectual soul being "created on the borderline of eternity and time." (*Ibid.*)

These Christian philosophical formulations correspond to some intuitive sense we have that, if eternal life is to be all-fulfilling, it must, on the one hand, encompass somehow both our desire for absolute unity and timelessness; on the other hand, it must also include our *growing* in our love for God and for creatures in God, in the splendor of variety.

Yet, the references given above still leave some intellectual uncertainty. How exactly does a creature who moves in time from moment to moment experience the timeless? If we once entered what is timeless, would we not have to remain there in what is changeless? How could we ever "get out" to resume temporal succession? The next part of this exploratory paper will address these questions.

Foreverness and Timelessness: Reconciled?

To sharpen one of the questions: Can a being that is a body/soul composite in time as well as in eternity—can such a composite be, by virtue of the resurrected body, not only eternal in the sense of Eternity One, everlastingness or *foreverness*, but also participate in eternity in the sense of *timelessness*, Eternity Two? And, if so, how?

The best partial understanding I have found is in Thomas Aquinas' writings concerned with our future life. He thinks that our experience of eternity will be primarily timeless by virtue of our unity with God, who is ever-present and timeless. In our substance, we shall be changeless and timeless; but in our accidents, we shall be everlasting, in a changing state of response to the creatures who will be present in the promised "new heaven and new earth." This may be why in the *Summa contra Gentiles* (6), Thomas speaks of *a kind of* participation of the soul in the timeless eternity of God, rather than of the human person simply becoming timeless.

Here is Thomas' imagery of the reconciliation of timelessness and temporality as advanced in an article about agility of movement in our heavenly life: He is responding to the idea that some propose that there will be no movement in eternity, since the soul will be satisfied completely, and will not need anything. He replies that it is fitting that we glorify God by movement and be refreshed by the beauty of the creatures. "And yet movement will in no way diminish their happiness which consists in seeing God, for He will be everywhere present to them" (*S.T.*, II-II, 84, 1).

This splendid formulation shows the incorrectness of imagining that the soul in eternity would go back and forth between the timeless beatific vision and temporality. Rather it is somehow *simultaneously* enjoying timelessness with respect to God, *and* everlastingness as it enjoys redeemed creatures in succession.

Yet even with the aid of such philosophical explanations, there still remains a certain mystery about our participation in eternity. It still seems paradoxical to think that we can participate in the timeless without becoming ourselves timeless. Or that having done so, we would still be interested in experiencing anything else besides God.

Given the acceptance of limitations in our understanding, there still remains the possibility that, not by conceptualization, but by experience, we might gain some glimpse of how it might be possible to reconcile Eternity One and Eternity Two; to be everlasting and changing, and yet to be timeless.

First, consider a very common occurrence which is called doing two things at the same time. Is it possible to knit while watching television? Yes! Part of the person is engaged in manual labor, yet the eyes can simultaneously be gazing forward at something else. In a remotely analogous manner, could not the center of the soul in eternity be focused unchangingly, timelessly on God, while some other part of the soul was encountering changing creatures everlastingly?

Perhaps this analogy is not so remote when we recall the accounts of mystics who insist that it is possible to be in trance of rapturous union with God in the innermost part of the soul, and yet be able simultaneously to stir the soup!

Second, consider the nature of our own selfhood. On the one hand, we obviously move along in time, growing not only in body but also in spirit; we are aeveternal, having a beginning in time but no end in time. Yet, there is a part of us, our innermost created being, which is unchanging, a substratum which underlies all changes, making it possible to speak of baby-me as the same person as adult-me. This innermost core does seem to be something unchanging, fixed, *timeless*—eternal. Yet we know that our timeless unchanging self co-exists with our changing self in some paradoxical manner which we cannot deny, no matter how difficult it might be to explain this co-existence.

Third, consider those special moments when time seems to "stand still." Usually, these are connected with dazzling happenings, such as the sight of an exquisite ocean view, or the delight of seeing the beauty of another personality when we fall in love. Sometimes, time stands still, however, not in the face of something overwhelming, but rather in the ordinary course of life, when it can seem as if "being" itself speaks of its wonderfulness through any one of its parts, even a tiny spot of color. In this case, one might say that the richness of experience that stops the flow of temporality is really the very depth of being itself as opposed to non-being.

If we reflect on such privileged moments which seem timeless, we will be struck by various important truths. The greater the ontological reality of the object of experience, the more perfect its fullness, the more it "holds" us. Lacking an immediate craving for something else to fill the bottomless pit of our desires, we feel lifted beyond the temporal flow upon which we are usually fixated in the hope that something attractive might be coming to us along the conveyor belt of time! We are finally able to beg time to stand still.

Of course, in reality, at such moments, natural time is in fact proceeding. Our body cells are continuing their slow decay, etc. The clock is still ticking and time *is* elapsing. But, somehow, we were able to simultaneously experience some sort of psychological timelessness while all the while continuing our aeveternal, everlasting journey onward!

Might not our experience in heaven be analogous: simultaneously developing, growing, moving along the time continuum, yet caught up in a sense of timelessness? Certainly, such ought to be the case if you consider that of all objects, God must be the most ontologically rich, profound, and capable of causing us to cease moving forward in search of some "greater" satisfaction. Boethius thought that eternity included all time, "as in joy which is both a standstill, yet full of rushing energy, dynamic energy, infinite speed" (*Consolation*, v, 6).

In conclusion, let us return to our original question: Is it more correct, from a philosophical standpoint, to think of our experience of life after death in terms of Eternity One, *foreverness*, everlasting life? Or as Eternity Two, *timelessness*?

What I have tried to show is that it is impossible to choose between these two concepts. A gift of creation, *foreverness* is a state consonant with our human mode of being. Participation in *timelessness* is a further gift to be experienced in the unity of love of a timeless God, but it is not to result in some sort of fusion where there would be no temporality left to the creature. Within the participation in the unchanging God, we are to rejoice in a succession of responses to all other creatures *in* God, seen in the light of the Vision.

Finally we are left with St. Paul's ecstatic proclamation: "Eye has not seen, nor ear heard, nor the heart of man conceived, what God has prepared for those who love Him" (1 Cor 2:9).

Or, if we are looking for a more humanistic image, we could hope one day to be laughing at the eternal banquet, with St. Augustine and St. Thomas happily explaining to us what was missing in the philosophical tomes we pored over in our so ardent earthly search for wisdom!

MARCEL AND KIERKEGAARD ON HOPE AND DESPAIR

John Crosby

Balduin Schwarz knew and revered Gabriel Marcel, and he had a life-long love affair with the work of Søren Kierkegaard; it seems, therefore, appropriate to offer for this volume in his honor a brief study of these two great thinkers.

Of the writings of Marcel that I keep going back to, his great essay, "Sketch of a Phenomenology and a Metaphysics of Hope,"[1] holds a particular fascination for me. I propose to offer some reflections on what Marcel writes about despair (section 1) and the overcoming of despair by hope (section 2). I trust that I will not speak in the vein of those authors who, as Marcel complained, "throw handfuls of dirt" on his thought; perhaps the personal character of my reflections will protect me from committing this kind of impiety. I also propose to bring in the analysis of hope and despair in Kierkegaard (section 3), rubbing these two great authors against each other, to use the Socratic image. Kierkegaard in fact takes us well beyond Marcel in probing the drama of hope-despair, as we shall see.

1

Marcel writes, "There can strictly speaking be no hope except when the temptation to despair exists" (36). This is the aspect under which I would like to take Marcel on hope: hope as the overcoming of despair.

Now it is a definite circumstance under which I am tempted to despair and am challenged to hope; Marcel calls it the circumstance of experiencing a kind of "captivity." His examples of captivity include being imprisoned, being seriously sick, being separated from a beloved person,

---

[1] Gabriel Marcel, *Homo Viator: Introduction to a Metaphysic of Hope* (Chicago: Regnery, 1951), pp. 29–67. All page references to this work will be given directly in the text.

being distressed over the negative development of a beloved person, being an artist suffering from a time of dryness and barrenness. Undoubtedly we could enlarge this list of examples by drawing on other works of Marcel; I am thinking in particular of his papers on personal immortality, which he affirmed so passionately. There is an element of hope in the prophetic word spoken to a beloved person, "You will never die," and certainly in the longing to be reunited with that person. But it is remarkable that Marcel, at least in the essay on hope, does not include the captivity of being guilty, nor does he discuss hoping for forgiveness and despairing over being forgiven.

Let us look more closely at the captivity of a father anxiously awaiting word from his son, from whom he has not heard for a long time.

> Every day he awaits the letter which would bring his anxiety to an end. To despair would be to say, "I have been disappointed so many times there is every reason to expect that I shall be again today"; it would be to declare this wound incurable. . . . "I shall never be anything but the wounded, mutilated creature I am today. Death alone can end my trouble. . . ." The despairing man not only contemplates and sets before himself the dismal repetition, the eternalisation of a situation in which he is caught like a ship in a sea of ice. By a paradox which is difficult to conceive, he anticipates this repetition (42).

In this masterful description I discern two moments, which I propose to distinguish somewhat more than Marcel does. On the one hand, the circumstances of the father's captivity are experienced by him as "hardening" into fatalistic inevitability. This hardening reminds us of Buber's account of the confining way that causality is experienced in the It-world. Marcel says that such hardening includes a certain experience of time as "closed," as impervious to the eruption of anything new, of anything that might break the prison of the father's captivity. On the other hand, Marcel also expresses in this description something about the innermost gesture of despair, a gesture that he elsewhere in the essay on hope calls "capitulation."

> To capitulate, in the strongest sense of the word, is not only, perhaps is not at all, to accept the given sentence or even to recognize the inevitable as such, it is to go to pieces under this sentence, to disarm before the inevitable. It is at bottom to renounce the idea of remaining oneself, it is to be fascinated by the idea of one's own destruction to

the point of anticipating this very destruction itself (38).

We might accentuate the affinity with Kierkegaard in this last sentence and say that the despairing father ties his very self to being reunited with his son; in other words, he wills to be the self that he is only on the condition that he is delivered from his captivity; otherwise, he will give his self up, preferring annihilation to further existence. Marcel also remarks that this laying down of conditions for my selfhood expresses an excess of *Having* over *Being*.

I might just add here that there is a certain condition that one would be quite right in laying down for one's selfhood. If a person is weighed down with unforgiven guilt, he naturally looks for forgiveness as a *sine qua non* for his restoration as a personal self. It would not be right to take the same "distance" to his burden of guilt that he takes to the separation from his son, as if he were indulging in some kind of illegitimate Having by "going to pieces" at the thought of remaining forever unforgiven. If his guilt were really unforgivable, then the despairing capitulation of himself would correspond to the truth; there would be no hope here that he would be needlessly abandoning. Marcel's idea that one should never capitulate in captivity depends on the limited range of his examples of captivity.

And so, as I say, there is this double aspect of despair: the circumstances of my captivity hem me in more and more tightly, speaking a definitive "no" to my hopes; in addition I so tie my very self to being liberated that the "no" seems to be spoken to me personally and to be a final rejection of my self, so that I am tempted to capitulate as self.

There is another respect in which Marcel's thought on despair is deeply akin to Kierkegaard's; like the great Danish thinker he sees the religious dimension of despair. Despair is a metaphysical passion, which cannot be lived in a purely innerworldly way, without any intention towards God. The despairer cannot help thinking, however little he articulates it, "Since God is depriving me of that without which I cannot continue to be a self, He is abandoning me." Once the father in our example ties his very self to the reunion with his son, he can only think of God abandoning and rejecting him if God does not restore his son to him.

There is one other element in Marcel's description of despair that I want to bring into our discussion:

It must be noticed that the attitude of those who in the name of reason

> take up their position against hope is in all points comparable with that of the people who claim to avoid risks. In both cases what they want to avoid is disappointment (55).

It is not difficult to see how the father runs a certain risk in hoping against hope for news from his son; he continues to endure a certain vulnerable uncertainty and to expose himself to possible disappointment. By despairing he puts himself beyond such disappointment. Less obvious but no less real perhaps is the risk that he runs in not tying his selfhood to the reunion with his son, in willing to be a self unconditionally. But there is still more to the risks that are refused in despair; according to Marcel, the despairing person does not want to be in the risky and unprotected position of hoping for some good to *which he can lay no claim, to which he has no right*. Marcel is guided by a sound intuition when he suspects a connection between the overgrown rights-consciousness in which we all live and our incapacity for hoping—a point to which I shall return at the end. In various ways, then, one avoids risks by despairing rather than hoping. Nietzsche would rightly say that there is something spirit-less and slave-like in the readiness to despair.

2

So much on despair; now a word on the hope which drives out despair. "In hoping, I do not create in the strict sense of the word, but I appeal to the existence of a certain creative power in the world, or rather to the actual resources at the disposal of this creative power" (52). In making this appeal, the terms of my hardened captivity are loosened, rendered more "fluid," Marcel says. The ice around my ship does not confine it so tightly anymore. I break out of the realm of probabilities based on worldly calculations, such as the probability that a son who has not written for so long is no longer alive; I appeal to a certain goodness of being. And so I do not just expect the eternal return of what has already been in my life, but am ready for something new to break into my life, which I now experience as a story that is not yet finished.

Marcel clarifies the nature of this appeal by finding a certain element of patience in all hope. In dealing patiently with another we are "placing our confidence in a certain process of growth and development," and are showing "a subtle respect for the other person's need of time to preserve his vital rhythm, so that it [patience] tends to exercise a transforming influence upon him" (40). In practicing patience, I do not just take account of what the other person has in fact done with his life and what empirical condition he is presently in; on this level the other person may be dismal, hopeless; instead I break through to a deeper level in the other, to a level at which mysterious processes of growth are at work in him and unsuspected possibilities are close to breaking through.

And I do not just *recognize* these processes and possibilities, but in patiently hoping, I *appeal* to them, as was said, thus empowering the other to become what without my patient hope he might never have become. This is an important point. We must not, according to Marcel, over-intellectualize hope; we must not take it to be only the truthful recognition of the hidden creative powers of good in the world and in other persons. This would draw hope in the direction of a certain kind of rational optimism, which Marcel sharply distinguishes from real hope. No, in hoping we work with these creative powers, lending them support. To refuse to hope in them is not just to commit an intellectual error, but to be disloyal to them, unfaithful, and in some sense even to interfere with them. Hence the element of risk in hoping; in recognizing what is the case I do not take risks as I do when I cooperate with the creative forces of good, for no one can predict just what will come of this cooperation.

Marcel shows himself to be sensitive to the charge that in hoping we indulge in wishful thinking and flee irresponsibly from the hard realities of our condition. I interpret him as in the end rejecting this charge on the ground that there really is this goodness of being with its mysterious creative powers; it really is there to appeal to. We live in only one dimension if we live only in the midst of the empirical, the causal, of that which shows itself in "catalogued experience" (52), as Marcel says. We become narrow dogmatists if we fail to realize how non-definitive this dimension is and how much room there is in fact for the good to work behind and between and through the most hopeless patterns of human life.

It is perhaps to the point to mention here for comparison a profound idea of Max Scheler's about love for another person. He sees in each person the mystery of an unrepeatable self, which is the basis for the special moral tasks that one person has and another does not have. Now this real self of a person is commonly obscured by what the person has made of his life; we may see in some other only patterns of failure, only predictable bad behavior, only vicious circles. It is the accomplishment of love to find the real self and real vocation of another, however little in evidence it may be, and to affirm it in such a way as to empower the other to come to himself. This act of love, whereby we reach beyond the empirical mess that a person has made of himself and attain to the mystery and beauty of the person, is profoundly akin to Marcel's act of resisting all the temptations to despair of some person, and of finding those creative forces at work even in him that let us hope for him.

Corresponding to the two aspects that we distinguished in despair, there are the two aspects of hope. We have been speaking of hope as removing the fatalism from the circumstances of our captivity; now a word on the willingness to be ourselves even in the midst of our captivity.

At the moment of crisis, challenged to choose between hope and despair, tempted to "go to pieces" in the midst of one's distress, one can hold fast to one's self, refusing to capitulate. One can resolutely will to stay intact as personal self. This may seem to be the stirring of hope in the tempted person—it is very significant that Marcel distinguishes all such Stoical self-possession from hope. It coheres fully with Marcel's entire philosophy of communion to object that the person remains too solitary in resolutely holding on to his endangered self, and that as a result, his self remains too much a self in the sense of *moi*; it remains too little connected with the other. Hope belongs not to man in solitude but to man in communion. Hence Marcel repeatedly makes statements like this: "It is to a consciousness of these reciprocities, of this mysterious and incessant circulation, that I open my soul when I hope" (61). I have to put myself in a position to receive my endangered self back as a gift, only then does the danger of despair pass and give way to hope; in other words, I have to will to be myself in a way essentially different from the Stoic, that is, with less self-sufficiency and more grateful receptivity.

The communion that belongs to hope becomes especially clear when Marcel explains that the hope that lays down no finite conditions for my selfhood is possible only in relation to God.

> The only possible source from which this absolute hope springs must once more be stressed. It appears as a response of the creature to the infinite Being to whom it is conscious of owing everything that it has and upon whom it cannot impose any condition whatsoever without scandal. From the moment that I abase myself in some sense before the absolute Thou who in his infinite condescension has brought me forth out of nothingness, it seems as though I forbid myself ever again to despair, or, more exactly, that I implicitly accept the possibility of despair as an indication of treason (47).

It is, then, not in solitude but only before God that I can renounce all Having (as opposed to Being), that I can refuse to interpret my captivity as the final destruction of my self. And let us add that the risk we take in hoping appears more clearly than before; in abandoning ourselves unconditionally to the living God in hope, we give up all the securities of Having. This is how Marcel would answer the objection that by making hope a religious act we are trying to find a level of security that is foreign to the human condition; he would say that before God there is security and risk all in one.

3

It is at this point that I would like to bring in the Kierkegaardian analysis of despair and of hope. Kierkegaard contemplates a possibility of despair that I am not aware of in this text of Marcel. He considers the case of the person who is offered some good that answers to the deepest aspirations of hope *and who nevertheless despairingly declines the good*. Marcel seems to assume that whoever is offered release from his captivity will of course gladly accept it; we can despair only as long as our release is not at hand and can only be reached for in hope. Kierkegaard studies a darker mystery of despair: being offered the release that one hoped for *but then despairingly refusing it*.

In *The Sickness unto Death*, Kierkegaard portrays in a well-known passage how we can decline the Christian offer of salvation, not so much on the grounds that it is not true, but on the grounds that it is "too much":

Christianity teaches that this particular individual, and so every individual . . . exists *before* God—this individual who perhaps would be vain for having once in his life talked with the King, this man who is not a little proud of living on intimate terms with that person or the other, this man exists before God, can talk with God any moment he will, sure to be heard by Him; in short, this man is invited to live on the most intimate terms with God! Furthermore, for this man's sake God came to the world, let himself be born, suffers and dies; and this suffering God almost begs and entreats this man to accept the help which is offered him! Verily, if there is anything that would make a man lose his understanding, it is surely this! Whosoever has not the humble courage to dare to believe it, must be offended at it. But why is he offended? Because it is too high for him, because he cannot get it into his head, because in the face of it he cannot acquire frank-heartedness, and therefore must have it done away with, brought to naught and nonsense, for it is as though it would stifle him.[2]

Now it might be said that this rejection of Christian salvation is not exactly a despairing rejection, for those who reject it seem to feel no need for it and therefore to have no hope that would be fulfilled by it. And this is true; the theme of despair is not yet fully present in the passage quoted. We have to add something that finds its place elsewhere in this book of Kierkegaard, namely that many of those who reject a life in Christ as "too much" for them are at the same time drawn to it; they glimpse in such a life something of the fulfillment, beyond all that they could have dreamed, of all their deepest aspirations, and so it is not without a sense of profound loss that they decline it. A darkness enters their hearts when they turn away, a darkness they are aware of bringing upon themselves. These are real despairers; they despair of themselves ever participating in the superabundance of Christian existence. By the way, I am not abandoning the philosophical focus of Marcel's essay by bringing in Christianity; I do so because it is just in being offered the greatest imaginable good that we find in ourselves the sharpest crisis of hope and despair.

Josef Pieper has found a good analogy for the divided mind of those who are drawn to Christian salvation and yet shrink from it. He mentions certain neurotic invalids who, while they want to get well, at the same time fear nothing so much as getting well. And why do they fear this? Because they cannot bear to give up the claim that they have as sick people on the pity of others, because they cannot bear to live like other people on their own and without the support of those special attentions that we show to the sick.[3] Now the question is, what is it that people have to give up but are unwilling to give up in order to accept that which fulfills and surpasses all their deepest hopes? How is it possible to hang back in despair instead of coming to Christ?

The one answer that we find in Kierkegaard is this: there is a deep spiritual laziness that afflicts us in our inmost parts; it is sloth in the

---

[2] Søren Kierkegaard, *Fear and Trembling and The Sickness unto Death*, trans. by Walter Lowrie (Princeton, 1941), p. 216. The subsequent references to Kierkegaard are given directly in the text.

[3] Josef Pieper, *On Hope* (San Francisco: Ignatius Press, 1986), p. 56.

sense of the *acedia* discussed by St. Thomas Aquinas and others before him. Kierkegaard expresses it above in the passage quoted, and also in a sentence like this: "The narrow-mindedness of the natural man cannot welcome for itself the extraordinary which God has intended for him; so he is offended" (217). Pieper refers expressively to this narrow-mindedness as the lack of *Hochgemutheit*,[4] that is, the lack of a certain high-mindedness. It is spiritual mediocrity, it is the lack of all audacity. We readily recognize here that slave-like fear of risks that Marcel ascribes to all despair. The despairer gets a hint of the fulfillment of his hopes in Christ, but he shrinks away, lacking the "humble courage," as Kierkegaard says, to make the venture, perhaps even resenting Christianity for upsetting his established way of life.

But Kierkegaard goes further and deeper. There is a much darker and more malevolent form of despair, which he says is the despair not just of weakness but of defiance. It is the one that really takes us beyond Marcel's study. Let me try to explain it like this. We are all aware of lacks and wounds and sins in ourselves; we suffer under them and long to be made whole; and to this extent, we are ready to accept the redemption offered to us in Christ. But we also want to hold on to our lacks and wounds and sins, *because we can appeal to them in making a protest against God.* They let us feel aggrieved before God, equipped with a claim against Him. If we let God heal our wounds, we can no longer complain of them. Someone says, for example, that his sins are too great to be forgiven; but if you look closely, you find him taking a perverse satisfaction in being a reproach to God for letting him come into this desperate situation. It is as if the sick person in Pieper's analogy were to want to remain sick, not so much because he fears the demands made on healthy persons, but because he wants to keep alive a grievance against his doctor. He does not like being sick, but even less does he like being without his grievance, and so he refuses to use the means that would make him well. Scheler has observed something similar in a certain kind of *ressentiment*-driven humanitarian love, which is not primarily a passion for relieving human suffering but rather a passion for accusing God. The very last thing this humanitarian wants is the elimination of human suffering, for then he would lose his grievance against God. Kierkegaard describes this defiant despair masterfully when he writes:

---

[4] Pieper, *Über die Hoffnung* (Munich, 1977), p. 60.

Revolting against the whole of existence, it [despair] thinks it has hold of a proof against it, against its goodness. This proof the despairer thinks he himself is, and that is what he wills to be, therefore he wills to be himself, himself with his torment, in order with this torment to protest against the whole of existence (207).

This despairer does not want to "hear about what comfort eternity has for him . . . because this comfort would be the destruction of him as an objection against the whole of existence" (207). In my opinion, which is also Kierkegaard's opinion, this defiant despair is not something rare, reserved only for a few Luciferian characters; every one of us knows it at least as a temptation in ourselves, at least as an attitude that makes itself felt in our inner lives, even if we have reason to hope that we are not completely dominated by it.

When, then, we are in some kind of captivity, to return to Marcel's image, we can be strangely ambivalent about being liberated; we can yearn in hope to be liberated from it, but at the same time we can shrink back in despair from being liberated. Here is a drama of hope and despair that Marcel does not consider. And yet we see here anew how right Marcel was to identify a certain consciousness of our rights as an impediment to hoping. If hope is to take over in us and drive out all despair, we have to give up all grievances, all claims to compensation, all the pleasures of victimhood, and bear to live without them. We have to be willing to live not by grievance but by gratitude.

APPENDIX

SELECTED BIBLIOGRAPHY OF THE WORKS OF BALDUIN SCHWARZ

[This bibliography includes all books Balduin Schwarz has authored and edited, as well as those articles he wrote in English. A complete listing comprises seven books written, three books translated, three books edited, 125 scholarly articles, fifty-seven book reviews, and six letters to the editor of various publications. Also, two "Festschriften" (books of essays in his honor) appeared, in 1974 and 1982. For a complete bibliography, see below, item # 6 under "Books Written."]

Books Written

1. *Untersuchungen zur Psychologie des Weinens* (An analysis of the psychology of tears). Ph.D. diss. München: Druckerei Studenten-haus, 1928.

   This book was translated into Spanish by José Ortega y Gasset and published as *La psicologia del llanto*. Madrid, 1930.

2. *Der Irrtum in der Philosophie: Untersuchungen über das Wesen, die Formen und die psychologische Genese des Irrtums im Bereich der Philosophie, mit einem Überblick über die Geschichte der Irrtums-problematik in der abendländischen Philosophie* (On error in philosophy: An investigation of the essence, the forms, and the psychological genesis of error in the area of philosophy, with a survey of the history of error in Western philosophy). Münster: Aschendorff, 1934.

   This book was extensively reviewed by Nicolai Hartmann in his *Kleinere Schriften* (Smaller writings), vol. 3. Berlin: Walter de Gruyter & Co., 1958, pp. 374–77.

3. *Ewige Philosophie: Gesetz und Freiheit in der Geistesgeschichte* (Perennial philosophy: Law and freedom in the history of ideas).

Leipzig, 1937. A new edition of this book, with a Foreword by Josef Seifert, is forthcoming at the Verlag Franz Schmitt, Siegburg, Germany.

4. *Über das innere Prinzip der Periodisierung der Philosophiegeschichte* (On the inner principle determining distinct periods in the history of philosophy). Salzburger Universitätsreden, no. 7. Salzburg, 1966.

5. *Antwort an einen Atheisten* (A reply to an atheist). Reden zur Zeit, vol. 26. Würzburg: Johann Wilhelm Neumann, 1968.

6. *Wahrheit, Irrtum und Verirrungen: Die sechs grossen Krisen und sieben Ausfahrten der abendländischen Philosophie—Gesammelte Aufsätze* (Truth, error and confusions: The six major crises and the seven journeys of Western philosophy—Collected essays) [posthumous]. Edited by Paola Premoli and Josef Seifert. Heidelberg: Universitätsverlag C. Winter, 1996.

Books Edited

1. *The Human Person and the World of Values: A Tribute to Dietrich von Hildebrand by His Friends in Philosophy.* New York: Fordham University Press, 1960.

2. *Wahrheit, Wert und Sein: Festgabe für Dietrich von Hildebrand zum 80. Geburtstag* (Truth, value, and being: Essays in honor of Dietrich von Hildebrand for his 80th birthday). Regensburg: Josef Habbel, 1970.

3. *Dankbarkeit ist das Gedächtnis des Herzens* (Gratitude is the way the heart remembers). Salzburg: Verlag Das Bergland Buch, 1983. Reprint, Munich: Don Bosco Verlag, 1992.

Articles

1. "Dietrich von Hildebrand on Value." In *Thought* 24 (1949). pp. 655–76.

2. "Aristotle: Politics, Book I." In *The Great Books: A Christian Appraisal.* Edited by H. C. Gardiner. Vol. 1. New York: 1949. pp. 28–32.

3. "Plato: Meno." In *The Great Books: A Christian Appraisal.* Edited by H. C. Gardiner. Vol. 1. New York: 1949. pp. 43–50.

4. "A Reply to Father William O'Connor" [Concerning Dietrich von Hildebrand on Value]. In *Thought* 25 (1950). pp 379–84.

5. "Some Remarks on the Philosophy of History." In *The Historian* 4, No. 2 (February 1955). pp. 5–11.

6. "The Need for a Christian Reappraisal of the History of Philosophy." In *Proceedings of the American Catholic Philosophical Association* 32 (1958). pp. 54–66.

7. "The Role of Philosophy in Religious Education." In *Religious Education* 53 (1958). pp. 505–11.

8. Introduction to *The Human Person and the World of Values: A Tribute to Dietrich von Hildebrand by His Friends in Philosophy.* Edited by Balduin Schwarz. New York: Fordham University Press, 1960. pp. ix–xiii.

9. "Some Reflections on Gratitude." In *The Human Person and the World of Values. A Tribute to Dietrich von Hildebrand by His Friends in Philosophy.* Edited by Balduin Schwarz. New York: Fordham University Press, 1960. pp. 168–91.

10. "The Role of Linguistic Analysis in Error Analysis." In *Proceedings of the American Catholic Philosophical Association* 34 (1960). pp. 127–32.

11. "The School: On Benedictine Spirituality in Our Time." In *Monastic Studies* 8 (1972). pp. 25–38.

12. "Ideological Sources of the Loss of Respect for Life." In *Respect for Human Life* (1974). pp. 75–82.

CONTRIBUTORS

Ronda Chervin taught philosophy at Loyola Marymount University in Los Angeles, and at Franciscan University of Steubenville, Ohio. She studied under Balduin Schwarz at Fordham University.

W. Norris Clarke, S.J. is Professor Emeritus of Philosophy, Fordham University. He was for many years a colleague of Balduin Schwarz at that University.

John Crosby is Professor of Philosophy at Franciscan University of Steubenville, Ohio. He studied under Balduin Schwarz at the University of Salzburg.

Thompson Mason Faller is Professor of Philosophy at the University of Portland, Oregon. He studied under Balduin Schwarz at the University of Salzburg.

Damian Fedoryka is Professor of Philosophy at Franciscan University of Steubenville, Ohio. He is a past president of Christendom College in Front Royal, Virginia. He studied under Balduin Schwarz at the University of Salzburg.

Peter Kreeft is Professor of Philosophy at Boston College. He studied under Balduin Schwarz at Fordham University.

Loretta Marra, daughter of William Marra, is an independent scholar. She studied under Josef Seifert, Damian Fedoryka, and John Crosby at the International Academy of Philosophy when it was in Dallas (before it moved to Liechtenstein).

William Marra (1928–1998) was Professor Emeritus of Philosophy, Fordham University. He studied under Balduin Schwarz at that university, and later taught there.

Mark Roberts is Professor of Philosophy at Franciscan University of Steubenville, Ohio.

Stephen Schwarz, son and only child of Balduin and Leni Schwarz, is Professor of Philosophy at the University of Rhode Island. He studied under Balduin Schwarz at Fordham University.

Josef Seifert is Rector of the International Academy of Philosophy in Liechtenstein. He studied under Balduin Schwarz at the University of Salzburg.

Ronald Tacelli, S.J. is Professor of Philosophy at Boston College.

Wolfgang Waldstein is Professor Emeritus, School of Law, University of Salzburg. He was for many years a colleague of Balduin Schwarz at that University.

Fritz Wenisch is Professor of Philosophy at the University of Rhode Island. He studied under Balduin Schwarz at the University of Salzburg.